BIBLICAL FOUNDATIONS OF SPIRITUALITY

BIBLICAL FOUNDATIONS OF SPIRITUALITY

Touching a Finger to the Flame

Second Edition

Barbara E. Bowe

**with contributions by
Laurie Brink and John R. Barker**

ROWMAN & LITTLEFIELD
Lanham • Boulder • New York • London

Published by Rowman & Littlefield
A wholly owned subsidiary of
The Rowman & Littlefield Publishing Group, Inc.
4501 Forbes Boulevard, Suite 200, Lanham, Maryland 20706
https://rowman.com

Unit A, Whitacre Mews, 26-34 Stannary Street, London SE11 4AB,
United Kingdom

British Library Cataloguing in Publication Information Available

Library of Congress Cataloging-in-Publication Data

Names: Bowe, Barbara Ellen, author.
Title: Biblical foundations of spirituality : touching a finger to the flame /
    Barbara E. Bowe with contributions by Laurie Brink and John R. Barker.
Description: Second edition. | Lanham : Rowman & Littlefield, [2017] | In-
    cludes bibliographical references and index.
Identifiers: LCCN 2016041394 (print) | LCCN 2016046054 (ebook) | ISBN
    9780742559608 (cloth : alk. paper) | ISBN 9780742559615 (pbk. : alk.
    paper) | ISBN 9781442262621 (electronic)
Subjects: LCSH: Spirituality—Biblical teaching. | Bible—Theology.
Classification: LCC BS680.S7 B69 2017 (print) | LCC BS680.S7 (ebook) |
    DDC 220.6—dc23
LC record available at https://lccn.loc.gov/2016041394

DEDICATED
In loving memory to my brother
TIMOTHY FINTAN BOWE
(1953–1995)

His life and death now rest forever
in the heart of the mystery of God.

CONTENTS

PREFACE TO THE SECOND EDITION

> But there are also many other things that Jesus did; if every one of
> them were written down, I suppose that the world itself could not
> contain the books that would be written.
>
> —John 21:25

Chapter 21 of the Gospel of John ends with an acknowledgment that
there is more to say. Ironically, chapter 21 is itself an appendix to the
gospel, which had earlier concluded:

> Now Jesus did many other signs in the presence of his disciples,
> which are not written in this book. But these are written so that you
> may come to believe that Jesus is the Messiah, the Son of God, and
> that through believing you may have life in his name. (Jn 20:30–31)

Our Bible is a repository of countless generations' theological reflection on God's presence experienced in the lives of the Israelites (Old
Testament) and early Christians (New Testament). But our Bible does
not contain all that was written about God's saving actions and manifold
blessings. In fact, to fully understand some of our canonical texts, we
need to have some familiarity with these other writings and the historical and social context out of which they emerged. For example, a prominent title for Jesus in the gospels is "Son of Man," a multivalent term
with roots in both canonical and intertestamental writings. The apocalyptic scene in Mark chapter 13 is best understood in light of the eschatology emerging as a reaction to Hellenism and the atrocities of Seleucid rule (second century B.C.E.). Peter's response to Jesus' query, "who do
you say I am?" (Mt 16:15; Mk 8:29; Lk 9:20) demonstrates that he
recognized Jesus as the messiah (anointed, Christ). But in the first-

century Palestinian context, "messiah" meant several different things: a king from the line of David, a prophet like Jeremiah, a warrior who would fight for political freedom. Knowing a bit of the backstory helps us to understand some key concepts in the New Testament.

The author of John chapter 21 knew of additional stories about Jesus, but recognized that the limits of space prevented his including them all. After the New Testament, Christians did not stop writing, and some of those late first and early second century texts were read in liturgy and considered authoritative until the close of the canon. These writings reveal how early Christians attempted to live their faith as they awaited Jesus' return, a return that had been greatly delayed.

The original edition of *Biblical Foundations of Spirituality: Touching a Finger to the Flame* rightly focused on the canonical texts. Its author, Barbara E. Bowe, hoped that her book would help readers to be informed and would shape their faith. "I am convinced that there is hardly a human emotion, hardly an aspect of the modern quest for God that does not have a precedent, a counterpart somewhere within the biblical story" (introduction, 3). Part of Bowe's goal was to provide a suitable textbook in which the whole of the Bible was surveyed for its spirituality. She certainly accomplished that goal. Winning the Catholic Press Association's first place award for the best spiritual book and the best scripture book in 2004, her publication was recognized for its outstanding scholarship and readability. Her book remains the one we most recommend when asked to suggest a good survey of the Bible that "regular folks can understand."

We both had the privilege of knowing Barbara Bowe first as students at Catholic Theological Union, and later as faculty members at that same institution. Here was a consummate teacher whose love of the word of God and passion for her students were evident both in the classroom and in her writing. But she was also a scholar and soon after *Biblical Foundations* was published, she began to consider how to improve the first edition. Her untimely death in 2010 saw her work uncompleted.

The second edition of *Biblical Foundations of Spirituality: Touching a Finger to the Flame* remains Barbara Bowe's gift to the people of God about the word of God she so loved. We have simply wrapped that gift in a new package. It is our intent that this new edition attends to the lacunae that Barbara hoped to address without altering her overall plan for the book. In addition, we noted that to fully understand the spirituality of the gospels the reader needed some familiarity with concepts that have their origin in the "intertestamental" period, the time between the Babylonian exile and the period of the New Testament. The first edition did not fully introduce these texts or theological concepts.

The new chapter on "Crisis and Hope" demonstrates both the continuity with the early biblical tradition and the development of new concepts (messianism, eschatology, Son of Man) that become significant for the New Testament's understanding of Jesus. In teaching the course that inspired the book, we noticed that students often asked about the period post–New Testament. "What happened next?" became an important question to help explain "how we've gotten here" in our own spiritual journey. The epilogue "The Church That Sojourns" introduces some of the postcanonical texts and shows how "biblical spirituality" was experienced and adapted for new generations of believers. The updated glossary and bibliography include information from these additional chapters. Together these new chapters enhance what remains an excellent resource for teaching and spiritual reading.

We stand on the shoulders of giants, heirs to the legacy of excellence in teaching and biblical scholarship at Catholic Theological Union. We hope that our contributions enhance your understanding of scripture and help deepen your spiritual life.

—Laurie Brink, O.P., and John R. Barker, O.F.M.

ACKNOWLEDGMENTS

I would like to offer a sincere word of thanks to the countless students at Catholic Theological Union (CTU) in Chicago over the last eight years who have been participants in the "Biblical Foundations of Spirituality" course. Their insights and questions about biblical spirituality have inspired me and influenced this project in many significant ways.

Special thanks are due also to Marianne Race, C.S.J., and to Therese Middendorf, C.S.J., who read earlier parts of the manuscript in its preparation and recommended helpful revisions. Special thanks, too, go to Lisa Buscher, R.S.C.J., who offered invaluable assistance in finding and correcting countless errors. Those that may still remain are solely my own responsibility. Finally, I owe a particular debt of gratitude to Jeremy Langford, editor at Sheed & Ward, now an imprint of Rowman & Littlefield. Without Jeremy's prodding, encouragement, and constant support this book might never have been written. His fine editorial hand has enhanced its content from beginning to end.

Finally, the concluding chapters of this book were finished during a fall quarter in Jerusalem as faculty director for the CTU Fall Biblical Travel Program. This holy city and this troubled land still eagerly await the biblical vision of justice and peace. I pray that both may soon be realized in their midst!

—Barbara E. Bowe, R.S.C.J.
Jerusalem

ABBREVIATIONS FOR BIBLICAL BOOKS

Gen	Genesis
Ex	Exodus
Lev	Leviticus
Num	Numbers
Deut	Deuteronomy
Josh	Joshua
Judg	Judges
Ruth	Ruth
1 Sam	1 Samuel
2 Sam	2 Samuel
1 Kings	1 Kings
2 Kings	2 Kings
1 Chr	1 Chronicles
2 Chr	2 Chronicles
Ezra	Ezra
Neh	Nehemiah
Esth	Esther
Job	Job
Ps	Psalms
Prov	Proverbs
Eccl	Ecclesiastes (Qoheleth)

Song	Song of Songs
Isa	Isaiah
Jer	Jeremiah
Lam	Lamentations
Ezek	Ezekiel
Dan	Daniel
Hos	Hosea
Joel	Joel
Am	Amos
Ob	Obadiah
Jon	Jonah
Mic	Micah
Nah	Nahum
Hab	Habakkuk
Zeph	Zephaniah
Hag	Haggai
Zech	Zechariah
Mal	Malachi
Wis	Wisdom of Solomon
Sir	Sirach (Ecclesiasticus)
Mt	Matthew
Mk	Mark
Lk	Luke
Jn	John
Acts	Acts of the Apostles
Rom	Romans
1 Cor	1 Corinthians
2 Cor	2 Corinthians
Gal	Galatians
Eph	Ephesians
Phil	Philippians
Col	Colossians

1 Thess	1 Thessalonians
2 Thess	2 Thessalonians
1 Tim	1 Timothy
2 Tim	2 Timothy
Tit	Titus
Philem	Philemon
Heb	Hebrews
Jas	James
1 Pet	1 Peter
2 Pet	2 Peter
1 Jn	1 John
2 Jn	2 John
3 Jn	3 John
Jude	Jude
Rev	Revelation

CHRONOLOGY

ca. 1800 B.C.E.	Ancestral narratives; promise made to Abraham
ca. 1250	Exodus from Egypt; Moses; Torah given on Mt. Sinai
ca. 1200	Entry into the land of Canaan and period of the Twelve Tribes
ca. 1000	David becomes king; Jerusalem as capital of monarchy
ca. 970–931	Solomon king; First Temple built in Jerusalem
ca. 930	Death of Solomon; the kingdom is divided between the North (Israel) and the South (Judah)
ca. 850	Elijah prophet in Israel
ca. 740	Amos, Hosea prophets in Israel; Isaiah, Micah prophets in Judah
721	Assyrians defeat Israel, destroy its capital, Samaria; end of northern kingdom
701	Assyrian King Sennacherib invades Judah; Jerusalem spared
621	King Josiah's reform; Jeremiah prophet in Judah
612	Babylonian destruction of Assyrian capital of Nineveh
598	First Babylonian capture of Jerusalem; first wave of exile

587	Babylonian destruction of Jerusalem and its First Temple; second wave of exiles taken to Babylon
538	Decree of Cyrus the Great of Persia ending the Jewish exile and instructing Jews to return to their land and to rebuild the Temple
520	Preaching of prophets Haggai and Zechariah to rebuild the Temple
515	Dedication of the Second Temple in Jerusalem
ca. 450–400	Restoration by Ezra (priest) and Nehemiah
ca. 400	Pentateuch completed
333–323	Reign of Alexander the Great; Hellenization of Alexander's Empire
167–164	Jewish Maccabean Revolt against the policies of the Greek Seleucid ruler, Antiochus IV
164	Rededication of the Temple in Jerusalem desecrated by Antiochus (commemorated on the Feast of Hanukkah)
63	Romans achieve world domination; Roman General Pompey conquers Palestine
37	Herod the Great becomes (puppet) king of Judea
ca. 4 B.C.E.	Birth of Jesus

New Testament Era

26–36 C.E.	Pontius Pilate, Roman procurator in Judea
ca. 27	Beginning of Jesus' public ministry
ca. 30	Crucifixion of Jesus by the Romans in Jerusalem
ca. 36	Saul (Paul) of Tarsus converted to faith in Christ
46–49	Paul's First Missionary Journey into Asia Minor
ca. 49	Apostolic Council in Jerusalem; Mission to the Gentiles confirmed
49–52	Paul's Second Missionary Journey (earliest Pauline letter to the Thessalonians—ca. 50)
54–57	Paul's Third Missionary Journey
58–63	Paul arrested, imprisoned at Caesarea, and then sent to Rome for trial

64	Emperor Nero; great fire of Rome; Christians' persecution
ca. 67	Martyrdom of Peter and Paul in Rome by Nero
70	Roman armies under Titus quell the first Jewish revolt and destroy the Second Temple
73	Final defeat of the Jewish rebels at Masada
132–135	Second Jewish revolt (led by Bar Kochba) against Rome crushed; Hadrian expels all Jews from Jerusalem and renames the city Aelia Capitolina

INTRODUCTION

Touching a Finger to the Flame

We all know that the Bible is an ancient and revered text. The word *bible* derives from an Egyptian word meaning "parchment scrolls" and was used to refer to the sacred writings preserved among Jews and, later, Christians. To their readers, these documents seemed to capture the fundamental stories and beliefs of their faith. The books of the Bible form a canon, or approved collection of authoritative texts deemed essential to the faith communities. Today, Jewish, Christian, and Muslim traditions rely on parts or the whole of the Bible as the foundation of their religious beliefs and practices. But how many of us relate to the Bible as a sacred text that speaks to us *today*? In my own life, one key experience helped me form a more intimate relationship with the Bible as a sacred text.

While in Korea, in the fall of 1988, a friend of mine took me to a Zen monastery on the outskirts of Seoul. She wanted me to meet a monk there who had befriended her and nurtured her faith. His name was Myoung Suk Ja. The brilliant fall day, with a blue, blue sky, made the sunlight play easily on the multicolored leaves and created against the blue sky a patchwork world of vibrant red and gold. The sheer beauty of the monastery grounds was breathtaking, and as Myoung welcomed us into his tiny cell I sensed the importance of the conversation that would follow.

Through my friend as interpreter, we talked for hours about the holy life and about the universal search for God manifest in every great religious tradition. He offered us green tea prepared with exquisite care from freshly picked leaves. Myoung's dark eyes spoke of a wisdom beyond his age. His whole demeanor exuded serenity and calm, and I knew I was in the presence of a holy man. After a second cup of tea, I pointed to the rows of books around us, and I asked him, "How do these help your search for God?"

His answer came slowly, deliberately. He took in his hands one of his treasured volumes, opened it carefully, caressing the page, and then handed it to me. "When you hold a sacred text in your hands," he said,

> and ponder its wisdom, it is not enough to learn the meaning of the words alone. A sacred text is like the flame of a candle. You can observe its color and height; you can describe its many properties. You can smell its fragrance, watch the way the flame constantly flickers in the air. You can measure the intensity of its heat and light, and calculate how rapidly the candle will burn. But that is not yet enough to know it. It is not until *you have touched your finger to the flame* that you can know the real meaning of the candle. This is how it is with sacred texts.

For the past eight years I have taught a course entitled "Biblical Foundations of Spirituality," as part of Catholic Theological Union's certificate program in biblical spirituality. My conviction in doing so is the belief that Christians, particularly Catholic Christians, have little idea of the profound spiritual resources for their lives and ministry waiting to be discovered in the Bible. Even if they have immersed themselves in a rigorous historical, critical investigation of the biblical texts and have mastered all the contemporary interpretive methods of Bible study, skills that are absolutely essential components of their training for ministry, I believe they rarely have, in the words of the Zen monk, *touched their fingers to the flame.* And so, for them and for anyone who takes this text in hand, there is a marvelous journey ahead where the deep questions of life, and death, and love, and ultimate meaning will be addressed. It is a journey one cannot afford to miss.

These biblical writings are texts that sear the soul. They invite us, for example, to stand with the Israelite ancestor Jacob as he wrestles against the nocturnal spirit at the Jabbok River, begging for a blessing (Gen 32:22–32). They ask us to experience Moses' sister Miriam's exuberant delight in leading the great liturgy of freedom—there by the Reed Sea (Ex 15:20–21). They compel us to weep at the death of the Israelite judge Jephthah's unnamed daughter (Judg 11:30–40) and to shake our fists at God with Job at our side. They challenge us to see that the coal that seared Isaiah's tongue (Isa 6:1–8) and the fire that burned in Jeremiah's heart (Jer 20:9) were not merely words but powerful prophetic images of our own journey with God. They beckon us to know Jesus, the Messiah, the Human One. They draw us to consider the faith of Paul and of the deacon Phoebe, the foibles of Peter, and the life of James the brother of the Lord. They summon us to lament at the divisive effects of intracommunity battles among Christians in ancient Corinth. They ask us to ponder, finally, the fiery words of the mysterious seer, John of Patmos, and to learn in all these encounters the identity of the invisible God as the Holy Other who speaks to our hearts. In short, these sacred texts convince us that the words of the author of Hebrews are profoundly true: "Indeed, the word of God is living and active, sharper than any two-edged sword, piercing until it divides soul from spirit, joints from marrow; it is able to judge the thoughts and intentions of the heart" (Heb 4:12).

My aim, therefore, is to give these words a hearing and to allow them to inform and shape our faith today. I am convinced that there is hardly a human emotion, hardly an aspect of the modern quest for God, that does not have a precedent, a counterpart somewhere within the biblical story. The people who produced these texts, we must remember, were *real* people—just like you and me. They struggled to understand their world and the divine presence within it—just like you and me. They had no blueprints, no recipes, no secret formulas, no easy answers for the ultimate questions of life—any more than we do. But their wisdom, their hopes and dreams, and their faith convictions constitute our heritage and the sacred, yes normative, text for our lives.

Today, with the renewed interest in all things spiritual, and as Generation Xers and Generation Yers and all those to follow search for spiritual wisdom in every conceivable corner of the world, in New Age phenomena of all kinds, in crystals, pyramids, and the like, there is an untapped resource, an often unknown wellspring of wisdom ready at hand. For Christian believers, and those open to the search for God, the Bible is our sacred text, a source of inspiration, a pathway to God, a vade mecum (manual) for life's journey—waiting to be discovered.

Each year I have searched for a suitable textbook (in addition to the Bible itself . . .) for the course I teach, and each year I find there is none. There is not, together in one volume, a textbook that surveys the whole Bible in order to open its treasure chest of stories, images, questions, and portraits of faith—one whose explicit purpose is to help readers *to touch their fingers to the flame* and so to be forever transformed by this divine encounter. I hope this will be such a book.

THE BIBLE AS A SACRED TEXT

It must begin with the simple affirmation that, for Christians like my-self, the Bible is our sacred text par excellence. In every sense, when we take this text in our hands, or hear it proclaimed in Christian assem-blies, we believe that we encounter the inspired word of God, mediated to us through the human words of these texts. Or, as Vatican II stated, "Sacred Scripture is the utterance of God put down as it is in writing under the inspiration of the holy Spirit" (Dogmatic Constitution on Divine Revelation—*Dei Verbum* #9). For Christians, moreover, the Bible is *the* sacred text that, more than any other, should sustain and nurture our faith. It is a repository that preserves the sacred memories and religious imagination of our Israelite and early Christian ancestors. It is a reservoir of "living water" that mediates to us the divine presence. It is no wonder, then, that we should turn to this living word as the privileged foundation of our life of faith, our spirituality for today.

But precisely *in what sense* may we speak of the Bible as the "word of God"? To make such a claim is, first of all, to speak not in a literal sense but *metaphorically*. Despite what some biblical literalists might say, the Bible did not fall literally out of the "mouth" of God. For, as our Christian tradition has always affirmed, the divine being we name as "God" is pure spirit, infinite being, and ultimately beyond our finite ability to comprehend. This God does not have a mouth, nor does God "speak" by means of any human language. Nor is this God limited by the constraints of human reason and conceptualization, which arise of necessity within the social, cultural, and historical boundaries of time and space. The language and concepts of biblical texts are, by defini-tion, finite and incapable of containing or capturing fully the infinite revelation of God.

At the same time, we are correct when we say that the Bible *medi-ates* God's self-revelation to us and is, in that sense, "word of God." For believers, then, the Bible is, indeed, a "revelatory text" and "a sacra-ment of the word of God."[1] Sandra Schneiders, a professor of Christian spirituality at the Jesuit School of Theology at Berkeley, offers both a helpful and a succinct description of the Bible's revelatory character:

> The real referent of the metaphor "word of God" is the entire mys-tery of divine revelation, God's received self-gift to us in and through such symbols as creation, sacred history, Jesus himself, and the life of the believing community. In all of these ways God "speaks" to us. . . . To say that the biblical text (as read and understood) is the sacrament of the word of God is to say that this mystery here comes to articula-tion with a clarity and transparency that focuses our attention on the

mystery of divine revelation and thus fosters our attentiveness to the
word of God wherever we encounter it.[2]

The truth of this statement should be understood to be the essential
starting point for all that will follow.

SOCIAL LOCATION OF THE READER

Holding the sacred text in our hands, every reader or interpreter of the
Bible brings to it her or his *unique* capacity for understanding and her
or his *particular* receptivity and openness (or lack thereof) to God's
self-disclosure. What we hear, what we see, what each of us understands to be the content of God's self-disclosure mediated by these
texts, is conditioned in no small measure by each one's "social location."
Or, to put it another way, where one *stands* (literally) determines what
one sees. This axiom is the core insight of our postmodern world.
Whereas, until about the mid-twentieth century, scientists and learned
teachers in every discipline believed that it was possible to discern
"objective truth" through scientific observation and rational analysis,
the postmodern perspective judges every opinion or "truth" as the limited product of a particular viewpoint and perspective. Postmodernity
has challenged the myth of continuous evolutionary progress and has
called into question the apparent stability of the social, scientific, religious, and moral order. Pure objectivity is not possible, only the fallible
judgments from different and particular social-cultural locations. It is
important, therefore, that I state my own specific "location" at the outset of this book.

I write and teach as a believing Christian, a "cradle Roman Catholic," as some would say. The existence of God, the authority of the
Church and its sacraments, and the credibility of the Roman Catholic
tradition were all "givens" in my life growing up in the 1950s and 1960s
in a small town in upstate New York. I write, furthermore, as a white,
middle-class, Harvard-educated woman, who for the past thirty-six
years has been a member of an international religious community of
women in the Church. These components of my social location mean
that I have benefited from a position of relative privilege in upbringing,
in education, and in racial and cultural identity. But at the same time, as
a woman, I have also experienced firsthand the discrimination and mar-
ginalization that, to a great extent, still define a "woman's place" in
society at large and especially in the Roman Catholic Church.

Three years in the late 1980s living and teaching in a school of
theology in Manila, the Philippines, changed forever my perspective on

the world and my reading of the biblical texts. In that Filipino context, more than any other, I learned that the Bible has extraordinary power to shape people's lives—both for good and for ill. Depending on how we read this text, either the biblical word can liberate and console those straining for human dignity or it can be, as Marx once wrote, the "opium of the people,"[3] lulling people into complacent disregard for *this* world and its strivings in favor of an undisclosed future world, unrelated to *this* world and wholly beyond *our* control. Whether the Bible becomes, for any reader, ultimately liberating or oppressive depends on our ability to "touch" the living, liberating God revealed therein and to be forever changed by the fire of this encounter. To do so is to know that the God of the Bible is the God who saves and the one who challenges us to respond. This God is the one who blesses and calls us to the fullness of life here and now.

PLAN OF THE BOOK

This book invites readers *to touch their fingers to the flame* of this sacred text we call the Bible. It begins by exploring the nature and meaning of that all-too-difficult word, *spirituality*, and then offers some ways in which we might understand what is meant by *biblical spirituality*. Following the order of the canonical texts and attentive to the varying social-historical contexts that they presume, the successive chapters of this book offer reflections on selected passages of the biblical tradition beginning with the book of Genesis and concluding with Revelation. In each case I connect the wisdom and witness of scripture with everyday life and spirituality. The official canon of scripture, encompassing both Old and New Testaments, was the result of three centuries of Christian reflection on the meaning of Christ's life and message. Gradually Christians recognized their own lives and faith experiences reflected in these many texts from Genesis to Revelation. They affirmed the continuity of the Christian message with the tradition of their Jewish forebears and embraced the scriptures of Judaism while claiming Christ as the fulfillment of Jewish hope and expectation. Therefore, biblical spirituality concerns this whole sweep of the biblical story. Admittedly, such an agenda is an ambitious one, foolhardy even, some might say. I choose it decidedly and with care, believing that there is a value in listening to the biblical story from beginning to end. There is wisdom in following the multiple threads of these voices of faith that, together, produce such a richly diverse biblical tapestry.

QUESTIONS FOR REFLECTION

1. What are the *sacred texts* of your life? What literature has influenced who you are and what you believe about life? What is it about these texts that has drawn you? Why?
2. If the Bible is one of the texts you have named, which parts of this biblical story awakened your imagination or captured your attention? Which ones angered you or spoke to your heart? Why?
3. How would you describe your own social location (gender, class, ethnic background, education, family history, etc.), and how has this location influenced your view of the world? How might it affect how you read the Bible?
4. How would you describe what it means in your life "to search for God"?
5. What are your hesitations in approaching the Bible as a sacred text?
6. Have you ever "touched your finger to the flame"? Which biblical passage mediated this sense of God to you? How?

I

WHAT IS SPIRITUALITY?

Surely the LORD is in this place—and I did not know it!

—Genesis 28:16

The quotation from Genesis that heads this chapter comes from the story of the early Israelite ancestors: Abraham and Sarah, Isaac and Rebekah, Jacob and Rachael. In Genesis 28 we find the account of Jacob's journey in search of a wife, a journey that brings him finally to the ford of the Jabbok River (a tributary flowing into the Jordan River from the east). There he encounters a mysterious stranger who wrestles with him through the night (Gen 32:22–32). Their conflict is fierce and fraught with potential danger. Jacob demands to know the stranger's name, to no avail. Through the night their wrestling continues. The stranger's blows wound Jacob for life, but he does not prevail. In the end Jacob is spared and receives the stranger's blessing, but he limps as he leaves the Jabbok. And in that struggle, he has come to know that the nocturnal stranger is none other than God.

It seems to me that the story of Jacob's nocturnal wrestling with the angelic figure at the Jabbok River is an apt paradigm for our struggle to live an authentically God-centered life today. We struggle to find and to know God in the midst of our complex and fast-paced lives. Paradoxically, the more we reject traditional patterns of organized religion, the more modern Western culture as a whole embraces an increasingly secular ethos—to that extent, the profound search for meaning, for the transcendent, for ultimate reality in our midst, seems to gain momentum. In such a cultural climate, the more real is the search for, and the wrestling with, our glimpses of the divine presence. But like Jacob in the Genesis story, we do not always know how to *recognize and name* this divine presence in our midst today or how to *live faithfully* in response to this mystery. In short, for many people in our contemporary world who are searching for an authentic spirituality, this search is sometimes a fierce struggle.

DEFINING OUR TERMS—*SPIRITUALITY*

First, it is important to define our terms. What comes to mind as you think about the elusive word *spirituality*? What aspect of your own life and search for God does this word signal? When I invite my students to give me a "spill" of words or phrases they most immediately associate with this term, the outpouring is both energizing and instructive. A stream of rapid-fire responses usually comes with words like *relationship, journey, intimacy, horizon, way of life, interconnectedness, Spirit engagement, embodied living, dance conversation*, and so forth. No two responses are ever exactly the same, and yet each student knows, intuitively and experientially, something about the relational character of this elusive word.

What does the term *spirituality* mean? Consult any ten recent books on the subject and you will find (at least!) ten different definitions of the term. For example, a popular study entitled *Christian Spirituality: Themes from the Tradition* gathers twenty-three different definitions of spirituality from articles and books published between 1984 and 1995 alone.[1] A few examples of these various definitions will suffice to show the range and character of this word:

> Philosophers speak of our human spirituality as our capacity for self-transcendence, a capacity demonstrated in our ability to know the truth, to relate to others lovingly, and to commit ourselves freely to persons and ideals. Psychologists sometimes use the term [*spirituality*] for that aspect of personal essence that gives a person power, energy, and motive force. Religious persons speak of spirituality as the actualization of human self-transcendence by whatever is acknowledged as the ultimate or the Holy.[2]

> Fundamentally spirituality has to do with becoming a person in the fullest sense.[3]

> A spirituality is the expression of a dialectical personal growth from the inauthentic to the authentic. Total authenticity of a human person would be her or his complete self-transcendence in love. Conversely, total inauthenticity would be complete self-alienation, self-centeredness in hate.[4]

> [Spirituality is] the experience of consciously striving to integrate one's life in terms not of isolation and self-absorption but of self-transcendence toward ultimate values one perceives.[5]

> [Spirituality is] the unique and personal response of individuals to all that calls them to integrity and transcendence.[6]

Or my personal favorite: "Spirituality is theology on two feet."[7]

The difficulty in defining this word precisely stems from the broad range of meanings that the term *spirituality* contains. Etymologically, the word derives from the Latin *spiritus*, meaning "breath, life, spirit." And so, in its broadest sense, *spirituality* has to do with the whole of our life grounded in ultimate reality, in the spirit, and attuned to the spiritual dimension of existence—that which both animates and transcends our bodily, physical selves. For someone who accepts religious categories, this spiritual dimension is what Rudolf Otto calls the sacred *mysterium tremendum et fascinans*, the awe-inspiring mystery that is at the heart of all life and is at once both fearful and irresistibly attractive. To use the term *spirituality*, then, first of all, assumes the existence of this transcendent reality, this spirit-filled dimension of life, and then argues further that we humans can and do experience this reality in our midst and that we are drawn to both name and respond to it.

In the broadest sense, therefore, *spirituality* is the human response to this transcendent reality, regardless of how we might name or experience that reality. Many would say that it is in the nature of human existence itself to sense (whether consciously or unconsciously) that there is something beyond ourselves, some ultimate reality, some mysterious presence that is responsible for and animates all of life. Theologians and philosophers of every age have tried to name this reality in universal terms. Contemporary theologians of the twentieth century have suggested the following phrases to name divine reality: "the ground of our being" (Paul Tillich), "the matrix surrounding and sustaining all life" (Rosemary Ruether), "the power of the future" (Wolfhart Pannenberg), "the beyond in our midst" (Dietrich Bonhoeffer), and the "holy mystery" (Karl Rahner). And despite its inadequacy, the simple word *God* serves, for most believers, as the traditional name for this mystery.[8] *Spirituality* is the dynamic term that points to a *lived* experience of this mystery in the day to day. It describes how we live our lives in response to this Ultimate Reality.

CHRISTIAN SPIRITUALITY

If spirituality is a *lived* reality, then it cannot exist in the abstract but only within specific individuals and groups of people who both name and respond to this Ultimate Reality in particular ways. Our concrete experiences and cultural contexts give us particular stories and symbols, boundaries of social awareness, different understandings of personal authority, modes of knowing and feeling, and a range of expectations regarding, for example, gender and race and every other aspect of our human lives.[9] In that sense, then, *Christian* spirituality describes a particular way of responding to the spirit of God mediated to the world and ultimately known through Jesus Christ. Christian spirituality concerns the progressive transformation that happens in us. It is the result of the cooperation of our whole lives with the power and presence of Christ's Spirit alive and working within the whole person—body and soul, thoughts and feelings, emotions and passions, hopes, fears, and dreams.

Michael Downey, one of the most prolific writers in the field of spirituality today, defines Christian spirituality in this way: "The Spirit at work in persons (1) within a culture, (2) in relation to a tradition, (3) in memory of Jesus Christ, (4) in the light of contemporary events, hopes, sufferings and promises, (5) in efforts to combine elements of action and contemplation, (6) with respect to charism and community, (7) as expressed and authenticated in praxis."[10] Downey's words highlight the multidimensional character of spirituality in general and of Christian spirituality, in particular. And, within the Christian tradition itself, there are numerous different traditions of Christian insight and ways of living and articulating the heart of Christian faith. One can think easily of the spiritual traditions associated with the early desert monastics, the varied theological and spiritual wisdom coming from the patristic writers who differed greatly in the East and in the West. Various modern schools of spirituality claim their origins in the traditions of the great saints: Ignatius Loyola (1491–1556; Jesuit); Francis (1181–1226) and Clare of Assisi (1193–1253; Franciscan); Dominic (1174–1221) and Catherine of Siena (ca. 1347–1380; Dominican); Benedict (ca. 480–550) and Scholastica (ca. 480–543; Benedictine); John of the Cross (1542–1591) and Teresa of Avila (1515–1582; Carmelite) to name but a few.

Given this enormous variety of both Christian and non-Christian forms of spirituality, anyone pursuing the spiritual life today is aware that there is great wisdom to be found in every spiritual path and that no one spiritual tradition can itself *totally* encompass or *fully* express the totality of the divine mystery.[11] The way of spiritual chauvinism that claims that *my* way is the *only* way to God and the path of spiritual ethnocentrism that falsely assumes that the Western faith tradition is superior to any other are both roads not to be taken.

BIBLICAL SPIRITUALITY

In some sense, for a Christian, all spirituality is fundamentally *biblical*. The life of faith of Christians has been and continues to be inspired and nourished by the encounter with the God mediated by the scriptures. In the words of the Vatican II document on Divine Revelation (*Dei Verbum* #21), "And such is the force and power of the word of God that it is the church's support and strength, imparting robustness to the faith of its daughters and sons and providing food for their souls. It is a pure and unfailing fount of spiritual life." The Bible is not only a fundamental source of Christian spirituality; it is also a touchstone by which we discern the authenticity of all spirituality within the Christian community. Biblical spirituality grounds a person in the experience of the infinite God acting in and through history. Through the scriptures one has access to the God revealed and known in the life of the covenant community of ancient Israel and in the fullness of the revelation in the person of Jesus, the Word made flesh—in his life, death, and resurrection. Our access to God is, of course, always a *mediated* access, communicated through religious language and symbol that stretch our powers of intellect and insight as we seek to understand. Pondering the scriptures we learn to embrace a God who is ever before us as the pillar of cloud, the one whose voice spoke through the prophets and whose wisdom permeates all created things. The God of the Bible is the Holy Presence in our midst, the One who calls us, a Friend and Protector who heals, forgives, and saves. We meet in the scriptures, ultimately, the God revealed in Jesus—the Human One who is *Emmanuel*, God-with-us.

A life of faith steeped in this biblical Word nurtures Christian seekers in the ways of God, plants deep within the human heart a love for all that God loves, a compassion for all God's people, and an ardent desire to hasten God's reign among us. With careful attention and discerning hearts, Christians draw deeply from this scriptural source the wisdom and spiritual insight necessary for a faithful Christian life. In short, our faith, our spirituality, is *biblical* because through the scriptures we are schooled in the ways of the biblical God.

This biblical foundation of all Christian spirituality is a wellspring for believers, a deep reservoir of images and ways of knowing God. Or as the prophet says, "With joy you will draw water from the wells of salvation" (Isa 12:3). At the same time, the Bible is a *human* word; it is therefore limited by the constraints of language, social-historical context, and the restricted metaphors of religious imagination in every age. Consequently, the Bible reflects the limited cultural norms and conceptual frameworks of its own time, incomplete and restricted as they are by their relevance to specific times and places. In short, this storehouse of images can both *form* and *deform* our ideas of God and our understanding of faith. Two examples of the positive and negative potential of the biblical text to shape our spirituality will suffice to illustrate the point.

When the anonymous prophet of the exile, whom tradition calls Second Isaiah (587–538 B.C.E.), spoke of God as the Holy One, he consoled an exiled people with the poignant portrait of a loving deity:

> Do not fear for I have redeemed you; I have called you by name, you are mine. When you pass through the waters, I will be with you; and through the rivers, they shall not overwhelm you; when you walk through fire you shall not be burned, and the flame shall not consume you. For I am the LORD your God, the Holy One of Israel, your Savior. I give Egypt as your ransom, Ethiopia and Seba in exchange for you. Because you are precious in my sight, and honored, and I love you. (Isa 43:1d–4c)

Here, the prophet comforts a weary people exiled from their land and grieving the loss of statehood and Temple. In the years between 597 and 587 B.C.E. the Babylonian armies laid siege to Jerusalem and in 587 finally succeeded in destroying the city completely. As I discuss more thoroughly in chapter 5, the exile was a moment when all was lost; the nation was destroyed. There was no hope. Against this disaster, Second Isaiah assures the people of God's concern and love and affirms their own dignity as God's favored ones. In a text like this, we hear God calling *each* of us by name, speaking words of love to *our* hearts. We meet a God who promises to be with *us* as a source of protection and care, guiding *us* through every sort of danger and fear. But, even in this text, the limits of the biblical language and perspective are clear. Is not the God portrayed here a cavalier deity who deems some people as "disposable" and offers them in exchange for others who are more favored? Is this a biblical portrait that is an adequate image of God or basis for contemporary spirituality?

What does one do, furthermore, with the even more graphic and frightful image of a God whom Joshua (describing events set in ca. 1200 B.C.E.) presents as condoning, even causing, the genocide of numerous peoples: "Joshua said: By this you shall know that among you is the living God who without fail will drive out from before you the Canaanites, Hittites, Hivites, Perizzites, Girgashites, Amorites, and Jebusites" (Josh 3:10). Violence, abusive power, unlimited destruction of property, a ravaging of the land, and genocidal policies, all presented as divinely sanctioned, mark the character of the book of Joshua from beginning to end. If this text is to be a resource for contemporary spirituality and Christian practice, then it requires of any reader a *hermeneutics of suspicion* and a thoroughgoing and serious social and historical critique.[12]

Shug, the wise and irreverent character in Alice Walker's novel *The Color Purple*, is a powerful literary voice expressing just such a suspicion and critique:

> Tell me what your God look like, Celie. Aw naw, I say. I'm too shame. Nobody ever ast me this before, so I'm sort of took by surprise. . . . Okay, I say. He big and old and tall and graybearded and white. He wear white robes and go barefooted. Blue eyes? She ast. Sort of bluish-gray. Cool. Big though. White lashes, I say. She laugh. Why you laugh? I ast. I don't think it so funny. What you expect him to look like, Mr. ——? That wouldn't be no improvement, she say. Then she tell me this old white man is the same God she used to see when she prayed. If you wait to find God in church, Celie, she say, that's who is bound to show up, cause that's where he live. How come? I ast. Cause that's the one in the white folks' white bible. Shug! I say. God wrote the bible, white folks had nothing to do with it. How come he look just like them, then? She say. Only bigger? And a heap more hair. How come the bible just like everything else they make, all about them doing one thing and another, and all the colored folks doing is gitting cursed? I never thought about that.[13]

As Walker's Shug convincingly attests, the biblical images of God have both *formed* and *deformed* our faith and spirituality. For this reason, then, a critical reading of the text, which is attentive to this negative potential, is always essential if the Bible is to be a trustworthy resource for authentic faith.

SPIRITUALITY AND THEOLOGY

In the classic definition from St. Anselm of Canterbury (d. 1109), theology can best be defined as "faith seeking understanding" (*fides quaerens intellectum*). Theology, therefore, results both from a critical reflection on one's lived faith experience and from the attempt to articulate this reflection in statements, formulas, and doctrines. It follows, then, that spirituality precedes theology. The life lived is the prior condition for our ongoing reflection on that life. Or, put another way, our experience of God and our daily response to this God we have encountered cause us to ponder the varied dimensions of what we have known. We struggle to name this experience we have had. Our spirituality gives rise to our theology, not the other way around.

As people of faith, we know that the revelation of God can come to us through a myriad of ways: through nature; through the witness of other people's faith and exemplary lives; through the sacred texts proclaimed and celebrated, in ritual moments, in personal prayer, in joy, and in sorrow, within the solitude of our own hearts. At any moment of our waking or sleeping God can break into our consciousness and invite us to respond to the gift of grace. These sorts of religious experiences are a universal phenomenon. At the same time, it is essential for us to distinguish between the religious *experience* and the *articulation* of that experience. The former is universal and timeless; the latter is limited and culturally conditioned. The former unites people of every culture in a common experience of the divine mystery at the heart of life, whereas the latter distinguishes among peoples and religious traditions based on their different and often unique, or even contradictory, ways of naming the divine.

Spirituality and theology, that is, experience and the articulation of that experience, are partners in the dynamic journey of faith. Our spirituality critiques our theology, and in that sense, "our lived religious experience is a valid authority for what we come to believe as true of God's revelation."[14] And our theology critically interprets our spirituality by offering a historical context and the philosophic and conceptual framework for naming our different experiences of God. The interplay of experience, reflection, and articulation is a constant movement within the lives of each individual person and within communities of faith. This dynamic process provides the context for integration of our experience of God within the contours of our daily lives. In short, this process is the stuff of our lived spirituality.

DISTINGUISHING DIFFERENT SPIRITUALITIES

In the history of spirituality it has been helpful to delineate different types of spiritual traditions according to their distinctive elements and characteristics. One such basic distinction recognizes two different types of spiritual traditions: the "apophatic" and the "kataphatic." Apophatic spiritual traditions (from the Greek *apophasis*, which means "denial, negation") affirm the absolute unknowability of God and reject all conceptual attempts to name, symbolize, or speak about God in concrete images. The apophatic way is the way to God through negation and abandonment of images, through darkness and surrender to the unknown.

There is considerable biblical warrant for such a spiritual path going back to the revelation of God to Moses on the holy mountain of Sinai/Horeb in Exodus 19 and 20. There YHWH spoke to Moses with the words, "I am going to come to you in a dense cloud" (Ex 19:9), and after Moses received the commandments we learn that "the people stood at a distance, while Moses drew near to the thick darkness where God was" (Ex 20:21). The classic proponents of this "way of negation" include the sixth-century theologian Pseudo-Dionysius (ca. 500 C.E.), who exhorted believers to "leave behind . . . everything perceived and understood" (*Mystical Theology*, 997B), and his anonymous fourteenth-century counterpart who wrote the famous spiritual classic *The Cloud of Unknowing*, which draws the imagery for its title precisely from the description of Moses and the thick cloud on Mt. Sinai.

In contrast to this well-developed apophatic tradition, the history of spirituality is also rich with examples of kataphatic spiritual traditions (from the Greek *kataphasis*, which means "affirmation"). These spiritual traditions affirm that God the Creator *can* be known, by way of analogy, through images, symbols, and concepts drawn from human experience in the created world. At the heart of these traditions, moreover, is the conviction that God is fundamentally a revealing God who seeks to make known the divine Self to the world. This spiritual way also has deep biblical foundations, especially in the Wisdom traditions of both testaments. In these texts, those who seek God are invited to discern the divine presence within all of creation, as in the Book of Wisdom: "For from the greatness and beauty of created things comes a corresponding perception of their Creator" (Wis 13:5).

For the Christian, of course, *the* revelation of the invisible God is ultimately knowable in and through the incarnate word who is Jesus. This is the claim especially of the Johannine tradition where Jesus says, in response to Philip's desire to see the Father, "Whoever has seen me has seen the Father" (Jn 14:9). Earlier in that same gospel, the prologue already emphatically affirms that "no one has ever seen God. It is God the only Son, who is close to the Father's heart, who has made him known" (Jn 1:18). Or as the author of the letter to the Colossians puts it, "He [Christ] is the image of the invisible God" (Col 1:15). Biblical texts such as these are grounded in the conviction that God can be experienced and known in and through Jesus the Christ, and it is principally this Christ-centered, kataphatic spirituality that supports and under-girds much of our contemporary Christian spirituality.

Another classic distinction in the history of spirituality is the diffe-rentiation that is often made between the contemplative and the apos-tolic dimensions of spirituality. In many ways, this is a false dichotomy but one that does point to the twofold character of the spiritual life. The term *contemplation*, or *contemplative spirituality*, refers to that trans-forming and unitive movement, in love, toward the mystery of God. It involves a person's desire or longing for God, together with the realiza-tion that God lives in all created things, and it implies the correspond-ing effort to make oneself present to and aware of this presence of God: "In contemplation, my subjectivity becomes one with the subjectivity of God, and I as a separate entity seem to disappear."[15] Isn't that similar to what Paul describes when he speaks of his faith experience as a trans-formative union with the death–resurrection of Christ: "And it is no longer I who live, but it is Christ who lives in me" (Gal 2:20a)?

Contemplative spirituality has often been linked with the mystical dimension of faith that sees the inner harmony of all things and denies any dualistic notion of life that opposes spirit and matter, the divine and the human, male and female, and so on. Contemplative spirituality strives to live in such a way as to deepen the awareness of this unity and divine presence at the heart of the world. Traditionally in Christian history, contemplatives have searched for God both in solitude (her-metic tradition) and in communal settings (monastic tradition); they have been men and women who have separated themselves from ordi-nary society or who have lived their contemplative lives in the midst of the city. Their names are legion, but among the more well known of the contemplatives we should name Meister Eckhart (1260–1327), Julian of Norwich (1343–1415), and Teresa of Avila and John of the Cross (al-ready mentioned above). Thomas Merton (1915–1968) is surely the best known among modern contemplatives. Regardless of their particu-lar setting, the core of their contemplative way has been the desire for union with God and their profound recognition of the unity of all life.

Apostolic spirituality, by contrast, denotes an active way of disciple-ship, a following in the footsteps of Jesus, in which believers participate in and further his saving mission. At the heart of apostolic spirituality is the assurance that one has been sent (from the Greek *apostello*, which means "to send") into the world to announce, in both word and deed, the saving power of God. The first apostles were witnesses of the resur-rection, those men and women to whom Jesus had said: "Go to my brothers [and sisters]" (Jn 20:17) or "Go therefore and make disciples of all nations, baptizing . . . , teaching" (Mt 28:19–20). Apostolic spiritual-ity continues the role of the first apostles. It implies a commitment to share Jesus' own saving mission of teaching, healing, reconciling, and calling all people to the fullness of life and to their full human dignity as creatures loved by God. This spiritual tradition draws its biblical inspiration from the great prophetic figures of Israel's past whose fierce commitment to God's justice challenged the people of their day. This is a spirituality whose fundamental belief resounds in the words of Jesus, the Good Shepherd, in John 10:10: "I came that they may have life, and have it abundantly." To give one's life daily, out of love, for the sake of the lives of others is the true way of holiness and the most fitting response to the Holy God.

The apparent distinction or dichotomy between apostolic and contemplative spiritualities is just that: a false dichotomy. Both approaches and ways of responding to God share a common core. Both reverence the mysterious otherness of God and recognize God's spirit and presence at the heart of all life. Both embrace God's design and purpose for the life of the world, manifest especially in the ministry of Jesus. Just as contemplative spirituality is profoundly apostolic in its concern for and union with all that God loves, so, too, apostolic spirituality discerns the mystery of God within the very heart of human engagement and contemplates the face of Christ in the faces of the brother and sister in need. These are not distinct paths to God but different aspects of one and the same movement that may find expression more clearly through one of these dominant modes of expression at one time or another. Authentic Christian spirituality, however, will necessarily be both contemplative and apostolic.

A third way of distinguishing different types of spirituality concerns the ways in which various spiritual traditions view the world. We have already noted the tendency in apophatic spirituality to turn *away* from the world outside of the self to an inner world of silence, darkness, and negation of images. Here the movement is a movement within to embrace a unitive love in the stillness of the presence of God. Apostolic spiritualities, by contrast, turn *toward* the outside world as the sacred locus of God's presence and the object of God's saving love. They actively confront the world and challenge those forces in the world that deny God's *shalom*, God's justice and compassion.

In the West, it is only in the recent past that the development of an ecological spirituality has revived this type of world-embracing stance that reverences the earth itself and all created life as sacred. The apostle Paul shares this perspective when he claims that not just human creatures but "the whole creation has been groaning in labor pains until now" (Rom 8:22), waiting to share the fullness of the spirit of God. And another contemporary theologian, Sallie McFague, for example, can even speak of the world, the entire universe, as "God's body" in constructing her ecological theology.[16] This insight, of course, is a wisdom that native peoples have intuitively known since the beginning of time but which the modern world is only now rediscovering. And yet, as we shall see, the boundary between world-renouncing and world-embracing spiritualities, both in the Bible and in our own lives, is never quite so neat.

CONCLUSION

Spirituality, as understood throughout this study, therefore, is an all-inclusive term to speak about a way of life lived in response to the divine spirit. It describes our human appreciation of the mystery at the heart of life, the mystery of God revealed and known. *Spirituality* is a dynamic, not static, term insofar as it points to our day-to-day engagement with the real world around us where God's presence meets our own. *Biblical spirituality*, moreover, defines our lived faith experience that draws on the special biblical treasure-house of stories, images, prophetic challenges, and prayers and on the ultimate example of the life and death of Jesus for its understanding of God and for its convictions about the meaning of human existence.

If we return to the biblical story of the ancestor Jacob wrestling with the mysterious figure at the Jabbok River, we see again an apt metaphor of the spiritual life: a search for God in our everyday lives, a wrestling to understand the manifestations of God's presence in persons and events, an earnest desire to name this mystery we have encountered, and the deep longing for a blessing. In our day especially we wrestle with myriad counterforces both within and outside of ourselves that hinder our quest for God. But, as in the case of Jacob, we encounter the face of God precisely within this daily struggle. And, day after day, perhaps we, too, will find ourselves able to say with Jacob, "Surely the LORD is in this place—and I did not know it!" (Gen 28:16).

QUESTIONS FOR REFLECTION

1. As you think about your life in light of the story of Jacob, what issues, questions, or forces are you wrestling with today? Why?
2. What characterizes that struggle for you? What blessing do you hope to receive? Can you find God in the midst of these encounters?

3. What is your personal definition of spirituality? How does your life reflect this search for and response to God?

4. Are you drawn to God more through the apophatic or contemplative way, or is your spirituality marked more by the kataphatic and apostolic dimensions? Where do you see that *both* dimensions might be present in your life?

5. Are there other contemporary novels, like *The Color Purple*, that have shaped your faith and knowledge of God? How and in what ways have these texts been influential for your spirituality?

6. If it is true that the Bible has both positive and negative potential to shape our ideas about God, then which biblical stories most draw you to God? Which ones do you challenge and critique? Why?

2

GOD BEYOND ALL NAMES

No one has ever seen God. It is God
the only Son who is close to the Father's
heart, who has made [God] known.

—John 1:18

The previous chapter explores the many layers of meaning of the term *spirituality*. It affirms the fundamental character of this term as *a life lived in relationship* with the divine mystery at the heart of the world, a mystery that we call "God." Put most simply, then, our spirituality is our lived relationship with the Other who is God. But unlike every other relationship we might share with persons (or even with animals) whom we experience with our senses and whom we call by name, our relationship with the ineffable, divine Other places us at the horizon of ultimate mystery. For, as the author of the Gospel of John reminds us again and again, "No one has ever seen God" (Jn 1:18).

And yet the God of the Bible chooses to be known and revealed among us, as the following fictional tale will suggest. There is a story that is told about a small Christian community. This community could be set anywhere in the world, and it gathered together ordinary people, like you and me, who wanted simply to share their faith together. As the story goes, it was their custom to assemble in the evening once a month and to invite the members simply to pray in silence together for a time. After a period of silence, anyone in the group was invited to share a comment, a prayer, or a petition. On one particular evening there was a guest in their midst, a great Shakespearean actor. During the evening he arose and asked to share a prayer. In his refined and stentorian voice he prayed from memory Psalm 23: "The Lord is my shepherd. . . ." When he had finished, the power and dramatic character of his prayer moved the assembly to spontaneous and enthusiastic applause. Somewhat embarrassed, the actor sat down, and the meeting continued. Just as they were about to conclude, one of their oldest members, a widow stooped and frail, stood to offer a prayer. She, too, prayed from memory Psalm 23: "The Lord is my shepherd," she prayed, "I shall not want. . . ." So moving were her words that this time the assembly remained in riveted silence as the woman took her seat. After a few awkward moments, someone found the courage to ask, "What has happened here? Why is it that we applauded after the actor prayed that same psalm and now we can only respond in silence to the woman's prayer?" Again there was silence, and then the actor replied, "I think I know the answer. As this woman spoke, we all suddenly realized that, yes, I knew the psalm, but *she* knows the Shepherd." How can we know, how can we name this God who is at once ineffable mystery and gentle shepherd in our midst? This is our question.

GOD, THE INEFFABLE MYSTERY

In the traditional language of the theologian, God is both infinite and pure spirit, a triune Godhead, a transcendent deity who is creator and sustainer of all life, the origin and goal of all human striving and of the universe itself. God is the One who was, who is, and who will be *in saecula saeculorum* (forever and ever), as the old Latin formula proclaimed. Throughout Christian history, moreover, theologians have reaffirmed the biblical insight of the fourth gospel and have reminded believers in various ways of this fundamental truth—that God is ultimately unknowable and that no one has ever seen God.

For example, one of the greatest North African Christian theologians of the fourth and fifth centuries, St. Augustine (354–430 C.E.), warned that if we think we have understood God, then what we have understood is, by definition, not God. John Chrysostom (347–407 C.E.), bishop of Constantinople and Doctor of the Church, was convinced that neither humans nor even angelic beings could know God:

> Let us invoke him as the inexpressible God, incomprehensible, invisible and unknowable. Let us affirm that he surpasses all power of human speech; that he eludes the grasp of every mortal intelligence; that the angels cannot penetrate him; that the seraphim cannot see him clearly; that the cherubim cannot fully understand him. For he is invisible to the principalities and powers, the virtues and all creatures, without exception. Only the Son and the Holy Spirit know him.[1]

Even Thomas Aquinas (ca. 1225–1274 c.e.), the "angelic Doctor" whose *Summa Theologiae* examined all that could be said of God by the greatest minds in the late medieval period, acknowledges that after all our theologizing, God remains unknowable: "All affirmations we can make about God are not such that our minds may rest in them, nor of such sort that we may suppose God does not transcend them."[2] For this reason then, speaking about God, or speaking to God, is learning to say (in the words of my Old Testament professor, William Holladay) "the least wrong thing about God," because anything we might say is, by definition, *always* wrong—wrong because our words can never fully capture or name adequately the infinite mystery we call God.[3]

Nevertheless, our finite minds still strain to know this mystery. We want both to know and to name God, but in this pursuit our language falters, words fail us, and our naming falls short of the mark. Because the infinite God is divine spirit, not reducible to finite human categories, the best we can do and the only way we can speak of God is to rely ultimately on metaphor and analogy. A metaphor is the application of a word or phrase to an object or concept that it does not literally denote in order to suggest a comparison. A metaphor points toward, but does not encompass or define. With respect to naming God, metaphorical language gives only a glimpse, an intimation of some aspect of the nature or character of God, but metaphor does not limit or define God. To sing, or to say, "a mighty fortress is our God, a bulwark never failing," is to speak of God's strength, God's solid and firm presence, God as our protective refuge, a safe haven in times of need. These metaphorical words suggest something about what we believe to be true of God; but they neither define nor limit God's being.

In the same way, our language for and about God relies on the use of simile. A simile is a figure of speech in which two unlike things are explicitly compared using the words *like* or *as*. The prophet Hosea (ca. 740 b.c.e.), for example, speaking in the words of God, gathers a string of similes as he tries to describe God's presence to wayward Israel: "So I will become *like* a lion to them, *like* a leopard I will lurk beside the way. I will fall upon them *like* a bear robbed of her cubs, and will tear open the covering of their heart; there I will devour them *like* a lion, *as* a wild animal would mangle them" (Hos 13:7–8). In the very next chapter of Hosea these violent animal images—these similes—give way to pictures of a gentle, forgiving God: "I will be *like* the dew to Israel. I am *like* an evergreen cypress; your faithfulness comes from me" (Hos 14:5a, 8c–d). In both sets of similes, Hosea reaches for words to describe adequately what he believes to be true of God. He draws his words and images from the world he knows, from the very world where he comes to know God.

The essential point is this: *All* our God language (biblical, theological, spiritual) is analogous and metaphorical. For if God is truly spirit, holy mystery, then it could not be otherwise. For this reason, moreover, we must hearken to the biblical injunction against fashioning images that become idolatrous: "You shall not make for yourself an idol, whether in the form of anything that is in heaven above, or that is in the earth beneath, or that is in the water under the earth. You shall not bow down to them or worship them" (Ex 20:4–5a). Walter Brueggemann, a prolific author, biblical theologian, and professor of Old Testament at Columbia Theological Seminary in Decatur, Georgia, explains the import of this commandment: "The temptation is not the creation of a rival that detracts from Yahweh, but an attempt to locate and thereby domesticate Yahweh in a visible, controlled object."[4] This biblical command against making images for God is a reminder to Israel, and to us, that God cannot be "captured" by our images, neither by objects nor by words. Instead we come to realize that the character of the biblical God is absolute freedom from all that seeks to limit or control divine presence in our midst. Whenever we claim that our words or our images are expressions of the *full identity* of God, we fall into idolatry. Whenever we claim that the metaphor is *synonymous with* the reality, we become idolaters.

From beginning to end, moreover, the Bible maintains an absolute distinction between ourselves as creatures and God as Creator. Again, the prophet Hosea provides an apt example. Claiming to be privy to the inner soliloquy of God, Hosea speaks of God's anger against an unfaithful people. But anger soon turns to anguish within the heart of God, and the prophet conveys God's singular, unique character: "I will not execute my fierce anger, I will not again destroy Ephraim; for I am God and no mortal, the Holy One in your midst" (Hos 11:9). God's character, God's very being, is utterly distinct from that of creatures. God is "God and no mortal."

So, too, are the ways of God beyond our comprehension. In the words of Second Isaiah, "For my thoughts are not your thoughts, nor are your ways my ways, says the LORD. For as the heavens are higher than the earth, so are my ways higher than your ways and my thoughts than your thoughts" (Isa 55:8–9). Many centuries later, the Jewish Pharisee turned Christian apostle, Paul, would echo the words of Isaiah in his letter to the Romans: "O the depth of the riches and wisdom and knowledge of God! How unsearchable are [God's] judgments and how inscrutable [God's] ways" (Rom 11:33). The starting point, therefore, of all our "God-talk" must be our acknowledgment that, in the final analysis, God remains unknowable.

BIBLICAL IMAGES FOR GOD

Despite this chasm of unknowing that separates creatures from the Creator, despite the biblical ban on creating images for the ineffable God, despite the utter inadequacy of all our God language—nevertheless, images and names for God abound, in the Bible and in our theological and spiritual tradition. The challenge for us always is to acknowledge the partiality and incompleteness of all that we say about God. We would be helped in this challenge if only we attended more carefully to the vast array of images and metaphors for God employed by the biblical authors themselves. One problem with the inadequacy of our God language is the fact that we have been so selective in our use of biblical (and nonbiblical) images for God. We have fixed on the few more dominant images of God in the Bible, many of which are exclusively masculine, coming as they do from the patriarchal world and culture of the time. The historical and cultural world of ancient Israel was patriarchal inasmuch as it focused on a male-dominant social and political system wherein women were subordinated to and dependent on the patriarch, the male head of the household in which they lived. Within such a patriarchal culture, God was imaged as a father, husband, warrior, judge, king, and the like. These images are all useful and to some extent also partly adequate and partly true, insofar as they communicate something of what we want to affirm about the God revealed to us. These images and metaphors are, at the same time, thoroughly untrue and inadequate because they can never capture fully the mystery who is God. There is always more; there is always mystery. No image or metaphor can fully satisfy. In Islam, Muslims pray by fingering a small set of beads while reciting the ninety-nine names of Allah. The litany of names envelops the suppliant, surrounding her or him with a profound sense of Allah's mysterious presence under such names as "Allah, the Subtle One, Allah, the Compassionate, Allah, the All Forgiving, Allah, the Guide to the Right Path," and so forth. This litany, like the Bible, draws on a vast array of ways to speak of God, each one offering some true dimension of the nature of the divine, but each one needing to be complemented by all the others. Therefore, the watch phrase I would always suggest is: "Multiply your metaphors!"

The Bible itself does just this. First, and most obviously, biblical images for God arise from the ready examples in the culture of different types of personal relationships: tribal, familial, marital, and interpersonal. So, the biblical God is at once *father* (Ps 68:5—"Father of orphans and protector of widows is God in his holy habitation"), *ancestral* God (Ex 3:6—"I am the God of your father, the God of Abraham, the God of Isaac, and the God of Jacob"), *mother to the people* (Isa 66:13—"As a mother comforts her child, so I will comfort you"), *husband* (Isa 54:5—"For your Maker is your husband, the Lord of hosts is his name"), *male and female lover* (Song of Songs, throughout), *helper* (Ps 54:4—"But surely, God is my helper; the Lord is the upholder of my life"), and *companion and friend* (Ex 33:11—"Thus the Lord used to speak to Moses face to face, as one speaks to a friend").

Many biblical images for God name the deity not only with personal, relational metaphors but also with political metaphors. Most prevalent, of course, is the enigmatic name of God spoken to Moses from the burning bush—YHWH, Adonai, the Lord (Ex 3:14). This is the God who pronounces commandments and calls Israelites to obedience as their only *Master* and *Lord*. But God is also addressed as *king* (Ps 10:16—"The Lord is king forever and ever; the nations shall perish from his land"), *savior* (Ps 106:21—"They forgot God, their savior, who had done great things in Egypt"), *redeemer* (Isa 60:16—"and you shall know that I, the Lord, am your Savior and your Redeemer, the Mighty One of Jacob"), *liberator* (Ex 6:7—"You shall know that I am the LORD, your God who has freed you from the burdens of the Egyptians"), *warrior* (Ex 15:3—"The LORD is a warrior; the LORD is his name"), *protector* (Ps 68:5—"Father of orphans and protector of widows is God in his holy habitation"), *prosecuting attorney* (Mic 6:2—"Hear, you mountains, the controversy of the LORD . . . , for the LORD has a controversy [lawsuit] with his people"), and *judge* (Gen 18:25—"Shall not the Judge of all the earth do what is just?").

The biblical portrait of God is also enriched by metaphors related to crafts and professions in ancient Israel. Perhaps the most familiar text in all of scripture (Psalm 23) praises the God who is *shepherd* to the flock, celebrating God's tender care for us, God's people. The prophet Jeremiah likens God to a *potter* working the lump of clay: "Can I not do with you, O house of Israel, just as this potter has done? says the LORD. Just like the clay in the potter's hand, so are you in my hand, O house of Israel" (Jer 18:6). God is also a *washerwoman* who cleanses us from our iniquity (Ps 51:2); a *healer* who restores us to health in mind, body, and spirit (Jer 17:14); the *midwife* who guided our birth (Ps 22:9); and even the *knitter* who fashioned us in the womb before we were born (Ps 139:13). God is both *construction worker* and *jeweler* setting precious stones (Isa 54:11–12), *blacksmith* (Isa 54:16), and *teacher* of Israel (Isa 30:20).

Animal metaphors for God also appear in scripture and show the imaginative creativity of the faith of ancient people. God can be likened to a *mother eagle* carrying its young on her wings (Deut 32:11; Ex 19:4). Perhaps this image of the eagle's wings shaped Jesus' words as he laments over Jerusalem: "Jerusalem, Jerusalem. . . . [H]ow often have I desired to gather your children together as a *mother hen* gathers her brood under her wings, and you were not willing" (Lk 13:34; Mt 23:37). To use again an example cited earlier, the prophet Hosea describes God's just anger against unfaithful Israel in fierce animal images: "So I will become like a *lion* to them, like a *leopard* I will lurk beside the way. I will fall upon them like a *bear* robbed of her cubs, I will tear open the covering of their heart; there I will devour them like a *lion*, as a *wild animal* would mangle them" (Hos 13:7–8). By the use of such a wide variety of different images for God, the biblical writers attest to the necessity and importance of multiplying metaphors.

This same intuition is at work in the multiple compound titles given to God in the scriptures. The ordinary Semitic word for a deity is *El*, a word common in both Ugaritic and Canaanite traditions. Israelite beginnings in Canaan naturally adopted both language and practices from their Canaanite neighbors. In order to speak of their God, whose unique name—YHWH—was revealed to Moses, they addressed and worshiped this deity under a variety of other titles. Abraham (Gen 14:22) worshiped YHWH under the name "El Elyon"—God Most High, the creator God whose sovereignty extends over all the nations. At Beer-sheba (Gen 21:33), Abraham knew God as "El Olam"—the Everlasting God. In Exodus 6:3 we learn that YHWH is "El Shaddai," a name with puzzling origins. Does it mean "God of the mountains," or is *shaddai* a metaphorical term pointing to God's manifestation in the mountain storms such as Moses or Elijah saw at Sinai (Ex 19; 1 Kings 19)? This same God is at once "El Roi" (God of Vision—Gen 16:13), "El Berith" (the God of the Covenant—Judg 9:46), and "El Elohe Israel" (El the God of Israel—Gen 33:19–20). And finally, the name "El Bethel" (Gen 35:7) illustrates a fundamental claim that Israel's God is the one who appears in certain specific places, like Bethel, where the ancestor Jacob first met God in a dream. This multiplicity of names and images speaks for itself. It reminds us that the biblical God cannot be adequately known by only one image. And this God is indeed a *God beyond all names*.

MATERNAL IMAGES FOR GOD

Masculine imagery for God may be more prevalent in the Bible because the Bible took shape within an androcentric culture in the ancient world. Nevertheless, maternal images for God appear much more frequently than we have ever recognized. The very first verse of the whole Bible, for example, speaks of a God whose presence is manifest in a creative spirit (the feminine Hebrew noun—*ruah*) hovering over the chaos waters. As the story of salvation history begins to unfold, moreover, God is revealed to Moses as a God who is "merciful and gracious" (Ex 34:6). Here, it is essential to realize that the English word *merciful* translates the Hebrew term related to *rehem*—meaning "womb." This fundamental affirmation about the character of God highlights God's motherly compassion, God's womb love. Over a hundred times, the biblical writers reiterate this feminine image of God through the use of the gender-specific term—*womb*—to describe God's compassion, mercy, and tenderness. So, for example, Moses can remind the Israelites: "Because the LORD your God is a merciful [*rahum*] God, he will neither abandon you nor destroy you; he will not forget the covenant with your ancestors that he swore to them" (Deut 4:31). Later the prophet Isaiah would echo the same conviction about God when he gives voice to God's question: "Can a woman forget her nursing child, or show no compassion [*rahem*] for the child of her womb? Even these may forget, yet I will not forget you" (Isa 49:15). The same prophet can describe God's passionate distress at the suffering of the people with these words: "For a long time I have held my peace, I have kept still and restrained myself; now I will cry out like a woman in labor, I will gasp and pant" (Isa 42:14).

Jeremiah's (ca. 630–587 B.C.E.) vision of God's covenant love is replete with feminine imagery, as, for example when God asks: "Is Ephraim my dear son? Is he the child I delight in? As often as I speak against him, I still remember him. Therefore I am deeply moved for him; I will surely have mercy [motherly compassion] on him, says the LORD" (Jer 31:22b).[5] These few examples point to the rich biblical tradition that freely uses maternal images to describe and name the unseen God. Images such as these function as fundamental symbols for the mercy and tender compassion that characterize Israel's God. Not simply a God of vengeance and warlike wrath, as some have wrongly thought, but a mother God surrounding the children of her womb with warm mercy—this, too, is the God revealed to ancient Israel.

CONCLUSION

Who, then, is the God of the Bible? And how shall we name this God? Even this brief survey of such a vast array of names, images, and metaphors for God in the Bible should teach us that the biblical God can never be captured in a single title, metaphor, or name. Rather, this God can be known only in the continual unfolding of revelation day by day, a revelation that in the biblical story will finally bring us face to face with Jesus, "the only Son . . . who has made [God] known" (Jn 1:18).

QUESTIONS FOR REFLECTION

1. Which are your favorite names or images for God? Why do these images capture your attention and imagination?
2. For each of the images you named, what are their strengths, and what are their weaknesses? How are they adequate metaphors for God, and where are they inadequate? Why?
3. Of all the biblical images discussed in this chapter, which do you prefer, and why? Which do you reject, and why?
4. Have your images for God changed over time? What factors contributed to these changes?
5. Why, do you think, does the Bible contain so many different ways of speaking about and naming God?
6. Muslims pray with the ninety-nine names of Allah. How would you compose your own list of ninety-nine names for the God who has touched your life and called you to follow?

3

THE RIDDLE OF THE WORLD

When I look at your heavens, . . . what are human
beings that you are mindful of them,
mortals that you care for them?

—Psalm 8:3–4

Who among us has never looked up into the spectacular beauty of a
clear night sky and wondered, as this psalmist did long ago, "Who am I,
and what is the meaning of my life?" This basic, essential human question lies at the heart of every religious quest. The answer to the question resides deep within us and provides the foundation of our spirituality. The answer grounds our identity in the relationship we claim to
have with the Holy Mystery who is God. This relationship is an ongoing
personal dialogue, an "I . . . Thou" encounter, as the Jewish philosopher
Martin Buber (1878–1965) once said. Buber taught that human beings
have two kinds of relationships: those in which they enter into dialogue
and communion with another (I–Thou: subject–subject) and those in
which they are passive observers (I–it: subject–object). God, for Buber,
is the eternal Thou with whom we humans are always in dialogue. In
the context of this encounter, gradually we come to know the truth of
who we are. Slowly, we begin to see what is most authentic in our
human existence. And finally, if we are people of faith, we recognize
that our lives find their ultimate fulfillment in response to the voice of
this mysterious Other. Or, as St. Augustine puts it: "You have made us
for yourself, O Lord, and our hearts are restless till they rest in You"
(*Confessions*, I.i[1]).

THE RIDDLE OF HUMAN EXISTENCE

In the previous chapter we explore some of the manifold ways the biblical authors named or tried to describe and understand God. Now we must ask the question about the other partner in this relationship with God that we call our spirituality—ourselves as human creatures. The British poet Alexander Pope (1688–1744) might provide a starting point. In his poem "Riddle of the World," Pope reflects on the great paradoxes of human existence:

> Know then thyself, presume not God to scan,
> the proper study of Mankind is Man.
> Plac'd on the isthmus of a middle state,
> a Being darkly wise and rudely great:
> With too much knowledge for the Sceptic side,
> With too much weakness for the Stoic's pride,
> He hangs between; in doubt to act or rest;
> In doubt to deem himself a God or Beast;
> In doubt his mind or body to prefer;
> Born but to die and reasoning but to err;
> Alike in ignorance, his reason such,
> Whether he thinks too little or too much:
> Chaos of thought and Passion, all confus'd;
> Still by himself abus'd, or disabus'd;
> Created half to rise and half to fall;
> Great Lord of all things, yet a prey to all;
> Sole judge of truth, in endless error hurl'd;
> The glory, jest, and riddle of the world![1]

Pope's poem captures well the ambiguities that we experience in our quest for authentic living. He has put his finger on the paradox of our capacity for both knowledge and ignorance; he has named the struggle we often have between our rational and irrational selves. He has described our ultimate fate: "created half to rise and half to fall." He has, in short, captured something essential about the human dilemma.

A contemporary Catholic theologian, Richard McBrien, borrows from the work of the German existentialist philosopher Martin Heidegger (1889–1976) to address the same question of the nature of human existence in our day. McBrien explores and comments on Heidegger's helpful listing of the so-called polarities of human existence.[2] The first polarity he names is the tension we experience between our *freedom* and *finitude*. On the one hand, as both the psalmist and the poet also note, we are created with seemingly limitless possibilities, with immense potential and capacity for greatness. "You have made us little less than a god," the psalmist says. But that potential is tempered and constrained by our finite reality. For each of us, our particular, concrete reality (race, gender, culture, intelligence, health, temperament, life experiences, etc.) places limits on us.

A second polarity in human existence is the tension within us between rationality and irrationality and between truth and error. Or, as Pope describes us, we are "sole judge of truth, in endless error hurl'd." We recognize within ourselves a tendency toward the good and the true. Our minds lean toward truth, and yet we know ourselves as fallible in every way. We are often seduced by falsehoods, led astray by competing claims, and often unable to discern between good and evil. Especially in our contemporary world we are becoming increasingly skeptical about the reliability of any "truth claims" at all. Even more, there are times when reason itself eludes us and the irrational powers that are part of our nature seem to take the upper hand, or, as Pope has said, we are "chaos of thought and Passion, all confus'd."

A third polarity that describes our human existence is that between responsibility and impotence. Within us often there is an intuitive sense of what is required of us, of what we ought to do in a given situation. At the same time, we know ourselves as weak and impotent, incapable of doing that very thing that we feel called to do. The apostle Paul seems to describe this dilemma exactly when he writes: "For I do not do the good I want, but I do the evil I do not want" (Rom 7:19). Haven't we all shared Paul's same quandary?

A fourth polarity exists between *anxiety* and *hope*. On the one hand, there is a gnawing uncertainty that often disturbs us and causes great anxiety in our day-to-day lives. It can be summed up in the questions: What and whom can I trust? Is life really just absurd? Am I deceiving myself to think there is a purpose to all this? And yet those who live with hope reject such questions and reaffirm their conviction that life has meaning and that they participate in a whole totality of existence that is ultimately good and worthwhile. Human existence, moreover, for these people makes sense because it strains toward the goal of everlasting life.

Finally, there is a fifth polarity McBrien names that manifests itself in the tension between *individual existence* and our participation in *society*. Human beings, together with many animal species, are essentially social creatures. This means that we find our fulfillment in relationships and in human community. Our sexuality and our capacity for language and intricate patterns of communication, as McBrien notes, "make this unmistakably clear."[3] But death marks a boundary of our human existence, and we cross that boundary alone: "Authentic existence requires that we come to terms with our own death and that we recognize it for what it is: the boundary and limit of our own personal existence."[4]

For each one of us, then, the search for an authentic spirituality happens in the context of these polarities or paradoxes of our human existence. We are creatures, not the Creator. We exist as finite, fallible, limited beings, not as those who are infinite and all-knowing. We are dependent and interdependent on one another and on all the rest of creation itself; we are not autonomous. Our search for authenticity invites us to intimacy, vulnerability, and ultimately self-transcendence.

"WHO ARE WE, THAT YOU ARE MINDFUL OF US?" (PS 8)

Let us return now to the psalmist's question set at the beginning of the chapter. The Bible, as a whole, offers a variety of responses to this query, but three affirmations stand out as the core of biblical anthropology: (1) human beings are created—male and female—in the very image of God, (2) human beings are interdependent with all other created beings and find our fulfillment in human community, and (3) human beings are touched to our very core (in the language of the theologian) by both sin and grace.

"LET US MAKE HUMANKIND [ADAM] ACCORDING TO OUR IMAGE" (GEN 1:26)

Set at the very beginning of the biblical narrative in Genesis, two distinct creation stories (the postexilic, Priestly account in Gen 1:1–2:4a and the earlier, preexilic, Yahwist account in Gen 2:4b–3:24) stand side by side and together establish in different ways some fundamental convictions about the nature of the created order and the nature and place of human beings within that order.[5] The Yahwist account is so named because it prefers always to refer to God by the name YHWH. The Priestly account gets its name from the cultic and priestly concerns that have a prominent place in its story. (Chapter 5 discusses these distinctions more fully.) In the narrative structure of Genesis, the chronologically later "P" account stands first, with its "compressed and repetitive structure of announcement and execution":[6] "God said, Let there be . . . ; and there was. . . ." Central to this story are the theological convictions of the Priestly writer that affirm (1) the dependence of all creation on the divine commitment to create life; (2) the measured, intrinsic order and harmony in all of creation—"Evening came and morning followed . . ."—established by divine command; and (3) the creation of *adam*, the human species, as the crowning act of the week of creation.[7]

Essential to the Bible's revelation concerning human beings is the divine statement and resulting narrative report in Genesis 1:26–28:

> 26 And God said:
> "Let us make *adam* in our image, according to our likeness,
> and let them have dominion over the fish of the sea and
> the birds of the air,
> and the cattle and all the earth
> and everything that creeps upon the earth."
> 27 And God created *adam* in his image,
> in the image of God he created him;
> male and female he created them.
> 28 And God blessed them,
> and God said to them:
> "Be fruitful and multiply and fill the earth and subdue it,
> and have dominion over the fish of the sea and the
> birds of the air
> and every living creature that creeps upon the earth."

First, the essential affirmation of the text is the claim that humanity, the human species as a whole, has been created by God's express intent "in the divine image" and "according to the divine likeness." This unique claim concerns human creatures alone as the crown of God's creative act and implies that human beings have a particular identity that marks their existence. As the image and likeness of God (the *imago dei*), we human beings are not God, but we do share the divine stamp. We manifest a resemblance to the divine that shows itself in our relationship to God and to the rest of creation.

The biblical language in this text, particularly the verbs of *subduing* and *having dominion over* the earth, are rightly distasteful to modern ecological sensibilities, but for the Priestly writer they point more to the royal prerogative of *adam*'s character than to humanity's destructive or abusive license. What is most essential and definitive about this first creation story is its insistence that *adam* reflects in some significant, though unspecified way, the very *image* of God. This status attributes to *adam* a dignity unsurpassed by the rest of creation. And the fact that Genesis 1:27 explicitly defines *adam* as "male and female" means that our contemporary claims about the mutual dignity of women and men in their capacity to image God are entirely correct and faithful to the biblical revelation. Moreover, this affirmation of human dignity, male and female, is essential to the very fabric of creation itself and to its enduring permanence. Therefore, according to this fundamental biblical insight, whatever jeopardizes or diminishes the dignity of *adam*, male and female, violates God's created order.

Bishop Irenaeus of Lyon (ca. 130–200 C.E.) understood this claim about human dignity when he wrote, in the oft-quoted Latin phrase, *Gloria dei vivens homo*, the "glory of God is the human person fully alive." By this phrase, therefore, he maintains that God's very being is at stake in the full flourishing of creation and in human creation as its summit and crown. This is the first and most essential biblical claim about the nature of human beings. We alone are created in God's image; but we alone also bear the awesome responsibility to live as God's "image and likeness" in the world.

"THIS AT LAST IS BONE OF MY BONES AND FLESH OF MY FLESH" (GEN 2:23)

The Priestly creation story of Genesis 1, however, says little about questions of human sexual identity and the divine intention concerning the relationship of male and female in human creation. We must turn to the Yahwist creation story in Genesis 2–3 to discover clues to help us in this quest. The Priestly creation account in Genesis sees sexual identity in strictly biological terms, related to procreation and to the permanence of human creation itself. The Yahwist writer, by contrast, explicitly addresses the psychosocial character of human sexuality.[8] And these important insights add to our understanding of what, according to the biblical witness, it means to be "human."

This Yahwist story of creation lacks the solemn, rhythmic tone of the Priestly tale. Instead God appears here as the avuncular friend who, later in Genesis 3:8, walks and talks with the first couple in the garden in the "evening breeze." In the opening of the story, however, God is the divine artisan, the skillful potter, who fashions out of the dust of the earth (*adamah*) the earth creature (*adam*) and then breathes life into the creature, provides a garden home for this *adam*, and places *adam* in its midst.[9] In this creation account, *adam* is not the last to be created but, rather, the first. But *adam* in this Yahwist story is at first a creature without sexuality who must wait for full personhood (and full sexual identity) as the narrative unfolds. The same affirmation and dignity exist here for *adam* as in the previous narrative, but there is even more to learn in this second creation story.

The garden habitat for *adam* is indeed lush and well watered and provides every kind of fruit-bearing tree (Gen 2:9–14). As the story makes plain, however, God recognizes that all this is not yet enough.

For God sees that *adam* is alone and this is "not good" (Gen 2:18). So the divine artisan once again intervenes to provide a "helper/companion" (*ezer*) for *adam*.[10] God formed all the other living creatures out of the *adamah*: the beasts, the birds, the cattle (Gen 2:19–20). *Adam* gives names to all these creatures, but for *adam* "there was not found an *ezer* fit for him" (Gen 2:20). And so the story moves to a new and pivotal moment.

This moment is clothed in utter mystery, as the Lord God first "caused a deep sleep to fall upon *adam*" (Gen 2:21a) and by divine intent decides to "make an *ezer* fit for him." Now portrayed as the divine "anesthesiologist and surgeon," God removed a portion of the body of *adam*, a rib, built the rib into woman (*issa*), and brought her to *adam*. And then, for the first time, we hear *adam* speak. The words convey a truth so profound that it can only be expressed in poetry, not in prose: "This, at last, is bone of my bone and flesh of my flesh. This shall be called woman [*issa*] because she was taken out of man [*is*]" (Gen 2:23). Only now, with this poetic exclamation and the introduction of these two new terms, do we learn that the earth creature has become complete: "woman and man, female and male." The uniqueness of this creative act, the mystery and deep sleep clouding its exact contours, and the poetic affirmation of mutuality all alert us to its profound importance. The narrative comment that ends this unit also makes this plain: "Therefore, a man [*is*] leaves his father and his mother and cleaves to his wife [*issa*], and they become one flesh" (Gen 2:24).

The new creature, now defined as woman and man, becomes that fitting "companion/helper" (*ezer*) for each other, and together they are one flesh. This divinely intended partnership is the bedrock and essential fabric of human existence, established by God in creation, as Phyllis Bird so clearly states: "Companionship, the sharing of work, mutual attraction and commitment in a bond superseding all other human bonds and attractions—these are the ends for which *adam* was created male and female and these are the signs of the intended partnership."[11] Contrary to much traditional commentary on this text, its tone stresses mutuality and equality, not subordination of female to male. And if we attend to this text in the manner outlined by Bird and Trible we find another biblical affirmation of the innate dignity of our human existence and one that affirms explicitly the equality and interdependence of male and female in the plan of God.

A LOVE STORY GONE AWRY

As we have seen, the biblical writer in Genesis 2 reflects on the power and promise of the divine intent for human existence, male and female. But this story does not have the last word. Tragically, the love story has, as the Old Testament scholar Phyllis Trible says, "gone awry."[12] Genesis 3, accordingly, narrates the account of the "Fall." Here, we encounter the sobering reality of the consequences of human freedom and our frightening capacity to thwart divine intent.

As noted above, both creation accounts in Genesis highlight the theme of the dignity bestowed on human creation by God's explicit intent. Both affirm that the human species, male and female together, has been gifted with the same dignity and status as God's image and likeness on earth. But it is the Yahwist writer who sees the darker side of human potential and portrays the desire of the first couple to usurp their creaturely status and to "be like God" (Gen 3:5). This writer employs Israelite wisdom and the rich traditions of other ancient Near Eastern myths to answer the puzzling questions of his day. What is the origin of evil? Why is there such pain in childbirth? Why are human life and striving so difficult? What is the source of the enmity between humans and the serpent world? In the context of these questions and ponderings, the Yahwist writer weaves a story at once tragic and profound.

The story actually opens at the very end of Genesis 2 with the idyllic picture of the man and woman in the garden, naked but without shame (Gen 2:25). The picture is one of innocence and harmony, the "love story" filled with delight. But immediately in the next verse the serpent enters, and trouble begins. In the mythic world of the text, the serpent symbolizes evil, and cunning, that sets itself against God. In the conversation that ensues between the serpent and the woman, they speak *about* God as if God were an outsider and not the One who created them both. They claim to know the mind of God and pretend to interpret God's ways. There is pathos and futility in this picture.

The only negative command God had given in the garden concerned a certain tree in its midst: "But of the tree of the knowledge of good and evil you shall not eat, for in the day you eat of it you shall die" (Gen 2:17). The woman knows, understands, recalls, and even repeats this command to the serpent. But the serpent is a wily sort, twisting the words around and denying their intent. And so, as the story goes, the woman weighs the options, considers the tree and its fruit, and desiring to have wisdom, takes the fruit and eats. The man is a weak and willing accomplice, saying nothing, as he, too, eats the forbidden fruit. Only when both have eaten is their shared transgression clear. Suddenly, the innocence is gone, and they cower in the shame of their nakedness.

The interrogation by God that follows is almost pathetic, as both the woman and the man point the finger of blame elsewhere: "Not I . . . , the woman did it," he says. "Not I . . . , the serpent did it," she says (Gen 3:12–13). Compromising their dignity, they appear as no more than bickering children. But the story is not about child's play; and it has forbidding consequences. To the serpent God pronounces a curse that it must crawl in the dust of the earth. But on the woman and the man God bestows a punishment: for the woman, pain in childbearing and subordination to her husband; for the man, toil and drudgery in tilling the unproductive soil. And God then banished them from the garden.

This timeless story attempts to capture the tragic side of human existence: creature set against Creator, willful in disobedience, and with unchecked hubris, desiring to be "like God." Both the woman's assertive tactics and the man's passive complicity receive an equal measure of blame and of punishment. Their punishments rupture the harmony God had ordained between human beings and the earth and, even more tragically, between the woman and the man, *is* and *issa*. What began as a partnership of equals in the garden ends in alienation from each other and from the earth. This is not God's intent for creation but the tragic consequence of sin in which, by virtue of our humanity, every human being participates.

CONCLUSION

In its own marvelous and limited way, this story comes to us with profound truth about ourselves. It lays out for us, at the very beginning of the Bible, both the promise and the limits of our own humanity and the degree to which our very freedom can deal death to us and not life. Finally, it sounds a caution at the outset and reminds us of our need for God. Left only to ourselves, we are sometimes a very sorry lot. As Paul the apostle would write many, many years later describing the human condition: "All have sinned and fall short of the glory of God" (Rom 3:23).

But what do these realizations about humanity have to do with a spirituality that leads to being whole, loving, and fully alive? First they reaffirm for us the conviction that human origin and destiny are bound closely to the earth and the whole created universe. The earth, this garden into which we have been placed, is ours to revere, to tend, and to care for as cocreators with God. If we jeopardize this essential harmony by our rapacious actions, disaster follows. Second, these stories hold out for us the divine vision and intent for human living in the relationship of male and female. Surely without a thought for our modern feminist questions, the ancient authors nevertheless preserved for us a vision of humanity as one creation, living in mutuality and mutual responsibility as the very image of God. It was our sinfulness that disrupted these harmonious relations with the earth and with one another. And so our fulfillment as "whole, loving, and fully alive" persons is bound up with our striving to restore these harmonies once again. *Our well-being deepens as we learn to reverence the rest of creation and to treat all others with the profound respect due to them as creatures, like us, fashioned in the image of God.*

And as we continue to ponder today the meaning of our lives as human beings, the words of Alexander Pope keep resounding in our ears, and we cannot escape the truth. We know all too well the riddle that we are:

> Created half to rise and half to fall;
> Great Lord of all things, yet a prey to all;
> Sole judge of truth, in endless error hurl'd;
> The glory, jest, and riddle of the world!

QUESTIONS FOR REFLECTION

1. Recall an experience like that of the psalmist when you, too, have "looked at the heavens" and wondered about the meaning of life and your own personal existence. What thoughts fill your heart and mind at such moments? How would you compose your own personal psalm?
2. Which of the human polarities described in this chapter do you most experience? When, and how? How does your faith help you to cope with these?
3. Which lines of Pope's poem most ring true for you today, and why?
4. As you read the creation stories of Genesis, what do these stories have to say to *your* life? How have they shaped your understanding (negatively or positively) of the relationship between male and female?
5. In what ways do you experience your own sinfulness, your own experience of this "love story gone awry"? What does this story of the "Fall" in Genesis 3 teach us about ourselves and about God?

4

THE GOD OF BLESSING AND SALVATION

On that very day, they ate of the
produce of the land. . . . And the
manna ceased on the morrow.

—Joshua 5:11–12

How does God interact with creation? What can the Bible tell us about
the character of God's dealings with the world? In our concrete human
lives, where and how is God to be found? These are some of the questions we explore in this chapter. How we answer these questions, or
how others before us have answered them, depends in large part on the
particular situation and concrete historical circumstances in which we
find ourselves.

It is more than a simple and self-evident axiom to say: "Where we
stand determines what we see." The corporate executive, for example,
will perceive the world and God very differently from the day laborer
eking out existence on the edge of survival. These two will see the world
differently, imagine differently, and hope differently. The homeless
man or woman will relate to a God whom the millionaire can scarcely
comprehend. The disabled find God in places, both physical and spiritual, where the able-bodied cannot go. The rich and powerful often
know the world as a place of favor and delight and God as the great
provider. The poor and powerless, on the other hand, see only misery
around them, and they cling to meager fragments of hope in God and in
a future yet to be. The *place* where we stand, literally and figuratively,
shapes the way we see the world and the way we experience and name
God within it.

In the "good times" of our lives, when all seems to be going well, we
are likely to experience God as a supportive companion and friend who

is the source of life and of all the good gifts that come to us. But in moments of brokenness, in times of sorrow and pain, the only God we know is the One to whom we desperately cry out for help and comfort. These examples illustrate a basic principle that underlies all our contemporary theology and our attempts to articulate what we believe about God. The principle simply stated is this: Our beliefs about God did not drop out of the sky or come to us in a prepackaged form. They are the fruit of our ongoing reflection on our experience of the world *where we are* and where we believe God is revealed to us.[1]

These daily experiences are the "raw data" of our theology. These data include also the reservoir of wisdom that comes down to us from previous generations, the explicit teachings and sacred texts of our faith tradition, our experience of the beauty and power of the natural world around us that speak to us of God, and all the day-to-day interactions of our lives that are revelatory of God to us—to name some of the most obvious sources of God's disclosure. It was exactly this process, of experience and ongoing reflection on experience in the community of faith guided by the Spirit, that produced the sacred books we call the Bible.

"IN MANY AND VARIOUS WAYS GOD SPOKE OF OLD TO OUR ANCESTORS" (HEB 1:1)

One of the first observations any student of the Bible makes is to recognize the great diversity of theological perspectives contained within this multifaceted text. But among these multiple traditions two principal, overarching perspectives seem to dominate. Like the harmonic voices of a melody and its counterpoint, they play *with*—and sometimes *against*—one another throughout the whole of the biblical story. In terms of dominance, one "sounds" more loudly and with greater insistence than the other, but both are essential—no, indispensable—for an integral and comprehensive understanding of the biblical God. Biblical interpreters have called these two different perspectives and theological tendencies "saving theology," on the one hand, and "blessing theology," on the other.[2] Each conveys essential insights about God and God's relationship to the world. Both are utterly "true," and together they offer fundamental biblical wisdom about the ways of God.

SAVING THEOLOGY

In order to explore the contours of each of these theological approaches it will be necessary to look at them in sequence, one by one. But, in fact, they cannot really be separated like that, either in the experiences of our contemporary lives or in the biblical story. Their value rests precisely in their complementarity. But, so that we might understand each perspective better, we will explore their distinctive insights separately and will begin with the more dominant tradition, called "saving theology."[3] For each perspective, the saving and blessing theologies, I note its distinct origin in human experience, its images of God and of humanity, its dominant goal, and the way in which it has differing implications for our contemporary spirituality.

First, then, let us attend to the Bible's saving theology. When our biblical ancestors set about to tell the story of their faith, they began with some "preliminary" matters that serve as a prelude to their history as a people. These preliminary narratives constitute the book of Genesis and include the creation accounts, the primeval legends of the flood and its aftermath, and the ancestral sagas of the families of Abraham/Sarah, Isaac/Rebekah, Jacob/Rachael, and Joseph. But the real "history" (if we may call it that) of this people begins with the Exodus—with the story of their salvation, their dramatic rescue at the sea (which I deal with in greater depth in chapter 5). This story depicts Israel's God as the deity who had rescued them from bondage under Pharaoh in Egypt.[4] They saw their beginnings as a people in being saved from slavery and oppression, and—from the perspective of saving theology—their understanding of their God originates in that event.

This foundational event, furthermore, shapes in its entirety the great biblical drama we call "salvation history." This story traces the journey of God's people from slavery in Egypt under a hostile pharaoh to freedom in the promised land (ca. 1250–1100 B.C.E.), from social and political insignificance to their short-lived dominance as a great nation (1050–587 B.C.E.). This salvation story survives through the experience of the Babylonian exile (587–538 B.C.E.), when many inhabitants of Jerusalem were taken off into exile, and in the rebuilding of the Temple in Jerusalem after they returned to their land (ca. 515 B.C.E.). This same story of salvation history traces the journey of the postexilic community of Jews up to the time of Jesus. All through these biblical stories we hear the memory of God's saving deeds on Israel's behalf, not once but again and again throughout their history. God, in this perspective, therefore, is the God who acts, the One who is their savior and redeemer. Through this lens of saving theology, God's very name and identity are synonymous with these saving deeds, as Joshua will remind the

Israelites after they entered into the land: "For it is the LORD our God who brought us and our ancestors up from the land of Egypt, out of the house of slavery, and who did those great signs in our sight" (Josh 24:17).

It is almost as though God's very name for them is hyphenated as the "God-who-brought-us-up-from-the-land-of-Egypt." Like the great *deus ex machina* (literally, "the god from the machine") of Greek drama in which the deity entered the drama by means of a crane from off stage, so, too, the savior God of ancient Israel comes from nowhere to intervene and rescue God's needy people. The power of this image of God rests in its element of surprise and unpredictability. At any moment, this God can break into our lives as our savior. But there is something contrived, as well, in such an image, making God into a magic miracle worker, not a constant presence in our lives.

The implication for what it means to be human from this perspective of saving theology, therefore, is to know ourselves as impoverished and bereft apart from God's saving power. It means recognizing our poverty and radical need of God's mighty power. Once rescued, we desire to spend ourselves in rendering homage and service to this God who saved us. Faithful obedience to God, expressed in fidelity to covenant demands, we are convinced, is the only fitting response. In this view, the memory of God's saving deeds shapes human consciousness and ought to instill in human beings an abiding sense of gratitude and solidarity with others in need of rescue like themselves. The goal of human existence, in this perspective, is liberation and freedom. It is ultimately to find *life*—life lived to each one's full human potential. From this vantage point, realizing one's human dignity depends on faithful obedience to God; there is no other way. These ways that Israelites understood God and the world are the consequence and outgrowth of their dramatic rescue by God in the Exodus event. As we will see in a moment, this theological viewpoint has significant implications for our spirituality today.

BLESSING THEOLOGY

There are other circumstances in our lives, however, when we experience God primarily as the source of blessing and providential care. These are the times when we see the world as a hospitable place, when our lives are marked by satisfaction and success, when we have good health, the sustenance we need, and can live freely in happiness—these experiences open us to know God as constant protector and the provider of all good gifts. In ancient Israel, it was the elders and parental guardians of the tribes, the royal counselors, the scribes and sages, and the priestly leaders of the people who became the guardians of the traditions associated with blessing theology. Their positions of authority and power gave them a vision of life that saw God as their friend and kingly counterpart. Blessing theology originates from these positive experiences of giftedness and blessing.

In the Bible, this strain of theological reflection envisions God predominantly as a king who governs the world with power and right judgment and who establishes all things in order and harmony. This is the God, for example, of Psalm 96:10: "Say among the nations, 'The LORD reigns! Yea, the world is established, it shall never be moved; he will judge the peoples with equity.'" The God of blessing establishes cosmic order and holds the world in existence at every moment. This is the view of God as Creator and source of all wisdom about the mysteries of life. Through the lens of blessing theology God is not a deity who intervenes only at dramatic moments of crisis and need but, rather, is ever present in the midst of the world, creating and sustaining it.

From the perspective of blessing theology, to be human means to share kingship and wisdom with God. It means to see oneself, not as deprived and needy, but as created fully in "the image and likeness of God." This insight is perfectly expressed in the words of another psalmist: "You have made them [i.e., human beings] a little lower than God, and crowned them with glory and honor. You have given them dominion over the works of your hands; you have put all things under their feet" (Ps 8:5–6). And because of this royal status human beings must care for the world and for all creation as God does. They share God's wisdom and knowledge of the world and exercise their God-given "dominion," as the psalmist says. Understood through the lens of blessing theology, therefore, the goal of human striving is also the fullness of *life*—but life now understood as the rightful exercise of power and the sharing of divine privilege. This perspective breeds an awareness of noblesse oblige (literally, "nobility obliges"), which fosters a sense of responsibility for creation in those who share this view. As we continue to listen to the wisdom of the biblical story, we will encounter both these viewpoints in the theological perspectives expressed by the terms *saving* and *blessing theology*. It remains now to explore their implications for our contemporary spiritual lives.

IMPLICATIONS FOR CONTEMPORARY SPIRITUALITY

As people of faith, surely we can identify with both of the perspectives outlined above. We can, no doubt, recall moments when we have experienced God as the One who has saved us *and* as the One who blesses our lives day by day. This is, of course, the point. Both these ways of understanding God capture something essential in our experience of faith. But there are tendencies in each perspective that have both positive and negative consequences for our faith lives.

The popular hymn "Amazing Grace" captures at once the power and the danger of saving theology: "Amazing grace, how sweet the sound that saved a wretch like me! I once was lost, but now am found, was blind but now I see." The human experience of being "lost" and "blind," unable to find our way, powerless in the face of forces beyond our control (whether political, economic, physical, or psychological), is a shattering feeling. And when we sense that God has intervened to rescue us, to save us and put us again on the path of life, our lives are radically changed by that encounter. In these moments we know our need for God, in the marrow of our bones. And, because of our personal experience of rescue, we trust the God who saves us. Gratitude can be our only response, and our one desire is to place ourselves, in humble obedience, in the hands of a saving God. This is the strength and grace of saving theology.

And yet a spirituality grounded exclusively in this view of saving theology risks exaggerating the one dramatic moment of God's saving presence at the exclusion of the constant daily closeness of a God who is always with us. This saving perspective, with its heightened awareness of our human frailty, our sinfulness and need, can leave us with a twisted sense of human depravity, a distrust of self, and an unhealthy notion of our own lack of self-worth. An exaggerated focus on the dramatic *before* and *after* of the saving event loses sight of the fact that our lives, and our faith journeys, are lived as the gradual process of coming to greater maturity and wholeness as human beings and as people of faith.

Through the lens of saving theology, our attitudes toward the Church and the world around us can also be misplaced if we tend to see the world exclusively as an evil, sinful place where no good can be found, and the Church as the perfect haven where we seek refuge from this dangerous world. Armed with this conviction of "having been saved," we can too easily and falsely divide the world into exclusive categories of the "saved" and the "sinners." Focusing on the dramatic power of our *personal* experience of grace we can forget that God saves us together as a *people*. Through the lens of saving theology, we tend to lean toward others who possess strong authority and who, like God, can save us from our weak and needy selves. We look for wisdom more often outside ourselves and, because we distrust our own "truths," place great confidence in the sure, confident prophetic voices in our midst. We like to see the world in categories that are white or black; things are much easier that way. All these are dangers if the perspective of saving theology is the *only* attitude we have.

The implications for a spirituality grounded exclusively in blessing are also double-edged. The Jesuit poet Gerard Manley Hopkins, in his poem entitled "God's Grandeur," captures the energy, vigor, and grace of a faith that sees God's splendor everywhere: "The world is charged with the grandeur of God. It will flame out, like shining from shook foil; it gathers to a greatness like the ooze of oil Crushed." This optimistic view of the world looks on all of creation as a sacrament of God's presence. It recognizes that in God "we live and move and have our being" (Acts 17:28) at every moment each day. When we live in the certainty of God's blessings, we know that our lives are steeped in a constant flow of divine grace and goodness to us. And even if we fail, it is only a momentary lapse from God's gracious love. In this view, our fundamental conviction is that we are made in the very image of God. We are, therefore, thoroughly good and the object of God's creative love. With this God-given dignity we believe that we have been called to be cocreators with God, entrusted by God with the care of the universe and of human society. Things are less black and white. Instead, we are more aware of the mysteries at the heart of the world, mindful that there are ambiguities in life that we can never fully comprehend. Our ministry is, therefore, more tentative and less sure, always open to be corrected by new insights and daily wisdom.

From this blessing perspective, we tend to see the Church as the communal setting where we search together for God's truth and where we celebrate the presence of God in our midst. From this viewpoint, the Church is not immune to the weakness and sinfulness of life but, in fact, participates in both the sin and the grace of the world. We can recognize God among us in the simple but profound signs of reconciliation between enemies, forgiveness of those who harm us, heroic lives of simple duty, daily done, the generosity of those who care for others, and all the many ways in which we demonstrate our lives of faith today.

In discussing these two strands of biblical theology, Michael Guinan poses the question: "Am I blessed or am I saved?"[5] The answer to this question, of course, is yes. In the biblical tradition, and in our own lives, it is the *combination* and *complementarity* of these two insights about God and the world that together lead us to a balanced and fruitful life. If the danger of saving theology is its excessive claims to absolute certainty, then the danger of blessing theology is its tentative character, its constant questioning, and its lack of certainty. With respect to their differing sense of what it means to be human, Guinan has again described well the implications of these theological perspectives: "The saving tradition needs a sense of dignity and worth; the blessing tradition, a sense of humility, weakness, and limits. Neither alone adequately represents the biblical tradition."[6]

THE BREAD OF DELIVERANCE BECOMES THE BREAD OF BLESSING

> While the Israelites were camped in Gilgal they kept the passover in the evening on the fourteenth day of the month in the plains of Jericho. On the day after the passover, on that very day, they ate the produce of the land, unleavened cakes and parched grain. The manna ceased on the day they ate the produce of the land, and the Israelites no longer had manna; they ate the crops of the land of Canaan that year. (Josh 5:10–12)

It was the Old Testament scholar Claus Westermann who pointed out the perfect biblical text to capture the interrelationship of these two biblical themes. He notes this text in the book of Joshua that describes the moment at the end of the people's sojourn through the desert from Egypt to the promised land. In that journey they had encountered hardship, temptation, hunger, and thirst. But always the saving God had rescued them, despite their murmurings and complaints. The manna, the bread from heaven, coming miraculously to sustain them in their journey, was the most dramatic sign of their saving God.

But as this text of Joshua narrates, once in the land, God provided for their needs in a new way. The people received daily sustenance in the fruit of the land. Or as Westermann puts it, "The bread of deliverance becomes the bread of blessing."[7] For Westermann, this sign, precisely *within* the story of salvation history, signals the interrelationship of the saving and blessing traditions. It is not that we must choose one or the other in order to know and understand God properly. Nor is it the case that we move in our spiritual journeys always from a saving God to a God of blessing or the other way around. The movement is not linear but cyclic, moving back and forth between dramatic experiences of salvation and daily encounters with the God of blessing. As we shall soon see, this was exactly the case with the Israelite and early Christian experience.

One further caution for contemporary spirituality must be noted. We can all too easily fall into the mistaken notion that if we have experienced ourselves as being saved by God, then that status somehow separates us from others as "superior" and should exempt us from obligations and responsibilities for our neighbors. Nothing, of course, could be farther from the truth. The corresponding danger of people who see God as the one who has blessed them is the mistaken assumption that they have earned or deserved their special status. Worse still, the wealthy can mistakenly see their riches as "proof" of God's favor on *them* and not on the destitute who struggle for survival. Both judgments fall very far from the mark.

CONCLUSION

If this brief survey of these biblical perspectives teaches us anything, it should convince us that spiritual growth and maturity rest in the integration of all the insights of both saving and blessing theology for our lives. It means that we will come to know both the God who, at times, rescues us from danger and sin and the God who, at other times, walks with us as friend and companion sustaining us throughout our lives. We will be as suspicious of the easy certainties of "black and white" labels as we are of an excessive tolerance, a moral relativism, or a lack of commitment that takes no sides at all in the life-and-death questions of our day. And with our ancestor Joshua, we will come to know that, in our lives also again and again, "the bread of deliverance becomes the bread of blessing."

QUESTIONS FOR REFLECTION

1. Recognizing that "where we stand affects the way we see" the world, God, and ourselves, what factors in your own present setting have especially shaped your ideas and your faith?
2. In this contrast between "saving" and "blessing" theology, which do you experience now most powerfully, and what life experiences have led you to this conviction?
3. In your lifetime, how has God rescued or saved you? What have these experiences taught you?
4. From what do you pray to be saved by God? Why?
5. When you "count your blessings," what things, people, and experiences do you name? Why?

5

I HAVE HEARD THEIR CRY

Then the LORD said, "I have seen the misery
of my people . . . , I have heard their cry.
I know their sufferings, and I have come
down to deliver them."

—Exodus 3:8a

Now with this chapter, building on all that has been said to this point, we will begin in a more systematic way to "touch our fingers to the flame." We will follow the narrative sequence of the biblical text from Genesis to Revelation, selecting for comment some "key" biblical passages that might serve as the grounding and foundation for contemporary faith experience. The reader will need to have a Bible itself close at hand and to read each section to be discussed as we trace the ongoing, gradual disclosure of Israel's God, culminating in the new vision of God-in-Christ in the Christian proclamation. In choosing such a broad agenda and one that covers such an extensive historical time span, one runs the risk, I realize, of sacrificing depth in the interest of breadth. Nevertheless, I remain convinced of the importance of such a broad overview and of the valuable lessons it can teach us. Accordingly, the reader will be invited along the way to make more concrete the particular lessons and wisdom for his or her own life.

THE EXODUS AS A FAITH PARADIGM

In the previous chapter I note that, in many ways, the legends and stories collected in the book of Genesis are really the preamble and setting for the "history" of the Israelite people that actually begins in the book of Exodus, with the account of their liberation from slavery in Egypt. As noted in the previous chapter, this dramatic event is the statement of saving theology par excellence. Often, when we hear the word *Exodus*, however, we might think just of the one, climactic moment in the biblical story when God stretched forth a mighty hand, and the waters parted, allowing the Israelite band to escape, only to recede again, engulfing the Egyptian riders. This is the moment we recall each year in the liturgical readings of the Easter Vigil when we repeat the words of their song of celebration:

> Then the prophet Miriam, Aaron's sister, took a tambourine in her hand; and all the women went out after her with tambourines and with dancing.
>   And Miriam sang to them:
>   "Sing to the LORD, for he has triumphed gloriously; horse and rider he has thrown into the sea." (Ex 15:20–21)

And this is the moment that perhaps captured our childhood imaginations most or was nurtured by Hollywood films.[1] In fact, if we look more closely at the biblical narrative, then it becomes clear that the Exodus event is not one, single event but, rather, several key moments, spread out over the first seventeen chapters of the book of Exodus and even beyond. Each piece of this story is essential, and together they establish the foundation of biblical faith for all time, up to and including our own generation.

Rather than view the Exodus experience as a single event, then, I would suggest that we see this foundational story in five interrelated parts: (a) the cry of the people (Ex 3:1–7); (b) the theophany at the burning bush, with its distinctive elements of the call of Moses (Ex 3:10–12) and the revelation of God's name, YHWH (Ex 3:13–15); (c) the long struggle with Pharaoh in the cycle of plagues (Ex 7:8–14:4); (d) the victory at the sea (Ex 14:5–31); and (e) the aftermath and wilderness wanderings (Ex 15:22–17:7). Each section has its own wisdom to impart.

A. THE CRY OF THE PEOPLE (EX 3:1–7)

As the story begins, we see our leader and hero, Moses. He had been spared at birth by the courageous and clever collaboration of five women: his mother and sister, the two midwives, and Pharaoh's own daughter (Ex 1:15–2:10). Now, the adult Moses is "running from the law," having slain an Egyptian in anger. The narrator tells us that he is "keeping the flock of his father-in-law Jethro, the priest of Midian; he led his flock beyond the wilderness, and came to Horeb, the mountain of God" (Ex 3:1).[2] Here, Moses has what in contemporary language would be called an extraordinary "God experience." The technical term is *theophany*, a manifestation of God—mediated through natural phenomena or by visual or auditory experiences. These biblical theophanies (and there are many of them throughout the scriptures) convey the mystery and power of God.[3] They attempt to describe the writer's conviction that God has "appeared" and has revealed something to the recipient. The modern reader can never know for certain "what happened" in these encounters, just as we can never completely explain our own contemporary experiences of God. They happen; they touch our minds and hearts—as people of faith we are certain of that. They change our lives forever just as they did for Moses, or the prophet Jeremiah, or the apostle Paul, or Francis of Assisi, or the martyred bishop of El Salvador, Monsignor Oscar Romero.

In the case of Moses, here in Exodus 3, there is a mysterious natural phenomenon. The bush nearby is burning but without being consumed. And then a voice speaks to him from the bush: "'Moses, Moses!' he said. 'Here I am.' Then he said, 'Come no closer! Remove the sandals from your feet, for the place where you are standing is holy ground. . . . I am the God of your father, the God of Abraham, the God of Isaac, and the God of Jacob.' And Moses hid his face, for he was afraid to look at God" (Ex 3:4–6). Moses must remove his sandals as a sign of reverence and respect. These moments of encounter with the divine mystery, when we are privileged to "see God," are awe-filled and holy. The "holy ground" can, in fact, be anywhere, in both familiar and (as here in the case of Moses) unfamiliar places. God's presence and our receptivity, that is, our openness to this divine disclosure, hallow the ground, as they do here for Moses. The voice who speaks to Moses from the bush identifies the divine presence by its continuity with what has come before: "I am the God of your father. . . ." Though a dramatically new moment, for God will have a new name and there will be a new relationship between God and the people, this encounter is part of an *ongoing revelation*. It is therefore connected to all that has come before in the biblical story.

This lesson is an important one for our contemporary lives as well. Our journeys of faith, though integral to our own growth in maturity and personal integration, are sometimes marked by dramatic moments that can be revelatory of God in an extraordinary way and, therefore, life-changing for that very reason. Perhaps it is not insignificant, too, that Moses here in the story is "on the run." He is in a precarious and vulnerable position where, spiritual wisdom tells us, the intervention of God can be more effective.

Finally, in verses 7 and 8, the voice explains the purpose and reason for its appearance: "Then the LORD said, 'I have observed the misery of my people who are in Egypt; I have heard their cry on account of their taskmasters. Indeed, I know their sufferings, and I have come down to deliver them from the Egyptians.'" What brings the deity to this moment and this place, where God will intervene dramatically in human affairs, is the cry of the people. The word used here in Hebrew is *z/tsaaq*—an almost onomatopoetic deep guttural sound. This word, in its variant spellings and in both its noun and verbal forms, occurs over one hundred sixty-five times in the Old Testament, with significant reverberations in the New Testament. There are, for example, repeated allusions to the Israelites "crying out to God" in their need and God answering their cries as, for example, in Psalm 34:17: "When the righteous cry for help, the LORD hears, and rescues them from all their troubles." There are other times when God seems deaf to their cries and they cry out all the more, as in Psalm 22:2: "Oh my God, I cry by day, but you do not answer; and by night but find no rest." There are severe warnings to the Israelites to treat others justly because God hears the cry of the alien in their midst, just as God heard their cry in Egypt: "If you do abuse [the alien], when they cry out to me, I will surely heed their cry" (Ex 22:23). This fundamental biblical affirmation about God's relationship with creation stands at the opening of the story of salvation, and it resolutely affirms that Israel's God is not immune to the cry of human misery. The God of the Bible "hears the cry" and comes with compassion to rescue the people.

Walter Brueggemann sees this first movement of the Exodus drama embodied in the cry of the people as a highly political act, as the "critique of ideology."[4] In the story, Pharaoh presided over a political arrangement that dealt death, not life, to the Hebrew people. Their enslavement was brutal, and their very lives were in jeopardy. In their outcry, we can see an act of public protest against the oppressive policies of the Egyptian state. The cry is a resounding "No!" to that order of things. It resembles, in our day, the courageous protests in the Plaza de Mayo in Argentina of the "Mothers of the Disappeared" who (like their biblical ancestors) raised a great public outcry against the unjust violence done to their husbands, fathers, sons, and brothers at the hands of those in power. In the Exodus story, the people's cry shakes a fist in Pharaoh's face and screams, "This must not be!" The cry protests the inhuman treatment and loss of human dignity suffered by the Hebrew people. It thereby hearkens back to the creation story's affirmation of humanity created in the image and likeness of God, destined for life and honor.

Often, perhaps, we have understood salvation history as the story of God's divine initiative, God's decisive act to intervene and liberate the people from slavery and lead them into the promised land. What we might fail to notice in this view, however, is that the compelling factor that almost wrests God's action to intervene on their behalf is the people's own *cry*. This moment of human outcry, the desperate, gut-wrenching cry of a people oppressed, seems to move the heart of God to come to their rescue: "I have seen their misery, . . . I have heard their cry." Reading this first part of the Exodus story, then, we see that in the drama of our salvation history, the engine that drives this entire biblical narrative is not at first the lone initiative of a distant God to come near to us but, rather, the reality of human anguish brought to collective, public expression in the people's lament, in their great outcry.

B. THE THEOPHANY AT THE BURNING BUSH (EX 3:10–15)

Appearance of heavenly figure

A second moment in the Exodus drama builds on the first and continues the ongoing dialogue between Moses and the Lord. God not only announces to Moses the divine intent to rescue the people because of their cry; God also enlists Moses as the divine agent of liberation: "So come, I will send you to Pharaoh to bring my people, the Israelites, out of Egypt" (Ex 3:10). Here, we have what will become in the biblical narrative the classic paradigm of the "call narrative." These are stories of individuals who experience a divine call. They are common especially in the prophetic literature of ancient Israel and in the call stories of the disciples of Jesus. Here, with the call of Moses we see some of the essential elements and theological convictions that lie behind these scenes.

First is the obvious but striking claim that God collaborates with and utilizes human creatures in the work of salvation. This divine–human "cooperation" will remain a constant theme throughout the Bible, with various individuals at different times enlisted to do the work of God on earth.[5] This theme seems to affirm, according to the discussion in the last chapter, the basic tenet of blessing theology: that God takes human beings seriously and that God has indeed entrusted them with the care of creation and of God's people.

Moses' response throughout this encounter would be comical if it were not so poignant. Five times God announces that Moses will go to Pharaoh as God's ambassador, and five times Moses raises legitimate

fire: cleanse, warmth, destroy, light, comfort, fear, awe
→ symbol for God

objections to God's call. Each time, like the superior fencer in a great duel, God parries Moses' objections, but, in the end, God's plan for the liberation of the people moves ahead with Moses as the reluctant leader. To the initial announcement of his call, Moses responds: "Who am I that I should go to Pharaoh, and bring the Israelites out of Egypt?" (Ex 3:11). For each part of this dialogue, it is easy to see contemporary analogies in our own lives as we struggle to respond to God today. Who among us, when feeling called by God to do an impossible task, does not say: "Who am I to be the one?" On rational grounds, this is a very legitimate objection Moses raises. Remember, in anger he had killed an Egyptian (Ex 2:11–15) and was *persona non grata* in Pharaoh's sight. God's reply is shocking in its simplicity: "I will be with you" (Ex 3:12a). By these words, God seems to say, "This is not about *you*, Moses, but about my determination to set my people free." The only assurance needed is God's promise to be with him, but God adds the promissory sign that Moses would be successful and return to the holy mountain of his encounter with God (Ex 3:12b).

The dialogue might have ended there, but Moses persists: "But Moses said to God, 'If I come to the Israelites and say to them, "The God of your ancestors has sent me to you," and they ask me, "What is his name?" what shall I say to them?'" (Ex 3:13). Ah, here is the real catch. Moses wants to "name" God. As in the childhood story of Rumpelstiltskin, to know the name is to have power over, to control and possess for one's own. As *adam* had called each of the animals by name and so could tame them for his use (Gen 2:19–20), to name God is to have a domesticated deity, and the God of the Exodus will have no part of this. The response that God gives in verse 14 is perhaps the most enigmatic verse in all of scripture. It is untranslatable really, much debated among Old Testament exegetes, and the puzzle of Jews and Christians through the centuries. In Hebrew the text says: *Ehyeh asher ehyeh*. The standard English rendering is: "I AM WHO I AM." He said further, "Thus you shall say to the Israelites, 'I AM has sent me to you'" (Ex 3:14). The twice repeated verbal form, *ehyeh*, is part of the Hebrew verb *hayah*, "to be." Some maintain that its form here is "causative" and should be rendered "I cause to be." Others stress the open-ended character of the phrase and suggest a translation similar to God's words in response to Moses' first objection, "I will be with you." The later Greek translation of the Old Testament rendered this in almost philosophical language as an ontological statement: "I am the One who exists." But God's reply does not convey philosophical certitudes. It points to God's identity as bound up in *relationship*; God's self-identity is to be in relationship with creation.

All these attempts to translate the untranslatable name point, perhaps, to the real meaning of the divine response. When asked for a name, Moses receives a reply that seems to say, "My name is that I have no name. You cannot know my name." God's only "name" is mystery, presence, and life. Insofar as it can be known at all, it will be revealed in the ongoing relationship with God's people. The four Hebrew consonants that became synonymous with the divine name, YHWH (the tetragrammaton, probably vocalized as "Yahweh"), are always rendered in our English Bibles by the word LORD, spelled in all capital letters. This became Israel's name for their God, but in fact, it is a name that preserves God's utter freedom and namelessness. As we have seen in chapter 2, despite our attempts to name and control God, the biblical God is always a "God beyond all names."

Moses' objections to his call, however, do not stop here. Despite God's continuing promises to uphold his mission to Pharaoh, Moses tries again to thwart his calling: "Then Moses answered, 'But suppose they do not believe me or listen to me, but say, The LORD did not appear to you'" (Ex 4:1). This time, he argues that his word alone will not be believed. The people will question his alleged claims to have seen the LORD and will distrust his report of his religious experience. He needs some *hard proof*. And so it is with ourselves as well. Often, perhaps, we are the ones who mistrust our own experiences of God, demanding proof where it cannot be found. But this time God relents and even gives Moses a "bag of tricks" (the snake that becomes a walking staff, a tunic that will make leprosy appear and disappear at will, the ability to turn river water to blood [Ex 4:3–9]). All these were the powerful deeds that should convince the disbelieving. But still, Moses quibbles with God.

Moses said, "O my Lord, I have never been eloquent, neither in the past nor even now that you have spoken to your servant; but I am slow of speech and slow of tongue" (Ex 4:10). With this fourth objection, Moses points to his own shortcomings, his lack of skill and unsuitability for the job. Here again we can, no doubt, see ourselves when faced with a forbidding task or project, a life choice we feel called to follow but are afraid to embrace. But God continues to stave off Moses' reply with a question that puts his silly banter to shame: "Then the LORD said to him, 'Who gives speech to mortals? Who makes them mute or deaf, seeing or blind? Is it not I, the LORD? Now go, and I will be with your mouth and teach you what you are to speak'" (Ex 4:11–12). With a promise that God will make again and again in the scriptures, namely, to put God's own words within the mouth of the messenger, this response ought to have been enough, but Moses tries one last time.

In the fifth and final objection, Moses at last reveals his true self. His words sound almost desperate: "But he said, 'O my Lord, please send someone else'" (Ex 4:13). When all is said and done, it is clear that Moses' real objection is simply that he *does not want* to cooperate. He does not want to be the Lord's messenger. He wants no part of it; it is as simple as that. Go away, he seems to say, as we might say to a pesky street vendor trying to sell us his wares. But God's persistence is greater than Moses' refusal or reluctance: "Then the anger of the LORD was kindled against Moses and he said, 'What of your brother Aaron, the Levite? I know that he can speak fluently; even now he is coming out to meet you, and when he sees you his heart will be glad'" (Ex 4:14–17). And so, with the help of Aaron as a companion, Moses finally relents and returns to Egypt to do God's bidding.

What lessons do we learn for our spiritual lives from this part of the story? We see first, I think, that the ways of God with the world oblige us in a divine–human collaboration. The biblical God is not a remote deity but, in fact, a God who is involved with the joys and pain of human existence, who "hears the cry." Although the implications of the divine name show that God promises to be with us as life-giver, we can never control God for our own purposes. Nevertheless, God takes us seriously as partners in the work of salvation and will not let us "off the hook." If we are serious about our lives in response to God's presence in our midst, then we must be prepared both to "take off our sandals" in reverence and to embrace this formidable challenge.

C. THE STRUGGLE WITH PHARAOH IN THE PLAGUE CYCLE (EX 7:8–14:4)

The Exodus drama moves next to its longest, most repetitive portion. The plague cycle makes up nearly seven chapters of the book of Exodus and purports to be the story of the dramatic struggle between Moses and Pharaoh. In fact, it is a story not really about Moses and Pharaoh at all but about the larger, cosmic forces of life and death, good and evil, God and Satan. It is a story "writ large" in dramatic and mythic proportions. On the one side is "Moses," who, together with his assistant Aaron, relentlessly proclaims God's command for the life of the people: "Thus says the LORD, the God of Israel, 'Let my people go, so that they may celebrate a festival to me in the wilderness'" (Ex 5:1, repeated in 7:16, 8:1, 8:20, 9:1, 9:13, 10:3). On the other side is "Pharaoh," who, with hardened heart, relentlessly refuses to comply: "But Pharaoh said, 'Who is the LORD, that I should heed him and let Israel go? I do not know the LORD, and I will not let Israel go'" (Ex 5:2, repeated in 8:32, 9:7, 11:10). And so it goes, back and forth and back and forth: "Let my people go!"—"No, I will not let the people go!"

Through the full cycle of ten plagues, like a great tug of war, it goes. God's determination for the life and freedom of the people, on one side, wrestles with "Pharaoh's" death-dealing policies of oppression and human degradation, on the other. It is only with the horror of each successive plague that Pharaoh relents for a brief moment, only to resume his deadly game with its renewed harsh treatment of the people. The plagues are as follows:

FIRST PLAGUE: Water Turned into Blood	Ex 7:14–24
SECOND PLAGUE: The Frogs	Ex 7:25–8:14
THIRD PLAGUE: The Gnats	Ex 8:12–19
FOURTH PLAGUE: The Flies	Ex 8:16–32
FIFTH PLAGUE: The Pestilence	Ex 9:1–7
SIXTH PLAGUE: The Boils	Ex 9:8–12
SEVENTH PLAGUE: The Hail	Ex 9:13–35
EIGHTH PLAGUE: The Locusts	Ex 10:1–20
NINTH PLAGUE: The Darkness	Ex 10:21–29
TENTH PLAGUE: The Death of the Firstborn	Ex 11:1–14:4

Scholars have attempted to read these "plagues" as natural phenomena that can be explained by various climatic and natural cyclic forces in the Nile Delta of lower Egypt. And so, for example, some argue that in the first plague the waters of the Nile could "appear" blood red because of the yearly cycle of flooding its banks that happened regularly before the building of the Aswan Dam. But I think this line of questioning completely misses the point. If this story communicates primarily a *theological*, and not a *historical*, truth, which I am convinced it does, then our questions must move in a different direction.

If you read slowly through this entire plague cycle, by about the third or fourth plague you begin to say to yourself, "Okay, I see. I get it." But the story will not let *you* go. It persists, ten times, with this larger-than-life struggle and forces you to ask the question: "What is this story trying to tell me? What, if anything, has this struggle between Moses and Pharaoh to do with me, with my life and faith?" Several responses come to the fore. First, this powerful drama says something about the intransigence of *evil* itself or, as Brueggemann prefers to say, the intransigence of the "dominant ideology."[6] The responsibility for Pharaoh's "hardness of heart," though announced as fixed by God at the beginning of the encounter (Ex 4:21), rests ultimately with Pharaoh himself. Evil, in this sense, digs in its heels and makes a conscious choice for death, not life. Second, the almost monotonous repetition and redundancy in the story may be suggesting something about the character of redemption itself. It may be warning us that the movement from "bondage to freedom" (however we construe these terms) does not happen quickly or without a struggle. In the Exodus narrative, the voice from the bush records God's determination to set the people free in chapter 3. The *actual* escape from the Egyptian pursuers, however, comes only in chapter 14. And even there, as will be clear in the next section, we will need to see the victory at the sea as both a climactic ending and a new beginning.

The plague cycle forces us to contend with reality. It reminds us that our redemption (personal and communal) sometimes entails real conflict with real people whose self-interest is served by perpetuating the bondage of others. It also reminds us that, in this struggle of life over death, God is with us. God intends our life and freedom, but we must cooperate with God.

D. THE VICTORY AT THE SEA (EX 14:5–15:21)

Finally, we come to the moment of rescue by the sea. The horror of the final plague—the death of the firstborn among the Egyptians—is matched in the story only by the deadly policies of Pharaoh. In the violent world of the ancient Near East, these are violent symbols the biblical writer employs, and they must not go without critique by the modern reader. But the point and climax of his story is the people's escape to "freedom." Again, the storyteller builds the suspense as the motley band of Hebrew slaves, taking their staffs in hand, flee in the dead of night from Pharaoh's power: "So the people took their dough before it was leavened, with their kneading bowls wrapped up in their cloaks on their shoulders" (Ex 12:34). At this point in the story they leave familiar, albeit hostile, territory behind and, with Moses and Aaron at their lead, venture out into the unknown. It is a moment of true crisis, and it comprises both the "danger and the opportunity" that a crisis entails. The text is careful to point out that the God who had called out to Moses from the bush was still at their side:

> The LORD went in front of them in a pillar of cloud by day, to lead them along the way, and in a pillar of fire by night, to give them light, so that they might travel by day and by night.
> Neither the pillar of cloud by day nor the pillar of fire by night left its place in front of the people. (Ex 13:21–22)

And so, at YHWH's bidding and with YHWH in their midst, they went out from Egypt—but with Pharaoh's armies in hot pursuit! Terror grips them, and they want to turn back. They challenge Moses and prefer slavery in Egypt to death in the wilderness (Ex 14:11–12). In these complaints we already have a preview and hint of what to expect in the final scene. But with words of reassurance Moses presses them on: "But Moses said to the people, 'Do not be afraid, stand firm, and see the deliverance that the LORD will accomplish for you today; for the Egyptians whom you see today you shall never see again. The LORD will fight for you, and you have only to keep still'" (Ex 14:13–14).

And so, they come at last to the sea, to the place of their rescue. And the drama builds again as the Egyptian pursuers come closer and closer. But at the command of God and with God's own power, Moses stretches forth his hand and the waters part!

> Then Moses stretched out his hand over the sea. The LORD drove the sea back by a strong east wind all night, and turned the sea into dry land; and the waters were divided. The Israelites went into the sea on dry ground, the waters forming a wall for them on their right and on their left. The Egyptians pursued, and went into the sea after them, all of Pharaoh's horses, chariots, and chariot drivers. At the morning watch the LORD in the pillar of fire and cloud looked down upon the Egyptian army, and threw the Egyptian army into panic. (Ex 14:21–24)

As the waters engulfed their pursuers, the prophet Miriam, sister to Aaron and Moses, took timbrel in hand and together with all the women led the celebration with dancing and song.[7] She sang the words of the joyous refrain that in later tradition would be ascribed to her brother Moses (see Ex 15:1–18): "Sing to the LORD, for he has triumphed gloriously; horse and rider he has thrown into the sea" (Ex 15:21).

So, at last, the long struggle is over! So, at last, they are free—or so it seems. Their "liturgy by the sea" celebrates this glorious moment. But we are led again to ask the question: "What is this story trying to say to us, today?" If, as I have argued in the case of the plague cycle, the point of the story is more theological than historical, then what is it teaching us about the God of the Exodus and about the God whom we encounter in our own lives? Surely, this dramatic rescue affirms the central insight of the saving tradition, namely, that our God is a God who saves us from death and is our champion on the side of life. We see in this powerful story that all of our life is gift, unmerited bounty from God, almost despite ourselves and our foolish complaints. This moment of rescue by the sea is indeed the climax and conclusion to the long, laborious plague cycle. But, as we shall see in the final scene, it is really only the beginning of the struggle of God's people to embrace God's gift of life.

E. THE AFTERMATH—WILDERNESS WANDERINGS (EX 15:22–17:7)

The final episode in the long biblical narrative we call the "Exodus story" is really still an open-ended story of which we, in our present generation, are very much a part. Living the demands of their freedom proved to be a formidable challenge. In the Exodus narrative, the aftermath of YHWH's rescue at the sea and the immediate sequel to the great celebration in song and dance is as puzzling as it is poignantly human. Exactly three verses (!) after their extraordinary rescue, the people begin grumbling and murmuring against Moses and (even more surprising) against the God who had saved them. They complain about the quality of water (Ex 15:22–26, 17:2–7); they long for the "fleshpots of Egypt" and complain that they have no food (Ex 16:2–6). Despite assurances, they doubt that YHWH is with them (Ex 17:7) and they would rather return to Egypt. When gifted with manna as food from heaven, they long instead for the foods of Egypt: cucumbers, melons, leeks, onions, and garlic (Num 11:4–6). They criticize Moses' leadership and challenge his prophetic status (Num 12:1–2, 14:2–3). They bicker among themselves like children wanting their own way (Num 16:12–14). They grumble incessantly about wilderness life (Num 21:4–5) and seem to prefer slavery to freedom.

CONCLUSION

Again, we must ask the question: "What are we to learn from this biblical story?" As the Hebrew band moved out of slavery and embarked on the road to freedom, the Israelites entered the vast wilderness in their search for the promised land. There, in the wilderness, they began to learn the demands of freedom, its costs and challenges. They came to know God as YHWH, the One whose name is nameless and whose freedom is absolute. The rest of the biblical story in its entirety will continue to pose this challenge to them: how to live out the demands of freedom, as a people claimed and saved by God. The accounts of their murmuring and grumbling point to another lesson, namely, that they were continually called to trust the gift of life that God offered to them. Again and again, they seemed to prefer the certainties of slavery to the fearsome risks of the wilderness way toward life. In short, we could say that they learned in the wilderness that "Pharaoh" was inside them. As their history (and ours) would tragically prove, they learned that the capacity for evil, the struggle for supremacy, abuses of power, rancorous bickerings, and willful deeds that enslave others—all these evils were within their own hearts. How God would continue to free them, and free us, from this "Pharaoh" is the heart and substance of the ongoing biblical story.

QUESTIONS FOR REFLECTION

1. As you think about the biblical story of the Exodus, in what ways does this story provide a paradigm for your faith journey? Which part of the story is for you the most important and compelling? Why?

2. Have you ever felt yourself "called" by God in any way? Through what particular circumstances was God revealed to you? What were your objections or resistances to your call?

3. The Exodus story speaks of removing sandals on "holy ground." Where is the "holy ground" of your life? What concrete places have been made holy for you, and by what events? How were these places and events "revelations of God" for you?

4. The Exodus story challenges us to imitate God's attentiveness to the human cry. What cries do you hear, whether from those close by or from those in other parts of the world? What must you do to respond?

5. Where, in our world today or in your life today, do you encounter "the intransigence of evil"? Is there anything that you would name as the "Pharaoh inside you"?

6

ROYAL POWER AND
THE COVENANT DREAM

I am the LORD your God. You shall not do as they
do in the land of Egypt, where you lived. . . .
My ordinances you shall observe and my statutes
you shall keep, following them: I am the
LORD your God.

—Leviticus 18:2–3

According to the Exodus narrative, when the Israelites left Egypt as a people saved by the mighty arm of God, they set out into the wilderness where they sojourned for forty years. They entered into that liminal place between what they had known in Egypt and what they would come to discover in the "promised land." The wilderness would be for them a place of testing and of encounter in which they would come to know themselves as God's own people. In the first step of their journey they came again to Sinai/Horeb, the holy mountain of God, as the Lord had promised Moses they would. And as they recount their faith story, it was at Sinai that they entered into a new relationship with YHWH their God.

A PEOPLE BOUND IN COVENANT WITH GOD

In the literary structure of the Pentateuch, that is, the first five books of the Bible, the mountain of Sinai looms as the central point of focus—the point toward which their rescue leads them and the point from which their life as a people begins. Table 6.1 may help to illustrate the centrality of this holy mountain and the traditions associated with it.

Table 6.1. Pentateuch

			Wilderness Wanderings		
			Sinai		
Gen 1–11	Gen 12–50	Ex 1–18	Ex 19–24 Leviticus Num 1–10	Num 11–36	Deut 1–34
Origins	Ancestors	Freedom	Covenant and Torah	Toward the Land	Final Warnings

At the Reed Sea, God had liberated the Israelites from slavery and set them on a path toward freedom.[1] But, as they tell their story, it was at Sinai that God sealed this relationship and established an everlasting covenant with them. We can scarcely exaggerate the importance of covenant theology in Israel's faith story. Built into the literary structure of the Pentateuch, this covenantal theme applies not only to the encounter between God and Moses at Sinai. It also provides the framework and the theological basis for understanding God's earlier promises made with Noah (Gen 9:8–17) and with Abraham (Gen 12:1–3, 15:5–7, 15:18–21, 17), as well as the continuing reinterpretation of covenant traditions with David in the period of the monarchy and with those who would rearticulate covenant theology in succeeding generations.

The Hebrew term berit—"covenant, binding agreement, fetter, bond"—is a rich term that captures the heart of Israel's religious beliefs. Covenants of varying kinds were common in the ancient Near East. Some were made between equal partners; others were made between unequal partners, such as those treaties common among the ancient Hittite peoples made between a sovereign and his vassals. The lord promised to guard and protect the vassals, who, in turn, would pledge fealty and obedience to their lord. This type may have provided a model for Israel's covenant theology and shaped its basic elements.

The biblical account of the covenant made at Sinai embodies the same kind of high drama that attends the Exodus story. With the people encamped at the base of the mountain, Moses ascends to the mountaintop, and there he hears again the same voice that had spoken to him from the burning bush:

> Then Moses went up to God; the LORD called to him from the mountain, saying, "Thus you shall say to the house of Jacob, and tell the Israelites: You have seen what I did to the Egyptians, and how I bore you on eagles' wings and brought you to myself. Now therefore,

if you obey my voice and keep my covenant, you shall be my treasured possession out of all the peoples. Indeed, the whole earth is mine, but you shall be for me a priestly kingdom and a holy nation. These are the words that you shall speak to the Israelites." (Ex 19:3–6)

The words of the Lord establish both covenant promises and covenant demands. Among all peoples, they would be God's own "treasured possession, . . . a priestly kingdom and a holy nation." In return, they must obey the voice of God and keep this covenant bond intact. So Moses repeated these words to the people, who with one voice exclaimed: "Everything that the LORD has spoken we will do" (Ex 19:8). And after three days of purification and preparation, the people went out to the base of the mountain as Moses ascended a second time to the top and heard the Lord's voice speaking in the midst of the thick cloud. Dramatic signs attend God's presence on the mountain as Moses and also the people below hear the words of God:

On the morning of the third day there was thunder and lightning, as well as a thick cloud on the mountain, and a blast of a trumpet so loud that all the people who were in the camp trembled. Moses brought the people out of the camp to meet God. They took their stand at the foot of the mountain. Now Mount Sinai was wrapped in smoke, because the LORD had descended upon it in fire; the smoke went up like the smoke of a kiln, while the whole mountain shook violently. As the blast of the trumpet grew louder and louder, Moses would speak and God would answer him in thunder. When the LORD descended upon Mount Sinai, to the top of the mountain, the LORD summoned Moses to the top of the mountain, and Moses went up. (Ex 19:16–20)

As it had been at the Reed Sea, the awesome power of the divine presence is again apparent in the Sinai event. But God's power is the kind that protects the people like a mother eagle carrying her young. Only one thing must they promise in return: fidelity to all that the Lord required of them. These stipulations of the covenant, which appear in the remaining chapters of Exodus, in the entire book of Leviticus, and in the first ten chapters of the book of Numbers, represent the collected traditions of laws and ordinances arising in the life of the Israelites over several centuries. The editors of the Pentateuch (writing probably in the time of the exile, 587–538 B.C.E.) collected and placed them all together here, in the narrative of the people's encampment at Sinai, in order to assert their foundational character in the life of the covenant people and to establish its new social and religious vision. No longer would Pharaoh's ways prevail; now they would live in the ways of YHWH.

The Mosaic covenant at Sinai articulated the values of Israelite faith that they believed God had revealed to them. First and foremost God called them to be a holy people, as their God was holy (Ex 19:5–6; Lev 19:1–2). But holiness must be manifest in concrete ethical principles demonstrated in reverent service to God and to neighbor. Covenant stipulations bound them to protect the weak and powerless: the orphan, the widow, strangers, the poor. The Decalogue, or the "Ten Commandments" (Ex 20:2–17; compare Deut 5:6–21) as we have come to call them, constitute the heart of covenant, ethical living. These commandments laid down the foundations for communal cohesion and integrity lived in the presence of their God.

Each commandment guarded a different dimension of covenant living. The first, "You shall have no other gods before me" (Ex 20:3), protected the oneness that must be at the heart of the community. Their God, YHWH, calls them to absolute, categorical, singular loyalty. The second, "You shall not make for yourself an idol" (Ex 20:4), guarded YHWH's freedom. No name, no image, could be used to domesticate God. Israel's God is dynamic, mysterious, and ever free. The symbols of YHWH's presence with the people in the wilderness are ephemeral, dynamic symbols: "the pillar of cloud by day and the pillar of fire by night."[2] Always with them yet just ahead of them, these were symbols of the God who reassured the people and led them forward into the unknown. The third commandment, "You shall not make wrongful use of the name of the LORD your God, for the LORD will not acquit anyone who misuses his name" (Ex 20:7), protected the sacredness of the divine Name and reserved it exclusively for use in solemn occasions.

Sabbath rest is the subject of the fourth commandment: "Remember the sabbath day, and keep it holy" (Ex 20:8). This stipulation had both a theological and a human rationale. Sabbath was the hallowing of time, a day set aside in observance of their special relationship with God. The Genesis creation story provided the origin for the Sabbath as an imitation of God resting on the seventh day, but it was as much a human practice to provide replenishment and rest for humans and animals alike. The fifth commandment, "Honor your father and your mother, so that your days may be long in the land that the LORD your God is giving you" (Ex 20:12), addressed a community of adults and, therefore, protected the honor of aged parents with their wisdom for the community. In the sixth, "You shall not murder" (Ex 20:13), God's word protected the value of human life itself and relegated the taking of life to war and self-defense. The seventh commandment, "You shall not commit adultery" (Ex 20:14), guarded the exclusive claims of the marital bond and, within the patriarchal culture that ancient Israel was, provided protection for the female and guarded male honor.

The eighth (Ex 20:15) prohibited stealing and was originally perhaps proscribed against kidnapping. In a culture where property (livestock, implements, clothing) amounted to life itself, this command safeguarded the survival of the people. The ninth commandment, "You shall not bear false witness against your neighbor" (Ex 20:16), prohibited the twisting of speech before a communal tribunal of justice in a way that would deny another member of the community access to justice. To protect the wholeness of the fabric of community life, Israel had to be able to trust the language of legal testimony that one member bore toward another. Finally, the tenth commandment, "You shall not covet your neighbor's house; you shall not covet your neighbor's wife, or male or female slave, or ox, or donkey, or anything that belongs to your neighbor" (Ex 20:17), recognized that the integrity of the covenant community demanded mutual respect for persons, their very life, and extensions of that life in one's primary relationships.

Through the centuries Israel would add numerous additional laws and ordinances, some universal (apodictic) law and others very specific case laws regulating social interaction among members of the community and prescribing penalties for violations of all kinds. All these laws and numerous cultic regulations, too, were gathered together and placed, in the story, here at Sinai. In that way their authority was grounded in the solemn moment of YHWH's establishment of the covenant bond. Concern for the proper ritual observance was a key element in the design of how Israel was to live appropriately in God's "tabernacling presence." The cult was viewed as the gift through which God gave Israel appropriate means for responding to the divine presence. To live rightly in God's presence was to abide by the requirements of ritual purity in the way they prepared foods, regarded normal bodily functions, and attended to the careful order God had established in creation. In the same way, the covenant was seen as a gift from YHWH and as an honor for the people. Its stipulations and laws were life giving, not burdensome, the object of meditation day and night. Much later, the psalmist would write of the beauty of the Torah:

> I will keep your law [Torah] continually,
>   forever and ever.
> I shall walk at liberty,
>   for I have sought your precepts.
> I will also speak of your decrees before kings,
>   and shall not be put to shame;

I find my delight in your commandments,
    because I love them.
I revere your commandments, which I love,
    and I will meditate on your statutes. (Ps 119:44–48)

A new moment was beginning; a new alliance was being formed. Promises were made by God and also by the people; stipulations were established. What, then, can we say of this covenant dream? It is clear in the Exodus story that this new moment resists the policies and way of life the people had experienced in Egypt. It is, therefore, a countervision. It invites this band of freed slaves into a new relationship with the powerful God who had led them to freedom. The covenant vision expresses what Walter Brueggemann aptly calls a "new social imagination."[3] This new imagination became possible because of their rescue at the sea, and it was celebrated in exuberant song by Miriam and the women with timbrels in hand. And now, at Sinai, it was given shape in the concrete ethical codes that the Torah enshrined. These people were to be a people chosen by God. But always we must ask: Chosen for what? Chosen for special privilege? No, not at all. It will become clear in the ongoing biblical story that they have been chosen *not* for special privilege but for special *responsibility*. But here, in the wilderness and as they gathered together at Sinai, the covenant people were born.

THE TRIBES OF YAHWEH

In the second year, in the second month, on the twentieth day of the month, the cloud lifted from over the tabernacle of the covenant. Then the Israelites set out by stages from the wilderness of Sinai, and the cloud settled down in the wilderness of Paran. They set out for the first time at the command of the LORD by Moses. (Num 10:11–13)

With these words, the book of Numbers recounts the beginning of the journey from Sinai to the promised land. As the people ventured again into the wilderness, their murmurings resumed (Num 11:4–15), their struggles for power intensified (Num 11:24–30, 12:1–16, 16:1–50), and their reliance on YHWH faltered. But despite these shortcomings, according to their story, God continued to lead them forward, and in the wilderness their structures for priestly and prophetic leadership took shape, laying the foundations for their life in the land.

Contradictory theories about the actual nature of Israel's beginnings in the land abound. A consensus would agree, however, that the political entity that came to be called "Israel" was probably forged by a combination of three main factors: (1) the possible entrance into the land of Canaan by a migratory group of Semitic people whose God, under the name of YHWH, had helped them escape from pharaonic power in Egypt, and who began to intermarry with the indigenous people of the land; (2) military conquests by the "Israelites" against the Canaanite cities; and (3) local uprisings by Canaanite peasants who aligned themselves with the Semitic minority under the banner of their God YHWH to resist the dominant power structures of the Canaanite city-states.[4] However we envision these beginnings, at some time around 1250 B.C.E. a new social-political and religious movement began to take shape in Canaan/Palestine. Archaeological studies have found evidence in this period of new agrarian settlements on the highlands of Judea and Samaria. These highland farmers developed new methods of terrace farming, introduced a typically styled "four-room house," and seem to have rejected the way of life in the highly stratified society of the Canaanite city-states.

According to the biblical story in the book of Joshua, this new movement was grounded in its common faith in YHWH (Josh 24) and rejected the gods of the Canaanite peoples. The people fashioned a loosely confederated union of tribes and clans, some united perhaps in kinship bonds but others coming from among the indigenous Canaanites who embraced a new allegiance to YHWH. The covenant renewal ceremony narrated in Joshua 24 suggests that these disparate tribes came together periodically for a religious ceremony to pledge their continued fidelity to YHWH and to their covenant bonds. Like the thirteen original colonies in American colonial history, these tribes also joined forces periodically for common defense. The book of Judges, in one of the oldest examples of Hebrew poetry in the Bible, narrates the judge Deborah's "call to arms" against the forces of the Canaanite King of Hazor (Judg 5).

They sought a different mode of social organization, as well, one that enfleshed a more egalitarian vision consistent with their covenant stipulations. Leadership was manifest in the hands of local elders and judges whose authority discouraged the centralization of power. Priestly leaders presided over cultic practices in the ancient shrines and sanctuaries dedicated to YHWH. The colorful biblical stories of this tribal period narrate both heroes (such as Samson, Deborah, Gideon) and villains (such as the power-hungry Abimelech, who wanted to be king, and Jephthah, who sacrificed his own daughter in fulfillment of a vow). Despite the humanness of the cast of characters, the story testifies to their attempts to live the covenant dream that called them to be "a people precious to YHWH" living in obedience to its new social vision.

Brueggemann aptly describes the character of this covenant dream as "a precarious social experiment based on a precarious theological vision." In this part of the story, precarious as its attempts were, we see evidence of risks taken to embody covenant norms and to reject social-political patterns that perpetuated slavery. We cannot help but be impressed listening to Joshua recount for the tribal assembly at Shechem all the saving deeds that YHWH had done on their behalf. And we cannot help but be challenged, as they must have been, by Joshua's strong summons:

> Now therefore revere the LORD, and serve him in sincerity and in faithfulness; put away the gods that your ancestors served beyond the River and in Egypt, and serve the LORD. Now if you are unwilling to serve the LORD, choose this day whom you will serve, whether the gods your ancestors served in the region beyond the River or the gods of the Amorites in whose land you are living; but as for me and my household, we will serve the LORD. (Josh 24:14–15)

What, then, does this text invite us to ponder? What wisdom does it offer for our lives today? Perhaps it tells us that an authentic spirituality always requires of us *daily choices* for God, not once and for all but regularly, daily chosen. These choices mean that we must put ourselves on the side of all that enhances life for others and for ourselves. It means that we make daily commitments to align ourselves with all that leads to freedom and communal responsibility. It means, furthermore, that we must contend with all those deadly forces, both within and without, that serve "other gods"—other values opposed to the ways of God. This was the challenge of the Israelite tribes as they moved into the land: how to live *faithfully* and *concretely* the values of the covenant vision. Even after 3,000 years this same challenge remains our own.

RISE OF MONARCHY

The "precarious social experiment" in the tribal period began to give way to a new moment in the life of the covenant people in the century between 1100 and 1000 B.C.E. Social, political, and economic factors affected the shifting historical context of covenant faith, continued to shape its religious and social imagination, and culminated with the establishment of the monarchy. Old Testament historian George Mendenhall describes these factors in this way: "Poor, isolated, fragmented elements of local society were becoming unified in larger social units necessary not only to what we are wont to call civilization (cites, social stratification, writing, urban specializations of all sorts), but also for the organization of an economic system larger than that of the agricultural/ pastoral village that is essential to the support of a growing population."[5] With an increase in the population of the Israelite tribes came the need for more agricultural and grazing land, space for the tribal clans and families to expand. This need created pressure for conquest of new frontiers. The consequent intensification of agricultural activity generated surpluses that in turn contributed to an emerging social stratification. Inter- and intraregional trade necessitated the rise of an advanced administration. All these factors marked the life of the tribal groups in the eleventh century B.C.E.

In this part of the biblical story, that is, in the books of Judges and 1 and 2 Samuel, another factor looms large as a cause for the emergence of the monarchy. As Israelite settlements expanded from the central highlands into the western coastal plain of Palestine they encountered the superior military threat of the Philistines, whose league of five cities (Ashdod, Ashkelon, Ekron, Gath, and Gaza) generally corresponds to the territory of the Gaza Strip today.[6] The Bible portrays the Philistines as Israel's archenemy, and certainly the consolidation of the tribal clans into a united political entity was due in large part to this threat.

Different assessments of this movement toward monarchy, and how it either supported or corrupted the covenant vision, stand side by side in the biblical texts. It is important to remember, though, that all of our Old Testament texts as we have them come from the priestly editors who assembled the traditions in the time of the exile in Babylon (587–538 B.C.E.) and shortly thereafter. Consequently, from a literary perspective, they all to some extent look backward from hindsight at the history and traditions of their ancestors and, through their *telling of the tradition*, comment on their successes and failures as they tell the story. And so, in the case of the rise of the monarchy, we find different assessments. The author of Judges, for example, recounts that when the people clamored for the judge Gideon to be named king, he categorically refused: "Then the Israelites said to Gideon, 'Rule over us, you and your son and your grandson also; for you have delivered us out of the hand of Midian.' Gideon said to them, 'I will not rule over you, and my son will not rule over you; the LORD will rule over you'" (Judg 8:22–23).

Gideon's response preserves the covenantal claim that YHWH alone rules; there can be no other—human or divine—who takes the place of YHWH. In the very next chapter of Judges, by contrast, we hear the story of Abimelech, who himself desired to be king and who was hailed as king by the people of Shechem. Abimelech's hubris receives a scathing critique by the writer, and he dies in dishonor at "the hands of a woman."

With Saul (1050–1000 B.C.E.), David (1000–960 B.C.E.), and Solomon (960–922 B.C.E.), the movement toward monarchy became a reality. The early "pro-monarchy" tradition found in 1 Samuel 9:1–10:16 recounts favorably the anointing of Saul by the judge and prophet Samuel: "When Samuel saw Saul, the LORD told him, 'Here is the man of whom I spoke to you. He it is who shall rule over my people.' Samuel took a vial of oil and poured it on his head, and kissed him; . . . he said, 'The LORD has anointed you ruler over his people Israel. You shall reign over the people of the LORD and you will save them from the hand of their enemies all around'" (1 Sam 9:17, 10:1). From this perspective the king was to be YHWH's own ambassador among the people who would guard and protect them as a shepherd guards the sheep. Moreover, the king's primary duty should be the protection of the covenant vision. Most of Israel's history as a nation proved this ideal to be a foolish hope. The repeated failure of leadership is a constant and tragic theme.

In general, the "revisionist" traditions reflected in 1 Samuel 7–8, 10, and 12 and Deuteronomy 17:14–20 all criticize the tribal insistence on a king and their desire "to be like all the nations" (1 Sam 8:20). From a later (exilic and postexilic) theological perspective, this desire reflected a movement toward religious assimilation and syncretistic practices, which implied a relaxation—even abandonment—of older covenant loyalties. The ensuing development of the royal bureaucracy—census and taxation, military conscription, forced labor, and the further stratification of society—moved in a direction different from the original vision of the covenant community, based as it was on the radical freedom of God and God's power of liberation for the people.

With the defeat of the Philistines and the establishment of the united monarchy under David (see 2 Sam 5–6), a new theology of covenant and people had to emerge. The earliest of the written sources of the Pentateuch, the so-called Yahwist source, shaped a story of Israel's beginnings that celebrates the promise made to Abraham in the ancient past that YHWH would give to Abraham and Sarah and to their descendants land, power, and progeny (Gen 12:1–3, 15:5–7). Perhaps reflecting the position and optimism of the Davidic empire, as some believe, the Yahwist source saw in the establishment of the Davidic dynasty the final fulfillment of the promises to Abraham of old. With Solomon, according to the biblical story, the move toward royal establishment was finally complete. The chilling "warning" by Samuel (actually a judgment from hindsight) describes the actual abuses of power later associated with Solomon's rule:

So Samuel reported all the words of the LORD to the people who were asking him for a king. He said, "These will be the ways of the king who will reign over you: he will take your sons and appoint them to his chariots and to be his horsemen, and to run before his chariots; and he will appoint for himself commanders of thousands and commanders of fifties, and some to plow his ground and to reap his harvest, and to make his implements of war and the equipment of his chariots. He will take your daughters to be perfumers and cooks and bakers. He will take the best of your fields and vineyards and olive orchards and give them to his courtiers. He will take one-tenth of your grain and of your vineyards and give it to his officers and his courtiers. He will take your male and female slaves, and the best of your cattle and donkeys, and put them to his work. He will take one-tenth of your flocks, and you shall be his slaves. And in that day you will cry out because of your king, whom you have chosen for yourselves; but the LORD will not answer you in that day. (1 Sam 8:10–18)

Whereas the Mosaic covenant traditions celebrated the freedom of YHWH's presence with the people symbolized in the pillar of cloud and fire in the wilderness, the Davidic expression embodied in Solomon's empire located YHWH's presence in the Davidic dynasty and in the permanent establishment of the Temple in Jerusalem as the house of YHWH. Religion and cultic practice were now servants of the state. No longer was Israel as God's people bound together on the basis of covenant allegiance to YHWH at the central sanctuary. Israel was now bound together politically, on the basis of a contract between king and people (2 Sam 5:3). As citizens of the state, the people of Israel now owed allegiance to a king who could (and did) take a census, exact forced labor, expropriate land, impose heavy taxes, assassinate his enemies, and require absolute submission.

CONCLUSION

What are the lingering questions from this part of the biblical story? Where is the wisdom for contemporary faith in all this? Where is the word for our time? Certainly, it becomes clear that we did not need to wait for the oft-quoted statement of the British historian Lord Acton (1834–1902), "Power tends to corrupt, and absolute power corrupts absolutely," to know the dangers and misery of the abuses of power. As we observed in the wilderness murmurings/grumblings, the "pharaoh inside them" reared its head once more. In an ironic and almost tragic way, for the Israelites the wheel had come full circle. At the Reed Sea,

YHWH had saved this people from the abuses of Pharaoh's harsh rule. Now, in the land, they themselves had embraced the very same modes of life they had rejected in Egypt. In their desire to be "like the other nations" they had been seduced by values contrary to the covenant dream. Isn't this always the risk for us? Isn't this the ever-present danger, that we will fail to live up to—and live *into*—the values that we have chosen, the commitments we have made?

And yet covenant faith was not destroyed; the dream had not died. It would be nurtured throughout the monarchy and during the time of exile and beyond by prophetic voices calling Israel back to its senses. It is to this prophetic tradition that we next turn.

QUESTIONS FOR REFLECTION

1. We make promises, agreements, and "covenants" of all sorts throughout our lives. What are the important promises and covenants of your life, with God or with others?

2. What demands and obligations do these covenants place on you and on those with whom you have made them? How can these experiences help you to understand the meaning of "covenant faith"?

3. We often learn by rote the Ten Commandments as children, but how do these ethical directives shape our adult lives? What are the values the commandments safeguarded, and how do these same biblical values affect your life today?

4. The cast of characters in the biblical story of the tribal and monarchy periods is filled with colorful characters, both heroes and villains. What does this very human story teach you about how God deals with us? Who are your heroes and villains, and what does their positive or negative example inspire in you?

5. In the story of the rise of the Israelite monarchy we come face to face with issues of power: both the right use of power and the abuse of power. Where in your life do you exercise authority and power, both *with* and *over* others? How does the Bible help you to reflect on the right use of power?

7

PROPHETIC SPIRITUALITY

See, I have set you this day over nations and over
kingdoms, to pluck up and to break down, to destroy
and to overthrow, to build and to plant.

—Jeremiah 1:10

Prophets, many would say, are very uncomfortable people. No matter
what the context, they claim to speak with an authority that tolerates no
dissent. Their power and influence derive from their claims of special
insight and "contact" with the divine. For this reason, they seem so sure
of what they see, so certain that their perspective about the present or
the future is the correct one, sometimes the only one. Perhaps we can
say best what prophecy is by saying what it is not. First, prophets, and
especially biblical prophets, are not crystal ball gazers peering into the
abyss of things yet to be so that they might "foretell" the future. Prophets are concerned primarily with the *present*, not with the distant future. They speak about present realities, the implications of present
actions, and their consequences in the immediate future. They read the
"writing on the wall," the "signs of the times," and declare to others the
certain consequences of their actions that they themselves seem not to
see. Second, prophets are not lone, solitary figures but, rather, individuals who speak for and represent the concerns and perspectives of different groups in society.

Known by various names in different cultures both ancient and modern, prophets are a common phenomenon in societies, and they serve
an essential social function.[1] Some prophets claim a place in the mainstream as spokespersons for the status quo. They lend so-called divine
legitimization to the dominant social-political group. Their words lend
affirmation and stability to those in power. Like the evangelistic preach-

er at a political prayer breakfast, such prophets are part of "the system." There are other prophets, however, who stand on the margins of society, on the periphery, and speak words that are often "out of sync" with the mainstream. These are those women and men who dare to challenge the status quo and who serve as essential agents for social change. These are the voices of challenge and social critique. Insofar as their message threatens those in power, these prophets often suffer abuse, arrest, and ostracism at the hands of the system. The Indian activist Gandhi (1869–1948), the African American woman Rosa Parks (1913–2005), who refused to take a backseat in the bus because of the color of her skin, or Nelson Mandela (1918–2013), jailed for nearly thirty years in South Africa for his opposition to the racist policies of apartheid, are among the many obvious contemporary examples of this type of prophet. Other persons will no doubt stand out for you as examples of modern-day prophets. It is important to keep these persons in mind as concrete examples of contemporary prophecy while we turn now to the biblical prophets.

THE TWOFOLD CHARACTER OF BIBLICAL PROPHECY

Prophecy in ancient Israel is a complex and multifaceted dimension of biblical faith. Before exploring the individual prophetic figures who spoke YHWH's message in diverse ways to Israel, it is important to review some of the elements that were common among the Israelite prophets. Taken together, the biblical prophets could be described as the custodians of the covenant dream. Again and again throughout Israel's history, they were the ones who continually called the covenant people back to fidelity to YHWH. Often they challenged even the king himself and all the royal bureaucracy. Their mission, however, was always twofold: to challenge covenant violators and to nurture covenant faith.[2] The account of the prophet Jeremiah's call offers the consummate statement of the "agenda" of the prophet's life:

> See, today I appoint you over nations and over kingdoms,
> to pluck up and to pull down, to destroy and to overthrow,<
> to build and to plant. (Jer 1:10)

The dual character of the prophetic task is more easily visible if we juxtapose the first and third cola (lines or phrases) in particular:

> A—to *pluck up* and to *pull down*—B
> B'—to *build* and to *plant*—A'

The agricultural images of "plucking up and planting" are reinforced by the construction images of "pulling down and building" in an A–B–B–A pattern that rounds out its message and comes to a conclusion (*inclusio*) by coming full circle. The message is clear and by this structure and rhetorical form receives special emphasis. Prophets must *both* criticize and energize, denounce as well as announce hope for the covenant people.[3] This dual role is not what we ordinarily associate with our image of the "prophet." We tend to focus more on their role as social critics and forget that prophets also bear the awesome responsibility to speak words of hope in times of despair. Which is more difficult, we might ask, to be a social critic and prophet of doom or to summon the energy to hope in a time of hopelessness? The biblical prophets did both.

The faith of the prophets rests on their unshakable conviction that God's word had entered into and taken possession of them. They stood on "middle ground," as it were, as the link between God and the people. On the one hand, they cried out to God on behalf of people; on the other, they pleaded with the people on behalf of God. Three Hebrew terms named these figures in ancient Israel: *hozeh* (visionary), *roeh* (seer), and *nabî* (prophet, one who announces, one who is called). These terms suggest that prophetic activity was characterized by both visionary and auditory experiences that provided access to the divine realm. These were figures of deep insight, fearless commitment, and unwavering fidelity to God's powerful word.

"WHAT MANNER OF [PERSON] IS THE PROPHET?"

When the great Jewish teacher of the last century, Rabbi Abraham Heschel (1907–1972), posed this question in 1962 in his now landmark book, *The Prophets*, he had in mind principally the prophet as the person on the margin, speaking a word from God to those in the center of society.[4] Heschel tries to get inside the prophetic consciousness, to touch the prophet's very soul. He succeeds with stirring power.[5] Like the poets and artists in every age, the biblical prophets had a heightened sensitivity to evil. They had a "breathless impatience with injustice" that prompted them to speak out.[6] The people's idolatrous ways and failure to live the demands of their covenant identity horrified them. Jeremiah offers again the perfect example: "Be appalled, O heavens, at this, be shocked, be utterly desolate, says the LORD, for my people have committed two evils: they have forsaken me, the fountain of living water, and dug out cisterns for themselves, cracked cisterns that can hold no water" (Jer 2:12–13).

These prophets were consumed with indignation and moral outrage. They stood aghast before the callous numbness of the people. They were convinced that even the "smallest" abuse of justice, the most minor violation of the covenant bond, was an affront in the eyes of God: "The prophet's ear is attuned to a cry imperceptible to others. . . . The prophet's ear perceives the silent sigh."[7] Others (especially those in power) are callous, unmoved by suffering or injustice, whereas the prophet, like YHWH, "hears the cry." Their mode of speech was often outrageous, desperate, or shocking. It is almost as if they try to take us by the shoulders and shake us into awareness of the horrors that they see. In words that we can barely stand to listen to, for example, the prophet Micah condemns the royal establishment of his day: "Listen, you heads of Jacob and rulers of the house of Israel! Should you not know justice?—you who hate the good and love the evil, who tear the skin off my people, and the flesh off their bones; who eat the flesh of my people, flay their skin off them, break their bones in pieces, and chop them up like meat in a kettle, like flesh in a caldron" (Mic 3:1–3). These grotesque images cut like a sword and speak as strongly today of contemporary horrors—in Afghanistan, in the Gaza Strip, or in Belfast—as they did in Micah's Jerusalem.

Neither did the Israelite prophets spare the religious establishment of their day. Priest and "court prophet" alike (those figures who were part of the royal establishment and in collusion with the king), they believed, had abandoned their covenant responsibility and had subordinated justice to the practices of "empty religion." Again, both Hosea's and Jeremiah's words are chilling:

> Yet let no one contend,
>   And let none accuse,
>   for with you is my contention, O priest.
> They feed on the sin of my people;
>   they are greedy for their iniquity.
> And it shall be like people, like priest;
> I will punish them for their ways,
>   and repay them for their deeds. (Hos 4:4, 8–9)

> For from the least to the greatest of them,
>   everyone is greedy for unjust gain;
> and from prophet to priest,
>   everyone deals falsely.
> They have treated the wound of my people carelessly,
>   saying, "Peace, peace,"
>   when there is no peace. (Jer 6:13–14)

This wholesale indictment of the establishment brought a harsh response from those in power. Consequently, another mark of prophets' lives is often loneliness, persecution at the hands of others, and mistrust of their own clarity and vision. But their message keeps on—relentlessly—calling Israel back to the heart of its covenant bond. The prophet Hosea (ca. 750 B.C.E.) captured the essence of covenant faith in conveying YHWH's words of love to a wayward people. Hosea sees that YHWH will once again lure the people into the wilderness and, there, will renew the covenant of love: "And I will betroth you to me forever; I will betroth you in *righteousness* [*sedeqah*] and in *justice* [*mispat*], in *steadfast love* [*hesed*], and in *mercy* [*rahamim*]. I will betroth you to me in *faithfulness* [*emeth*]; and you shall *know* [*daath YHWH*] the LORD" (Hos 2:19–20, Barbara Bowe's translation). These six terms recur, almost monotonously, throughout the prophetic writings, and they encompass the core of Israel's relationship with her God. These were the very attributes of the God who had rescued them; and these were to be the covenant commitments among God's people. The prophets would not let Israel, nor do they let us, forget.

PROPHETIC CHALLENGE AND VISION

Though there were prophetic precursors before the eighth century B.C.E., like the fiery prophet Elijah who was taken up in the "chariot of fire," the height of prophetic activity corresponds to the period from the eighth to the fifth century B.C.E. (see table 7.1). It was from this period that we have prophetic oracles that have been preserved in writing by the circle of those who heard and collected the words of the prophets. During these tumultuous years of the monarchy and its aftermath, the covenant people saw the destruction, first, of the Northern Kingdom of Israel in 722 B.C.E. and then of the Southern Kingdom of Judah, with its political and cultic center focused in the Temple in Jerusalem in 587 B.C.E. They endured fifty to sixty years of exile in Babylon, and when they returned to reestablish their life in the land, they were living as aliens under Persian rule. Through these years the words of the prophets kept their covenant vision alive. Let us listen now to some of these voices.

Table 7.1.   Prophetic Activity

Date	Israel—North	Judah—South	Exile (587–539 B.C.E.)	Postexilic
8th century B.C.E.	Amos	Isaiah		
	Hosea	Micah		
	722 Fall of Samaria			
7th century B.C.E.		Zephaniah		
		Jeremiah		
		Nahum		
		Habakkuk		
			Ezekiel	
6th century B.C.E.			Obadiah	
Exile 596/ 587–539			2nd Isaiah	
5th century B.C.E.				3rd Isaiah
				Zechariah
				Malachi
				Haggai
				Jonah
				Joel

THE NORTHERN KINGDOM OF ISRAEL: AMOS AND HOSEA

Amos

Of all the prophets in ancient Israel, none was more fiercely committed to covenant justice than Amos. Amos, who was "among the shepherds of Tekoa" (Am 1:1), heard God's call as he was about his business of "dressing his sycamore trees" (Am 7:14).[8] The voice of the Lord said to him: "Go prophesy to my people Israel" (Am 7:15). As a southerner (from Judah) he was sent north to the prosperous kingdom of Israel under its King Jeroboam II. Though the hostile Assyrian Empire was poised to strike at Israel's borders, Jeroboam continued his luxurious excesses and empty religious practices. Amos' vehement critique spared no one:

> Thus says the LORD:
>> For three transgressions of Israel,
>> and for four, I will not revoke the punishment;
>> because they sell the righteous for silver,
>> and the needy for a pair of sandals—
>> they who trample the head of the poor into the dust of the earth,
>> and push the afflicted out of the way;
>> father and son go in to the same girl,
>> so that my holy name is profaned. (Am 2:6–7)

YHWH's covenant promise that Israel would be a precious possession meant that they must live and conduct their lives in justice. Their failure to do so brought Amos' bitter condemnation:

Hear this word that the LORD has spoken against you, O people of Israel, against the whole family that I brought up out of the land of Egypt:
> You only have I known
> of all the families of the earth;
> *therefore* I will punish you
> for all your iniquities. (Am 3:1–2, emphasis added)

As we said earlier and Amos here makes clear, YHWH had rescued and chosen them for special responsibility, not for special privilege.

Amos regards the abuses of the powerful women of Bashan with particular disdain.[9] Calling them the "cows of Bashan . . . who oppress the poor, who crush the needy" (Am 4:1), Amos also reserves for them a particularly horrible fate:

>> The Lord GOD has sworn by his holiness:
>> The time is surely coming upon you,
>> when they shall take you away with hooks,
>> even the last of you with fishhooks. (Am 4:2)

Again the grotesque images convey the prophet's rage. Elsewhere Amos resorts to biting irony when he mimics the poetic rhythm of the Hebrew funeral lament and sings a dirge for Israel's death:

Hear this word that I take up over you in lamentation, O house of Israel:
> Fallen, no more to rise,
> is maiden Israel;
> forsaken on her land,
> with no one to raise her up. (Am 5:1–2)

This would have the same effect in his day as it might have in ours if we were to sing solemnly to the tune of "Taps" or "We Shall Overcome." The cadence of the Hebrew lament meter would bring chills to those who heard it. Thus, the prophet would use any method available to move the hearts of his hearers.

The core of Amos' preaching can best be summarized in a final example that preserves the very heart of the covenant vision:

> I hate, I despise your festivals,
>> and I take no delight in your solemn assemblies.
> Even though you offer me your burnt offerings and grain offerings, I
>> will not accept them;
> and the offerings of well-being of your fatted animals
>> I will not look upon.
> Take away from me the noise of your songs;
>> I will not listen to the melody of your harps.
> But let justice roll down like waters,
>> and righteousness like an ever-flowing stream. (Am 5:21–24)

Burnt offerings, fatted calves, and noisy songs are all meaningless without the core covenant values lived among the people: justice and righteousness pouring down like water. "Woe to those," Amos warns, ". . . Woe to those who are at ease in Zion, . . . [Woe to those] who lie upon beds of ivory, . . . [Woe to those who] eat lambs from the flock, who drink wine in bowls, and anoint themselves with finest oils, but who are not grieved over the ruin of Joseph!" (Am 6:1, 4, 6).[10]

Such fierce words from the prophet bring fierce reprisals from the powerful elite: "Then Amaziah, the priest of Bethel, sent to King Jeroboam of Israel, saying, 'Amos has conspired against you in the very center of the house of Israel; the land is not able to bear all his words.' And Amaziah said to Amos, 'O seer, go, flee away to the land of Judah, earn your bread there, and prophesy there; but never again prophesy at Bethel, for it is the king's sanctuary, and it is a temple of the kingdom'" (Am 7:10, 12–13). This exchange illustrates well the recurring struggle between the king, together with his priest who was part of the royal establishment, and the marginal prophet as guardian of the covenant.

Hosea

A very different prophetic voice in the Northern Kingdom came from the resident northerner Hosea, whose ministry spanned the years 750–724 B.C.E., ending just before the fall of the northern capital, Samaria, in 722 B.C.E. Unlike Amos', Hosea's message balanced both words of *disaster* and words of *hope*. His oracles draw on the central image of marriage as a symbol of YHWH's covenant relationship with the people. And just as infidelity destroys the marital bond, so Israel's infidelity and idolatrous practices have threatened their covenant status. The key text quoted earlier, "I will betroth you to me forever . . ." (Hos 2:19), imagines that YHWH will again renew the covenant relationship in love after a time of purification in the wilderness. But first the truth must be told. Like a prosecuting attorney in the courtroom, Hosea levels God's sweeping allegations against the people:

> Hear the word of the LORD, O people of Israel;
> for the LORD has an indictment against the inhabitants of the land.
> There is no faithfulness or loyalty,
>   and no knowledge of God in the land.
> Swearing, lying, and murder,
>   and stealing and adultery break out;
>   bloodshed follows bloodshed.
> Therefore the land mourns,
>   and all who live in it languish;
> together with the wild animals
>   and the birds of the air,
>   even the fish of the sea are perishing. (Hos 4:1–3)

Even the land and sea suffer from Israel's sin.

To a degree unparalleled in other prophets, Hosea seems to know the very heart of God and to be privy to the inner soliloquy within the divine psyche. His intimacy with this divine pathos produces some of the most profound passages in all of scripture. Hosea imagines YHWH's exasperated question, like that of a weary parent: "What shall I do with you, O Ephraim? What shall I do with you, O Judah? Your love is like a morning cloud, like the dew that goes away early" (Hos 6:4). Here, the prophet seems to have an ear on the very heart of God, listening to God's own anguish over the foolishness of the people's sin. Playing the harlot and seeking after other gods constitute one of their crimes. The monarchy itself seems to be another, as YHWH's word contends: "They [Israel] made kings, *but not through me*; They set up princes, *but without my knowledge*. With silver and gold, they made idols for their own destruction" (Hos 8:4, emphasis added).

In another passage Hosea again voices God's parental lament for these wayward children:

> When Israel was a child, I loved him,
>   and out of Egypt I called my son.
> The more I called them,
>   the more they went from me;
> they kept sacrificing to the Baals,
>   and offering incense to idols. (Hos 11:1–2)

And yet, as Hosea knows, divine anger always gives way to divine compassion. This is the very character of the covenant God; it cannot be otherwise. As with the generation of Noah in the ancient past, so God's fidelity is absolute. Therefore, the prophet consoles the people with assurances of God's own anguish and yet God's persistent determination to save and not to destroy:

> Yet it was I who taught Ephraim to walk,
> I took them up in my arms;
>> but they did not know that I healed them.
> I led them with cords of human kindness,
>> with bands of love.
> I was to them like those
>> who lift infants to their cheeks.
>> I bent down to them and fed them. (Hos 11:3–4)

> How can I give you up, Ephraim?
>> How can I hand you over, O Israel?
>> How can I make you like Admah?
>> How can I treat you like Zeboiim?
>> My heart recoils within me;
>> my compassion grows warm and tender.
>> I will not execute my fierce anger;
>> I will not again destroy Ephraim;
>> for I am God and no mortal,
>> the Holy One in your midst,
>> and I will not come in wrath. (Hos 11:8–9)[11]

Here, as elsewhere, God's mother-love, God's *rahamim*, "grows warm and tender."

Hosea's prophetic word ends in a great crescendo of hope: "I will heal their disloyalty; I will love them freely . . . , I will be like the dew to Israel; he shall blossom like the lily" (Hos 14:4–5). Despite the Assyrian threat that was soon to destroy the Northern Kingdom, the prophet affirms hope beyond defeat and destruction. But hope must be always grounded in a return to covenant fidelity, to intimate dependence on God:

> They shall again live beneath my shadow,
>> they shall flourish as a garden;
> they shall blossom like the vine,
>> their fragrance shall be like the wine of Lebanon.

> O Ephraim, what have I to do with idols?
>> It is I who answer and look after you.
> I am like an evergreen cypress;
>> your faithfulness comes from me. (Hos 14:7–8)

THE SOUTHERN KINGDOM OF JUDAH: MICAH AND ISAIAH

Micah

In the same turbulent eighth century B.C.E., while all of Palestine braced itself in the face of the threat of invasion and domination by the rising political power of the Assyrian Empire to the northeast, two prophets proclaimed a similar message in the heart of Jerusalem. Micah's words mix accusation and hope as he tries to bring Jerusalem to its senses. His desperate urgency drove him to outrageous acts: "For this I will lament and wail; I will go barefoot and naked; I will make lamentation like the jackals . . . for her wound is incurable; it has come to Judah, it has reached the gate of my people, to Jerusalem" (Mic 1:8–9).[12] Like his northern counterpart, Amos, Micah too leveled vehement criticism against those who violated covenant justice:

> Alas for those who devise wickedness
>   and evil deeds on their beds!
> When the morning dawns, they perform it,
>   because it is in their power.
> They covet fields, and seize them;
>   houses, and take them away;
> they oppress householder and house,
>   people and their inheritance. (Mic 2:1–2)

But even in the midst of international political upheaval and national violation of justice Micah finds the social imagination to dream of a different future. His familiar words, which are duplicated in Isaiah 2:2–4, envision a future time of peace. In our contemporary age of modern weapons and nuclear threats, they still resound in our ears but with an even greater urgency. Such is the power of the prophetic word, with its images that sear themselves on our souls:

> He [YHWH] shall judge between many peoples,
>   and shall arbitrate between strong nations far away;
> they shall beat their swords into plowshares,
>   and their spears into pruning hooks;
> nation shall not lift up sword against nation,
>   neither shall they learn war any more;
>   but they shall all sit under their own vines
>   and under their own fig trees,
>   and no one shall make them afraid;
>   for the mouth of the LORD of hosts has spoken. (Mic 4:3–4)

Micah also joins his prophetic voice to those who denounced empty and perfunctory worship devoid of covenantal living. Micah first poses the hypothetical question about proper worship and reverence of God: "With what shall I come before the LORD, and bow myself before God on high?" (Mic 6:6). Then, in escalating stair step fashion, Micah responds with five proposals only to reject them all in the climactic final verse. "Shall I come," he asks, "with:

> v7c—my first born, the fruit of my body?
> v7b—ten thousand rivers of oil?
> v7a—thousands of rams?
> v6d—Calves a year old?
> v6c—Burnt offerings?

Here, verses 6 and 7 each have separate phrases, labeled a, b, c, and d. Each phrase introduces a new thought in progressive steps, upping the ante each time. What does God require of us, what can we possibly give as propitiation for our failures and sin? What could be *enough*? Micah answers with a staggeringly simple response that encompasses the covenant demands completely:

> He has told you, O mortal, what is good;
>   and what does the LORD require of you
> but to do justice, and to love kindness,
>   and to walk humbly with your God? (Mic 6:8)

It is not the excess of sacrificial cultic offerings. It is not 10,000 acts of ritual devotion. It is not even the "fruit of our bodies" that YHWH demands. Only this YHWH asks—to do justice (*mispat*), and to love kindness (*hesed*), and "to walk" (that is, to conduct one's entire life) humbly *with* God. Here is the heart of the covenant—nothing more, nothing less.

Isaiah of Jerusalem

With the biblical book of Isaiah we have the proclamations and prophetic oracles not of a single prophet but, in fact, of several. These prophetic voices span the centuries from the eighth century B.C.E., in the prophet Isaiah of Jerusalem, a contemporary of Micah, to an anonymous prophet writing toward the end of the exile (ca. 545), to the postexilic prophecies coming from the early Persian period (538–500 B.C.E.). An anonymous editor gathered these traditions together because they shared to some degree a common vocabulary and theological vision. Our biblical "book of Isaiah" comprises, then, First Isaiah (chaps. 1–39), Second Isaiah (chaps. 40–55), and Third Isaiah (chaps. 56–66).

Because this work is so large we can at best only highlight some of the more significant passages, beginning here with First Isaiah.

In the case of First Isaiah of Jerusalem (ca. 742–705 B.C.E.) we can begin with a report of the prophet's extraordinary experience of his call from God. Isaiah 6:1–8 describes this moment in some detail and brings to mind the call of Moses from Exodus 3. As Isaiah describes the moment, he was in the Temple of Jerusalem and, with the same suddenness as Moses had experienced, he had a vision of the Lord "sitting upon a throne, high and lifted up." Above him there were seraphim (angelic beings), and they sang in chorus:

> Holy, holy, holy is the LORD of hosts;
> the whole earth is full of his glory. (Isa 6:3)

Dramatic signs signaled the awesomeness of the moment. The foundations of the doors shook, and the Temple area was filled with smoke. Isaiah was astonished and said: "Woe is me for I am lost; for I am a man of unclean lips, and I dwell in the midst of a people of unclean lips; for my eyes have seen the King, the LORD of hosts!" (Isa 6:5). These theophanies, these God experiences—whether those of Moses, of Isaiah, or of ourselves—are both humbling and overwhelming. God's majesty, holiness, mystery, exposes our littleness and the faults of our "unclean lips." But YHWH's response to Isaiah comes swiftly through the aid of the seraphim: "Then one of the seraphs flew to me, holding a live coal that had been taken from the altar with a pair of tongs. The seraph touched my mouth with it and said: 'Now that this has touched your lips, your guilt has departed and your sin is blotted out.' Then I heard the voice of the Lord saying, 'Whom shall I send, and who will go for us?' And I said, 'Here am I; send me!'" (Isa 6:6–8). A live coal sears Isaiah's tongue and so brands him for God's prophetic mission. This exchange, namely, of divine appearance, human reluctance, and divine empowerment, is the repetitive pattern we saw in the call of Moses and will see repeated in the call of Jeremiah. It signals for us an essential aspect of prophetic spirituality: the conviction that God not only calls but also sustains the messenger.

In Isaiah, we see the same fierce condemnations of injustice against the powerful royal establishment: "Your princes are rebels and companions of thieves. Everyone loves a bribe and runs after gifts. They do not defend the orphan, and the widow's cause does not come to them" (Isa 1:23). In short, they fail in their covenant obligations. In Isaiah, too, we see vehement opposition to empty religious practice: "Your new moons and your appointed festivals my soul hates; they have become a burden to me, I am weary of bearing them" (Isa 1:14). Instead Isaiah blurts out in rapid-fire verse what the people must learn to do:

> Wash yourselves; make yourselves clean;
> remove the evil of your doings
>   from before my eyes;
> cease to do evil,
> learn to do good;
> seek justice,
> rescue the oppressed,
> defend the orphan,
> plead for the widow. (Isa 1:16–17)

No matter how dire the circumstance, however, there is always the possibility of hope. Isaiah proclaims a hope grounded still in the Davidic monarchy and in YHWH's presence in the Temple in Jerusalem. But he envisions a monarchy purified by God's renewing Spirit:[13]

> A shoot shall come out from the stump of Jesse,
>   and a branch shall grow out of his roots.
> The spirit of the LORD shall rest on him,
>   the spirit of wisdom and understanding,
>   the spirit of counsel and might,
>   the spirit of knowledge and the fear of the LORD.
> His delight shall be in the fear of the LORD. (Isa 11:1–3)

ON THE EVE OF DESTRUCTION: JEREMIAH AND HABAKKUK

Roughly a century later Jeremiah, another prophetic "giant," emerged in Jerusalem in the days of King Josiah. Jeremiah is a towering figure in the history of Israel. If there were a competition for Israel's greatest prophet, Jeremiah would surely be a semifinalist, at least. His book of fifty-two chapters is a disparate collection of prophetic oracles that span the years circa 630 B.C.E. down to the time of the Babylonian exile in 587 B.C.E. All this while the Babylonian Empire was gaining strength, ready to devour the other nations of the Near East. Meanwhile Jerusalem seemed oblivious to its certain fate and placed foolish confidence in its Temple and its king. The people had forgotten YHWH: "But my people have forgotten me; they burn offerings to a delusion, they have stumbled in their ways" (Jer 18:15). Against this sin, Jeremiah's poetry is masterful, and he feels with such intensity that the pain of God can be heard in his message.

Jeremiah's ancestry linked him with the priestly families who traced their lineage all the way back to Moses, and his account of his prophetic call is modeled exactly on that of Moses. Like Isaiah's call in the Temple, Jeremiah too had an experience of God in which he "heard" God's word speak to him: "Before I formed you in the womb I knew you, and before you were born I consecrated you; I appointed you a prophet to the nations" (Jer 1:5). Like Moses before him, Jeremiah replied with a reasonable objection: "Ah, LORD God! Truly I do not know how to speak, I am only a boy" (Jer 1:6). But once again God's call could not, in the end, be resisted:

> But the LORD said to me,
>   "Do not say, 'I am only a boy';
>   for you shall go to all to whom I send you,
>   and you shall speak whatever I command you,
> Do not be afraid of them,
>   for I am with you to deliver you, says the LORD."
> Then the LORD put out his hand and touched my mouth;
> and the LORD said to me,
>   "Now I have put my words in your mouth." (Jer 1:7–9)

We saw how the seraph had touched Isaiah's tongue with a hot coal, purifying his speech. This image in Jeremiah is even more intimate. For the *Lord's own hand* touches Jeremiah's mouth and gives him the capacity, "though only a youth," to speak God's own words to the people. And like prophets before him Jeremiah's message combined both harsh censure and confident hope. Again, a few examples will suffice.

Despite the efforts for religious reform instigated by King Josiah (639–609 B.C.E.), which included repairing the Temple in Jerusalem and destroying all other altars and places of sacrifice, Jeremiah was a strong critic of the monarchy, and, after the death of Josiah, his oracles against Josiah's successors (Jehoiakim, 609–598 B.C.E.; Jehoiachin, 597–587 B.C.E.) contained bitter satire against the royal abuses. Against Jehoiakim's palace renovations he cried out: "Woe to him who builds his house by unrighteousness, and his upper rooms by injustice; who makes his neighbors work for nothing, and does not give them their wages; . . . Are you a king because you compete in cedar?" (Jer 22:13, 15). Then Jeremiah suggested that a most inglorious fate would be reserved for such a king: "With the burial of a donkey he shall be buried, dragged off and thrown out beyond the gates of Jerusalem" (Jer 22:19).

Jeremiah's accusations went to the very center of power—to the Temple itself, where the political and religious leaders had tried to convince the people that Jerusalem was invincible and that nothing could touch them—because they had the Temple of the Lord. To this foolish belief, Jeremiah replied by mocking their repeated claims:

> Do not trust in these deceptive words: "This is the temple of the LORD, the temple of the LORD, the temple of the LORD." For if you truly amend your ways and your doings, if you truly act justly to

one with another, if you do not oppress the alien, the orphan, and the widow, or shed innocent blood in this place, and if you do not go after other gods to your own hurt, then I will dwell with you in this place, in the land that I gave of old to your ancestors forever and ever. (Jer 7:4–7)

Instead, he warned them to embrace the covenant demands for justice, especially for the poor and weak in their midst. Only then would YHWH preserve them in the land.

More than any other prophet's, Jeremiah's career gives us a rare glimpse into the prophet's own reflection on his prophetic ministry. Suffering, harassment, persecution, and loneliness marked his life, as well as self-doubt. He felt called by God to deny himself wife and children (Jer 16:1–4). He resorted to outrageous acts, like wearing an ox yoke around his neck as a symbol of Judah's impending captivity (Jer 27:1–28:17). He was beaten and thrown into a cistern (Jer 37:6). His so-called confessions reveal the soul of the prophet. One in particular shows the heart of a true prophetic spirituality:

> O LORD, you have enticed [seduced] me,
>   and I was enticed [seduced];
>   you have overpowered me,
>   and you have prevailed.
> I have become a laughingstock all day long;
>   everyone mocks me.
> For whenever I speak, I must cry out,
>   I must shout, "Violence and destruction!"
> For the word of the LORD has become for me
>   a reproach and derision all day long.
> If I say, "I will not mention him,
>   or speak any more in his name,"
> then within me there is something like a burning fire
>   shut up in my bones;
> I am weary with holding it in, and I cannot. (Jer 20:7–9)

It is clear from this text that a prophet experiences an inner compulsion to speak the word of God—a fire—as Jeremiah says. Despite all obstacles and personal suffering, the fire remains and compels the prophet to speak. For the prophet, the word of God takes possession of his or her very soul. It cannot be contained. In another place, Jeremiah describes it this way: "Your words were found, and I ate them, and your words became to me a joy and the delight of my heart, for I am called by your name O LORD of hosts" (Jer 15:16).

This kind of confidence in YHWH's fidelity, both to the prophet and to the people as a whole, led Jeremiah to proclaim God's astonishing promise:

> The days are surely coming, says the LORD, when I will make a new covenant with the house of Israel and the house of Judah. It will not be like the covenant that I made with their ancestors when I took them by the hand to bring them out of the land of Egypt—a covenant that they broke, though I was their husband, says the LORD. But this is the covenant that I will make with the house of Israel after those days, says the LORD: I will put my law within them, and I will write it on their hearts; and I will be their God, and they shall be my people. No longer shall they teach one another, or say to each other, "Know the LORD," for they shall all know me, from the least of them to the greatest, says the LORD; for I will forgive their iniquity, and remember their sin no more. (Jer 31:31–34)

Certain that the "old" Sinai covenant had ceased to be effective, Jeremiah proclaimed a *new* covenant, not written on tablets of stone but grafted onto the heart of the covenant people. This was to be not simply a new printing fixing minor errors; this would be a reinvigorated *new* edition. For Jeremiah, God's fidelity, therefore, was not a static presence but a dynamic one constantly renewing itself in new and surprising ways among God's people. Jeremiah's contemporary, the prophet Habakkuk, counseled the people never to give up hope in this covenant vision. These are surely words that in our time we still need to hear:

> Write the vision;
>> make it plain on tablets,
>> so that a runner may read it.
> For there is still a vision for the appointed time;
>> it speaks of the end, and does not lie.
> If it seems to tarry, wait for it;
>> it will surely come, it will not delay. (Hab 2:2–3)

The disaster of the exile in Babylon would test this theological conviction as nothing had ever before, and once again it would be the prophetic voices that would show Israel the way.

SINGING THE LORD'S SONG IN A FOREIGN LAND: EZEKIEL AND SECOND ISAIAH

One only has to read the plaintive cries of the book of Lamentations to glimpse the horror and devastation suffered by the city of Jerusalem and its inhabitants in the Babylonian destruction of 587 B.C.E.:

> How lonely sits the city
>> that once was full of people!
> How like a widow she has become,
>> she that was great among the nations!
> She that was a princess among the provinces
>> has become a vassal. (Lam 1:1)

Jeremiah's repeated warnings had been to no avail, and the "foe from the north"—Nebuchadnezzar's armies from Babylon—razed the city to the ground and exiled the leadership of its people. Now, they had lost everything; now it was finished. They had lost the land. They had lost the Davidic dynasty that, God had promised and they had *thought*, was to be forever: "Forever I will keep my steadfast love for him [i.e., the king], and my covenant with him will stand firm. I will establish his line for ever and his throne as the heavens endure" (Ps 89:28–29). Worst of all, they had lost the Temple. The place of YHWH's holy dwelling in their midst, with its Ark of the Covenant (the portable box containing the tablets of the covenant) enshrined in the inner sanctum of the Temple, the Holy of Holies, was no more. Did that mean they had lost YHWH, their God, as well? Were the promises to Abraham now revoked? Had the savior "who brought them up out of the land of Egypt" now abandoned the people? Had the great dream of a covenant between God and a people crumbled? Was there any possibility of hope in a future beyond exile? These questions weighed heavily on their hearts.

As a people broken and exiled far from their homeland they cried out once again to their God in the midst of tears. In the words of the psalmist, "By the waters of Babylon, there we sat down and wept, when we remembered Zion" (Ps 137:1). As they had been in Egypt, so now they were strangers again in Babylon. "How shall we sing the LORD's song in a foreign land?" they asked. Once more, a prophetic voice would provide the answer.

Ezekiel

By his own report, "the word of the LORD came to Ezekiel the priest, the son of Buzi, in the land of the Chaldeans by the river Chebar; and the hand of the LORD was upon him there" (Ezek 1:3). [14] Probably, as a member of the priestly family of Buzi and most likely a priest himself, Ezekiel was among those Jerusalemites who were exiled to Babylon in the first wave of deportations in 597 B.C.E. Although Jerusalem "held on" for ten more years, it was, for all intents and purposes, a broken city that was finally razed by the Babylonians in 587 B.C.E. Ezekiel watched the catastrophe unfold and experienced the humiliation and despair of exile.

It is difficult for us to imagine the level of profound despair these events would have fostered in the exiled community. Only the horror of modern-day devastations of ethnic annihilations, or earthquake-ravaged cities, or thousands of people uprooted from their homes could compare with the desperation and hopelessness that must have been theirs. Then, by the river Chebar, Ezekiel saw a vision of Jerusalem. An angel took him by the hair of his head and brought him to Jerusalem. There he watched as a great chariot descended and the presence of YHWH went out of the Temple in the form of a cloud, like the pillar of cloud that had symbolized YHWH's presence with Moses and the people in the wilderness. And perhaps Ezekiel began to see and to understand that a new moment in their journey as a people was beginning.

Ezekiel saw that God had not given up on the people and they should not give up on God. There by the river Chebar, far from Jerusalem, Ezekiel began to understand that the God who had been with them in the wilderness was with them still—wherever they might be scattered throughout the world. God's voice came to Ezekiel with these words: "Therefore say: Thus says the Lord GOD: Though I removed them far away among the nations, and though I scattered them among the countries, yet I have been a sanctuary to them for a little while in the countries where they have gone" (Ezek 11:16).

But the prophet was convinced that God was calling them as a people to a new understanding of their covenant. Ezekiel believed that God would bring them back to the land where their family properties would be restored and where they would again live as God's people.[15] This new moment, however, required new energies and new imagination to live in a way that could survive disaster. It demanded that the people reexamine their priorities and theological convictions and that they recommit themselves to God's ways. It required, in short, a new heart:

> Therefore say: Thus says the Lord GOD: I will gather you from the peoples, and assemble you out of the countries where you have been scattered, and I will give you the land of Israel. When they come there, they will remove from it all its detestable things and all its abominations. I will give them one heart, and put a new spirit within them; I will remove the heart of stone from their flesh and give them

a heart of flesh, so that they may follow my statutes and keep my
ordinances and obey them. Then they shall be my people, and I will
be their God. (Ezek 11:17–20)

Only this divine "open heart surgery" could cure their hardness of
heart. "Hardness of heart," remember, had been the exact description
of Pharaoh's complicity with evil in the Exodus story. Here again we see
the ongoing struggle with the "pharaoh inside them" and God's determination to free them from that pharaoh by whatever means.

Like many prophets before him, Ezekiel laid the blame for the devastation of Jerusalem and for the exile of its people on the abuses of
power carried out by the "shepherds of Israel"—the kings. And yet he
still holds out hope for a renewed monarchy in the Davidic line that
would shepherd and feed the people *in justice*: "I will set up over them
one shepherd, my servant David, and he shall feed them: he shall feed
them and be their shepherd. And I, the LORD, will be their God, and
my servant David shall be prince among them; I, the LORD, have
spoken" (Ezek 34:23–24).

Ezekiel's most famous and perhaps best-known vision (Ezek
37:1–14), however, concerns, as the wonderful spiritual sings, "Dem
bones, dem bones, dem dry bones." The hand of the Lord brought
Ezekiel to a great valley, "and it was full of bones" (Ezek 37:1), and they
were very dry. As I read this text within an American cultural context, it
is easy to imagine the stark paintings of Georgia O'Keeffe's dry and
brittle animal skulls lying about in the southwestern desert of New
Mexico. For Ezekiel, the scene spoke only of death, corruption, and loss
of hope. YHWH then asked Ezekiel: "'Mortal, can these bones live?' I
answered, 'O Lord GOD, you know'" (Ezek 37:3). The question begs
for an answer and is a perennial question, not just for Ezekiel but for
the spiritual life. In all those moments of our lives that seem to be filled
with death, whether literal or figurative, we are drawn to ask the question: Will we survive? Is there any hope? How can we go on; how will
we endure? Can these bones live?

Ezekiel's vision imagines nothing short of a new act of creation! As
YHWH had fashioned *adam* out of the dry dust of the earth and
breathed life into this creature, so YHWH would do again with these
bones: "'Thus says the Lord GOD to these bones: I will cause breath to
enter you, and you shall live. I will lay sinews on you, and will cause
flesh to come upon you, and cover you with skin, and put breath in you,
and you shall live; and you shall know that I am the LORD.' So I
prophesied as I had been commanded; and as I prophesied, suddenly
there was a noise, a rattling, and the bones came together, bone to its
bone" (Ezek 37:5–7). Bone by bone, with sinews, flesh, and God's own

breath, these exiles would be re-created and called once more to be God's people. Ezekiel would prophesy their future restoration to the land with the Temple rebuilt as YHWH's eternal dwelling place among them (Ezek 40:1–48:35). His elaborate vision of the restored Temple imagined a great river flowing from the throne of God in the midst of the Holy of Holies (Ezek 47:1–12). The life-giving waters of this river would spill out from the Temple, flow out of its gates, and water the dry regions down even to the Dead Sea, restoring life to everything in their path. The desert would bloom; life would flourish, even as it had in the garden of Paradise. Many centuries later another visionary prophet would look to this text of Ezekiel for inspiration for his time. As we shall see in the final chapter, the seer John of Patmos would echo Ezekiel's words in his vision of the New Jerusalem that stands as the concluding word to the entire biblical story (Rev 21–22).

Second Isaiah

If Ezekiel proclaimed to the exiles a future restoration to the land, the anonymous prophet we call Second Isaiah would see that prophecy become reality in his day. Chapters 40–55 of the book of Isaiah contain the oracles of a prophet who, like Ezekiel, was with the exilic community in Babylon but at a time when Babylon's power was beginning to decline and was being challenged by the Persian armies of Cyrus the Great (539–530 B.C.E.), who conquered Babylon in 539. With that dramatic turn of events, suddenly the Jewish exiles found themselves at the mercy of the Persian ruler. But unlike the Babylonians, Cyrus followed a policy of repatriating conquered peoples. And so he sent the exiles home. Some returned to Palestine to rebuild their lives and reclaim their properties. Many did not. Instead these Jews became part of the vast community of the "Diaspora," the dispersed Jewish people living no longer in Palestine but in every conceivable part of the known world.

With his heightened prophetic insight, Second Isaiah "sees" this hopeful future about to unfold. He was convinced of YHWH's enduring fidelity to the people and even saw Cyrus as an anointed instrument of God's purposes to overthrow the Babylonian power. A central theme of this prophet would be the certainty that God had forgiven the people. And so, contrary to the pessimism of the book of Lamentations, which mourns that "[Jerusalem] has none to comfort her," he can announce to the people profound words of comfort:

Comfort, comfort my people says your God. Speak tenderly to Jerusalem, and cry to her
    that she has served her term,

that her penalty is paid,
that she has received from the LORD's hand
double for all her sins. (Isa 40:1–2)[16]

The prophet evoked ancient memories of God's mighty deeds in their Exodus from Egypt and proclaimed an escape through the wilderness, with all the mountains flattened out, and all the valleys raised up, and a straight "highway for our God" (Isa 40:3) from Babylon to Jerusalem. Their time of exile was finished; they would be going home!

Second Isaiah reminded them again and again that there was no reason to fear, that God the Holy One would be with them. He was more convinced, in fact, than some of his predecessors that God's word was immutable. In the face of the exigencies of life, only God could be relied on: "The grass withers, the flower fades; but the word of our God will stand forever" (Isa 40:8). If Jeremiah had seen the need for a new covenant, Second Isaiah proclaimed the eternal and effective character of God's word:

> For as the rain and the snow come down from heaven,
>   and do not return there until they have watered the earth,
> making it bring forth and sprout,
>   giving seed to the sower and bread to the eater,
> so shall my word be that goes out from my mouth;
>   it shall not return to me empty,
>   but it shall accomplish that which I purpose,
>   and succeed in the thing for which I sent it. (Isa 55:10–11)

This prophet, moreover, was one of the first to see that God's message of life was intended for all the earth and that, because of Israel's fidelity, the nations too would be drawn to God's ways. Central to Second Isaiah's message were his poetic visions of a "Servant of YHWH" who would be God's beloved, God's chosen one, on whom God's own Spirit would rest (Isa 42:1). The sufferings of this servant would be redemptive for others (Isa 53:4–5). Interpretive problems abound with these texts (Isa 42:1–4, 49:1–6, 50:4–9, 52:13–53:12): questions about the identity of the "Servant," whether prophet or king, an individual figure known or unknown, or a corporate personality representing the nation as a whole. Some see these songs as influenced by the prophetic career of Jeremiah, who suffered as God's righteous servant. Others claim that the songs envision the idealized servant, and from that vantage point it is not difficult to see how, many years later, Christians would turn back again to these texts to try to understand the message and identity of Jesus.

THE DECLINE OF PROPHECY

We have surveyed many, though not all, of the important prophetic voices of the preexilic and exilic times. These voices did not cease altogether once the people entered again into the land, but they competed with other leaders—priests and scribes—who saw the future of the covenant people in Palestine tied closely to the consolidation of their Torah teachings, the maintenance of cultic purity, the rejection of intermarriage with foreigners, and the rebuilding of the Temple. Other prophets continued to proclaim their visions of a new time when God's blessings would be shared by all peoples, as Third Isaiah declares:

> And the foreigners who join themselves to the LORD,
>   to minister to him, to love the name of the LORD,
>   and to be his servants,
>   all who keep the sabbath, and do not profane it,
>   and hold fast my covenant—
>   these I will bring to my holy mountain,
>   and make them joyful in my house of prayer;
>   their burnt offerings and their sacrifices
>   will be accepted on my altar;
>   for my house shall be called a house of prayer
>   for all peoples. (Isa 56:6–7)

The prophet Joel, writing in the late sixth or early fifth century B.C.E., saw a time when God's spirit would be poured out on "all flesh," and, although Joel was principally concerned with the Jewish community of his day, later generations saw in this text a promise of universal proportions, as Luke makes explicit in the Pentecost story of Acts 2:17–21. And so, as Habakkuk reminds us: "For there is still a vision for the appointed time. If it seems to tarry, wait for it; it will surely come, it will not delay" (Hab 2:3).

CONCLUSION

One thing especially should be clear from this long conversation with the prophets of ancient Israel. They were persons who had been touched by God in profoundly personal and intimate ways. They felt the coal sear their tongues (Isa 6:6), sensed God's hand touch their mouths (Jer 1:9), and felt the fire of God's word within them (Jer 20:9). They saw the world through God's eyes, felt its pain through God's heart, and challenged its abuses as if with God's mighty arm. Like YHWH, they could not be deaf to the cry of people in pain; their sensitivity to evil was raw and uncompromising. These were people who found the courage to hope beyond hope and who spent themselves to convey that hope in the face of despair. These were the poets and dreamers, the ones who could see beyond the surface of things into a deeper reality in the present and into a future time still to come. These were the faithful ones who endured affliction, distress, and persecution and who paid a heavy price for their courageous words.

What is the test of a "true" prophet? How do we distinguish between true and false prophets in our midst? These are questions asked in every age. Our biblical ancestors puzzled over these questions, too. The authors responsible for the book of Deuteronomy, for example, believed that the only "true" prophets were "prophets like Moses" (Deut 18:18) who had received the heritage of their wilderness leader. Others seemed to say that a true prophet was manifest only in the "proof" of his or her words. If his or her prophecies came true, then the prophet was authentic. We might suggest some features of authentic prophecy by summarizing the characteristics that we have seen displayed in the biblical figures discussed in this chapter.

First, and perhaps most important, there is no such thing as a self-appointed prophet. Prophets experience a deep call from God that seems irresistible. Their words are not their own; they speak words that they believe are God's own words within them. These words possess an inner authority that moves the hearts of others—even if only a minority, and not the "establishment," heeds their message. There is always something striking about their person. They command attention, display amazing creativity and often astounding courage. Prophets are not solitary figures but people engaged with others in a common vision that goes to the "heart of the matter" in every age. They are in "for the long haul"; their commitment is steadfast. They are not necessarily saintly folks, and we would perhaps prefer not to live with them at all. But we know we need their message. True prophets are sometimes plagued by doubts and reluctance. And in every age, true prophets often pay a heavy price for their prophetic message.

Spirituality marked by this prophetic spirit is, first of all, relentless in its struggle for justice. We see it in women and men who shelter and defend the homeless, who refuse to pay their taxes that support war and destruction, and who advocate for prisoners wrongly accused. Prophets in our day protest in public arenas, write letters to Congress, and question Church policy. Just as the prophets of old, contemporary prophets awaken people to the truth that they see, even the hard truth. Their willingness to suffer for their beliefs and their selfless concern for the *common good*, and not just their own well-being, lend authenticity and credibility to their lives and message. Prophetic spirituality, in this pattern, therefore, moves us to take risks, to say the unwelcome word, to follow the certainties of our God-inspired hearts. Faced with apparently insurmountable odds, prophets dare to look in the face of evil and to say, "No!" This kind of prophetic spirituality requires uncommon integrity and deep rootedness in God. And it means most of all that we *never, never* give up hope in God's promise of a future still to be.

QUESTIONS FOR REFLECTION

1. Who are the prophets in our time? How do we recognize them? Who has inspired you with her or his words and actions? How have these prophets shaped your faith today?
2. What are the prophetic dimensions of your own life? What God-given convictions motivate your words and deeds to strengthen the common good?
3. How do we discern authentic prophecy today? What are the signs you look for, and why?
4. As you think about the lives of these biblical prophets, what do they tell you about the relationship between religion and politics?
5. In a time of great crisis and despair, where do you look to discover the prophetic voices of hope?
6. On what situations in our world, in our country, and in your own life does God need to perform "open heart surgery"?

8

WISDOM HAS BUILT HERSELF A HOUSE

In every generation, [wisdom] passes into holy
souls and makes them friends of God,
and prophets.

—Wisdom of Solomon 7:27

In chapter 4 we explore the differences in two core biblical perspectives: the saving and the blessing traditions. In the context of that discussion I mention that, of the two, the saving tradition is the more dominant voice within the Bible. The last three chapters have concentrated on the dramatic unfolding of that story of salvation history—beginning with the Exodus and moving to the exile and postexilic period. Now it is time to turn our attention to that other viewpoint, that other way of understanding God, ourselves, and the world that we call the "blessing tradition."

WISDOM AND BLESSING

Jews today refer to their Bible with the acronym TaNaK. The three consonants T-N-K stand for, in Hebrew, the *Torah* (Law), the *Nebi'im* (Prophets), and the *Ketubim* (Writings). This threefold division of the Hebrew Bible corresponds in some ways to the distinctions made between the saving and blessing traditions. The "Law and the Prophets" (as Jesus would, in fact, later call them) contain the very traditions I have described as the saving tradition. The "Writings" is a catchall term to designate all the remaining books of the Jewish Bible not part of the "Law and the Prophets." These include texts such as Job, Proverbs,

Ecclesiastes, the Song of Songs, the Wisdom of Solomon, and Sirach. To these we could also add some of the Psalms that are explicitly "wisdom psalms," such as Psalm 133, which sings: "How very good and pleasant it is when kindred live together in unity!"[1] In these biblical books, which we will turn to in a moment, we find the concentration of that other perspective called the blessing tradition. Because this tradition has a fascination with the pursuit of "wisdom" as a central emphasis we can, therefore, also refer to it as the wisdom tradition.

As we have seen, the saving tradition affirms a God who acts in history, sometimes dramatically, to save and rescue the people. The wisdom and blessing tradition, by contrast, looks for God, not primarily in historical deeds or events, but in the daily ordinariness of life. The sages and all those who looked for wisdom went not so much to the sanctuary but to the marketplace in search of God in the midst of mundane human affairs. Wisdom typifies a way of viewing the world based on close observation and careful reflection in an effort to discern the harmony and order that is constitutive of it. Wisdom's goal is to develop strategies for life that will integrate the individual's existence with the perceived order of the world. Wisdom aims for a practical and comprehensive ethic and behavioral style adequate to the situations in which its followers live, labor, and interact with one another. And insofar as wisdom shapes our spirituality it does so by taking our everyday human existence with the utmost seriousness. Kathleen O'Connor, a professor of Old Testament at Columbia Theological Seminary in Decatur, Georgia, puts it this way: "[Wisdom] asserts that ordinary human life, here and now, in all its beauty, ambiguity and pain, are of immense importance to human beings and to their Creator. In wisdom's view the struggles and conflicts of daily life are not to be escaped but embraced in full consciousness of their revelatory and healing potential."[2] The documents of Vatican II drew on this same type of wisdom perspective in the Pastoral Constitution on the Church in the Modern World (*Gaudium et Spes*) when it wrote: "The joys and hopes, the griefs and the anxieties of the men of this age, especially those who are poor or in any way afflicted, these too are the joys and hopes, the griefs and anxieties of the followers of Christ. Indeed, nothing genuinely human fails to raise an echo in their hearts" (G.S. 1).[3]

COMMON FEATURES OF THE WISDOM BOOKS

The books of the wisdom tradition, enumerated above, exhibit many similar characteristics.[4] First, together they show a remarkable *lack* of interest in the great acts of divine salvation history, from Exodus to the postexilic period, that I have just traced in the previous chapters. That fact is hard to explain given the enormous importance the saving tradition places on these mighty acts of God. Second, and perhaps even more surprising, the wisdom books show almost no interest in the life of Israel as a *nation*, her kings and prophets, or her tumultuous history. Third, these books of the Bible manifest a questioning attitude about the problems and mysteries of life. They puzzle over the questions of suffering, inequality, and death. Jeremiah was not untouched by this perspective when he wrote: "Why does the way of the guilty prosper? Why do all who are treacherous thrive?" (Jer 12:1). Fourth, these wisdom books, each in its own unique way, search for ways of mastering life's exigencies and explore various modes of proper, "godly" human behavior in the midst of the world. Fifth, wisdom's concerns are the universal human concerns that affect the entire human race and not just the covenant community of Israel.

Sixth, these biblical books, as I have said in discussing blessing theology, ponder the mysteries of creation and relate to God most especially as Creator of the universe. Seventh, many of the wisdom books have a strong didactic tone and may have been used in the instruction of the young. They teach in the way that a father or mother might teach a child: "This is how the world works . . . this is what you need to know and to do to survive in the world." An eighth point describes the common mode of communication in many of the wisdom books: that of the *mashal, or riddle*, aphorism, saying, or proverb. This mode of speech is succinct and pithy. It tends to sum up wisdom in a few words. The apparent simplicity of these sayings is deceiving, however, and they convey perceptive wisdom about the deep mysteries of life. Wisdom is especially at home in ambiguity, and it resists mightily the "easy answer" or religious rote. Life is too complex for that; God is bigger than that. There is a home in the wisdom tradition for both the wary skeptic and the pious saint. As O'Connor says so well: "According to wisdom, life is not a simple set of truths to be followed scrupulously, but a continual encounter with conflicting truths, each making competing claims upon the seeker. Wisdom views life as paradoxical, requiring discernment from situation to situation of how, when and if one should act."[5]

As we shall see in our review of the many different types of wisdom books, all these diverse traditions of wisdom have been gathered and "hebraicized"—that is, brought under the great biblical umbrella of covenant faith in YHWH. And so, the author of Proverbs can begin with the succinct claim: "The fear of the LORD is the beginning of knowledge [wisdom]" (Prov 1:7).[6]

ORIGINS OF WISDOM

The traditions of biblical wisdom originated from a variety of sources. As such, we might say that wisdom is by nature eclectic, borrowing from wherever it can the best insights about life and how one lives life to the full. First, we can see the influence, and outright borrowing, from the sapiential wisdom traditions of Israel's neighbors in the Near East. Ancient Sumerian, Akkadian, and Babylonian influences can all be found in the book of Proverbs. For example, the Old Testament scholar Lawrence Boadt cites a Sumerian proverb, "A chattering scribe—his guilt is great!" that sounds very similar to Proverbs 18:13, which reads: "If one gives answer before hearing, it is folly and shame."[7] It is difficult to know always the exact origin or borrowing of a wisdom saying because all cultures share some of the same commonsense wisdom about life. Among the nations, Egypt was a principal source of influence on the wisdom of the Bible. Moreover, we can trace with certainty "borrowings" in Proverbs 22:17–24:22 from "The Instruction of Amen-em-opet," an Egyptian collection of wisdom sayings dating to the eighth and seventh centuries B.C.E. These parallels in the literature of other nations show that the biblical tradition did not develop in isolation from its neighbors but, indeed, in conversation with them.

A second source of wisdom is that coming from the ancient tribal and family wisdom that may go back to the early years of the Israelite tribes in Canaan. This is the collective ancestral wisdom passed on from father to son and mother to daughter over centuries. These are the stories about where the best grazing land might be found, or how to prepare foods in a certain way, or how to avoid reprimand from one's elders. This is the "down home" wisdom of *Poor Richard's Almanac*, which reminds us that "a stitch in time saves nine" or counsels us that "early to bed, early to rise, makes one healthy, wealthy, and wise." These are not just frivolous one-liners but, rather, bits of wisdom that make for a happy and successful life.

I was told once by an American who had lived with a Bedouin family that the Bedouin nomads, who still live in tents today on the outskirts of modern Jerusalem and tend their flocks of sheep and goats as they have since biblical times, possess a family memory going back centuries of exactly those places in the southern Negev desert where the geological earth crust is very thin, covering over underground streams. And if one takes a staff and strikes the crust layer, it will break, allowing access to the pure water and guaranteeing survival in the parched desert. There are no road signs to these places, no markers, just the *living* memory of family wisdom. Such "wisdom" may have been what Moses used when he struck the rock at Meribah (Ex 17:6)—who knows?

Another source of the Bible's wisdom tradition is the royal and courtly wisdom of the scribal class during the days of the monarchy. These were the educated state officials, the urban upper classes who were the professional wisdom teachers. These sages were the advisers to the kings and court officials, advising on matters of international diplomacy and internal affairs of the state. This was the most literate class in Israelite society. These may have been the "Dale Carnegies" of the ancient world, instructing others in how to "win friends and influence people," in short, how to survive in the affairs of state.

A fourth source of Israel's wisdom came from the scribal tradition of those learned in the Torah. We see an example of these figures very clearly in the book of Nehemiah (445–423 B.C.E.). Nehemiah was the scribal leader who together with Ezra (458–ca. 440 B.C.E.) directed the rebuilding of the Jewish community in the land of Palestine and guided the returning exiles in their repatriation in the land during the Persian period. Nehemiah 8 describes the character of their leadership as interpreting the Law for the people:

> All the people gathered together into the square before the Water Gate. They told the scribe Ezra to bring the book of the law of Moses, which the LORD had given to Israel. Accordingly, the priest Ezra brought the law before the assembly, both men and women and all who could hear with understanding. This was on the first day of the seventh month. He read from it facing the square before the Water Gate from early morning until midday, in the presence of the men and the women and those who could understand; and the ears of all the people were attentive to the book of the law. (Neh 8:1–3)

Standing together with Ezra were twenty-six other scribes who together "gave the sense, so that the people understood the reading" (Neh 8:8). The wisdom of these Torah scribes lay in their power to interpret the sacred texts for the people so that they might understand and come to know the Lord.

A final source for the wisdom traditions in the Old Testament is the figure of King Solomon, renowned in the ancient world for his wisdom. The biblical portrait of Solomon includes his prayer for wisdom that he prayed before his royal enthronement:

> And now, O LORD my God, you have made your servant king in place of my father David, although I am only a little child; I do not know how to go out or come in. And your servant is in the midst of the people whom you have chosen, a great people, so numerous they cannot be numbered or counted. Give your servant therefore an understanding mind to govern your people, able to discern between

good and evil; for who can govern this your great people? (1 Kings 3:7–9)

Other stories associate Solomon with wise legal judgments as, for example, in the famous case of the two women fighting over the same child (1 Kings 3:16–25). When to settle the debate the king cleverly ordered the child to be cut in two and one half given to each woman, the real mother of the child gave up her claim to save her infant. By this ruse the king knew which woman was the real mother and which the kidnapper—and thus returned the child unharmed to its own mother.

The tradition of Solomon's great wisdom brought a visit from the Queen of Sheba, who marveled at Solomon's prosperity and wise judgment. She saw the king's wealth as a sign of his wise conduct, as would be common in the ancient worldview. Health, wisdom, and prosperity were all considered signs of God's blessing and favor, as even "Poor Richard's" homespun wisdom seemed to know: "Early to bed, early to rise, makes one *healthy, wealthy, and wise.*" Several of the wisdom books claim dependence on Solomon, among them Proverbs, Ecclesiastes, the Song of Songs, and the Wisdom of Solomon. Almost no one, however, attributes real authorship of these works to Solomon, who reigned as king from the death of David in 962 B.C.E. to 922 B.C.E., but his name lends authority to their messages and verifies his legendary wisdom.

Together, all these different strains of wisdom converge to shape the very diverse contours of Israel's wisdom tradition. It will be impossible to present more than a brief glimpse at the diversity and particular characteristics of the various wisdom books. Some selected examples from each of the books will have to suffice to teach us the "ways of wisdom."

THE BOOK OF PROVERBS

The book of Proverbs is a great compendium of wise sayings of every kind. There are two main divisions of the book. Chapters 1–9, probably written after the exile, serve as a kind of theological prologue to the rest. In these chapters the metaphor of wisdom as a female figure is a central theme. Chapters 10–31 gather different sayings and aphorisms dealing with every dimension of life from the most exalted to the most mundane. These proverbial sayings were drawn from all the different sources mentioned above and gathered together, in no discernible order, to entertain, to instruct, and to edify. They teach ordinary good sense, as in: "Do not boast about tomorrow, for you do not know what a day may bring" (Prov 27:1). These sayings inculcate virtues to live by like diligence—"A slack hand causes poverty, but the hand of the diligent makes rich" (Prov 10:4); humility—"When pride comes, then comes disgrace; but wisdom is with the humble" (Prov 11:2); or truthfulness—"Deceit is in the mind of those who plan evil, but those who counsel peace have joy" (Prov 12:20).

The sheer number and diversity of these proverbs as well as even their sometimes contradictory character—for example, "It is senseless to give pledge, to become surety for a neighbor" (Prov 17:18) and "Whoever is kind to the poor lends to the LORD" (Prov 19:17)—suggest that the wise person is the one who can choose among competing ways of viewing life and discern among many possibilities the right action in a given moment. There is never one, simple, obvious path—there are always many. And the wise person regularly chooses which to take.

Some proverbs seem almost to make fun of human foibles and thereby to warn the wise not to take themselves too seriously. Who among us has never used these devious strategies to "get a good bargain" in the marketplace: "'[It is] bad, [It is] bad,' says the buyer; then goes away and boasts" (Prov 20:14). Or who has not fallen into excess with compliments toward those from whom we wanted favors: "It is not good to eat much honey, or to seek honor on top of honor" (Prov 25:28). We can laugh at ourselves, as the honey drips from our chins.

Proverbial wisdom divides the world between "the wise/righteous" and "the foolish/wicked." The wise exhibit humility, self-discipline, generosity, hard work, and prudence; while the foolish are arrogant, undisciplined, selfish, sluggardly, and lacking in judgment. And in the daily rhythms of life each one must choose between the ways of the wise and the ways of the foolish. In choosing the wise path we choose the path of life.

THE BOOK OF JOB

This example of biblical wisdom, the book of Job, takes a different course altogether. Job represents the gnawing questions of the postexilic period concerned especially with the meaning of suffering endured by the righteous. The opening prose prologue of the book may draw on a very ancient folktale. It introduces the man Job, a non-Jew who is upright and principled, without blame or reproach. But God's ambassador, *satan*, asks to test Job to see if his piety is real, and God agrees.[8] So Job endures every form of adversity: his animals and servants are killed, and the house collapses on his sons and daughters, killing them all. Job himself was struck with blistering sores over his entire body, and Job's wife in outrage urges him to curse God. But this Job refuses to do.

The rest of the book presents a rather different "Job," one who does not curse God but who does indeed curse the day he was born (Job 3). The speeches that follow are set in poetic verse. They contain the conversations, or better, the disputations, first between Job and his three "friends" (Eliphaz, Bildad, and Zophar—chaps. 3–27), then with a fourth "friend" (Elihu—chaps. 32–37), and finally with God (chaps. 38–42). These disputations are the wrestlings of one who seeks after wisdom and understanding about the perplexities and enigmas of life and who refuses to accept the old and tired answers of the past. In the midst of his misery and pain, Job asks, "Why?"

Job's friends have the standard, pat answer: suffering is the consequence of human actions and is the punishment for sin. With this reply they echo the customary theological assumption of the time. Good and righteous living brings reward, and sinful deeds bring punishment; this was the usual theological equation, or so they thought. But in Job's case the equation just did not work. Try as they might, his friends could not convince him that he had sinned and therefore deserved the misery that he suffers. A just God does not punish the righteous (Job 8:3), they say. They resort to derisive words mocking his "apparent" superior knowledge: "Can you find out the deep things of God? Can you find out the limit of the Almighty?" (Job 11:7).

With "friends" like Job's, who needs enemies? They are convinced he is hiding some sin or failing in self-knowledge. They make matters worse, not better, for Job because they compound his suffering by their persistent arguments. Job wants desperately to find meaning in his suffering—but there is none. Moreover, the very character of God is at stake in all of this. Is God just an uncaring, capricious deity playing havoc with people's lives? *Where* is this God? If God is all powerful, if God is all just, then *why* doesn't God act to relieve human suffering? These are not just Job's questions. These are our questions as well.

Finally, then, we hear God's reply:

Then the LORD answered Job out of the whirlwind:
"Who is this that darkens counsel by words without knowledge? Gird up your loins like a man,
I will question you, and you shall declare to me. (Job 38:1)

Out of the whirlwind God responds—not with answers but with questions. These speeches of God from the whirlwind are some of the most beautiful poetry in the Bible. In them, God questions Job—and questions us—about our pretensions of knowledge and our misplaced claims of truth:

> Where were you when I laid the foundation of the earth?
>> Tell me, if you have understanding.
> Who determined its measurements—surely you know!
>> Or who stretched the line upon it?
> On what were its bases sunk,
>> or who laid its cornerstone
> when the morning stars sang together
>> and all the heavenly beings shouted for joy? (Job 38:4–7)

Job's reply comes haltingly, first in the midst of the speech and again at the very end. God's words, God's presence, have overwhelmed him, and he feebly says: "Behold I am of small account; what shall I answer you?" God's questions persist, all the while displaying the divine care for the universe in all its beauty and power, the sea creatures, animals, and plants. Finally Job relents, exhausted and ashamed:

> I know that you can do all things,
>> and that no purpose of yours can be thwarted.
> "Who is this that hides counsel without knowledge?"
> Therefore I have uttered what I did not understand,
>> things too wonderful for me, which I did not know.
> "Hear, and I will speak;
>> I will question you, and you declare to me."
> I had heard of you by the hearing of the ear,
>> but now my eye sees you; therefore I despise myself,
> and repent in dust and ashes. (Job 42:2–6)

It is important to recognize that nowhere does God give Job an answer to his questions about the meaning of suffering. The answer seems to be that there is no answer. The only answer resides in the conviction that God cares for those who suffer, even comes to them and is *with them* in the suffering. And Job's final reply seems to say that this is enough. As another example of the search for wisdom in the biblical tradition, Job teaches us not so much about *why* we suffer but about how we must relate to God in our suffering. And this must be enough.

QOHELETH—ECCLESIASTES

Earlier I mention that the wisdom tradition has a place for both the wary skeptic and the pious saint. Qoheleth, certainly, is the wary skeptic, par excellence. He is a believer but a questioning, skeptical believer. This text comes probably from the third century B.C.E., and its title—

both in Hebrew (Qoheleth) and in Greek (Ecclesiastes)—means "one who assembles." Traditionally, the one who speaks in the text has been known as the "preacher/teacher," but twice the speaker claims to be a king (Eccl 1:1, 12) and so confirms the royal connections with its teachings.

The most characteristic and most oft-repeated phrase of this book is "Vanity of vanities, all is vanity!" The Hebrew word translated as "vanity" is literally "a puff of wind, breath, vapor." With this almost monotonous refrain, repeated thirty-eight times in the book, the speaker seems to be overcome by the realization that everything in life is transitory, ephemeral, and fleeting. Moreover, the cyclic patters of life, the day-in and day-out repetitions in both nature and human life, lull a person into satiety and weariness. The times and seasons are themselves locked into repetitive patterns set by decree:

> For everything there is a season, and a time for every matter under heaven:
>> a time to be born, and a time to die;
>> a time to plant, and a time to pluck up what is planted;
>> a time to kill, and a time to heal;
>> a time to break down, and a time to build up; . . .
> What gain have the workers from their toil? (Eccl 3:1–3, 9)

But what does it all mean? All this activity, toil, wealth, acquisition of property, pleasure and excess, cycles of days and nights and days again—what does it all mean? The reply comes again and again: all is vanity and "chasing after wind."[9] The reality of death makes this so, as "the wise man dies just like the fool" (Eccl 2:16). Death is the great leveler. Qoheleth is profoundly suspicious of the conventional answers that claim to affirm the rewards to the righteous and condemnation to the unjust. Qoheleth looks at the world around him and with the keen eye of the observant realist sees that, as the old song says, "it ain't necessarily so."

And so he questions the common wisdom. He risks saying, "Theology teaches X or Y, but the reality is something other." Qoheleth recognizes the ambiguities and contradictions of human experience, and, like Alexander Pope, the British poet cited in chapter 3, he too sees the human condition as a "riddle" to be *lived*, not a problem to be solved. Both his brand of wisdom and his brand of faith are deadly honest, and for this we must be grateful. And, though he wrestles mightily with the questions of life, he embraces life to the full. And so, Qoheleth counsels, must we.

SONG OF SONGS—CANTICLE OF CANTICLES

It has become almost customary in recent studies on the Song of Songs for scholars to begin by citing a quotation about the Song from the rabbis.[10] So I shall do the same:

> All the world is not worth the day that the
> Song of Songs was given to Israel; all the
> Ketûbîm [writings] are holy but the Song of Songs is
> the holy of holies. (Mishna *Yadayim*, 3.5)

This extraordinary collection of erotic Hebrew love poetry, the "holy of holies" as the rabbis called it, offers yet another glimpse of the many-faceted character of wisdom in the Bible. The Song of Songs was a favorite text of the Christian mystics, those many men and women who had extraordinary contemplative experiences of God's love and intimacy with them. Even so, some monastic regulations forbade the reading of the Song of Songs before one had reached a mature age. Jewish and Christian interpreters alike saw in the Song of Songs an allegorical message: depicting the love either between the Lord and the covenant people or, for Christians, between Christ and the Church. The basic intuition behind such an allegorical reading is sound. It recognizes that the experience of human love can be an adequate metaphor for divine love, as we saw earlier in our discussion of the prophet Hosea's use of the marriage/harlotry metaphor. But all scholars today would agree that the author of the text did not write an allegory. He wrote a meditation, in erotic poetic language, celebrating the joy and ecstasy of heterosexual love.

The Song praises the beauty, mutual attraction, and ecstatic delight of the male and female as they enter into the dance of love. There is not a hint of censure, caution, or disapproval. As Dianne Bergant, an Old Testament professor and specialist in the wisdom traditions of Israel, notes so clearly, "If anything, it characterizes heterosexual passion as noble and mutually self-transcending."[11] The female perspective is the dominant one in the poems, an unusual feature in a text coming from an androcentric culture and one that shatters conventional sexual stereotypes and roles.

That mutual, selfless human love and passion can reflect to us something of God is a truth the Song's wisdom teaches. Love alone teaches us to be truly other-centered. Love alone taps into the creative energies within us, freeing us to be playful and to be in perfect harmony with another. Love alone enables us to be vulnerable and to learn to trust another. Love alone forges "hoops of steel" bonding us together with the beloved even beyond death:[12]

> Set me as a seal upon your heart,
>   as a seal upon your arm;
> for love is strong as death,
>   passion fierce as the grave.
> Its flashes are flashes of fire,
>   a raging flame.
> Many waters cannot quench love,
>   neither can floods drown it. (Song 8:6–7)

The Song's wisdom, then, is the wisdom of love: divine love, yes, but also actual, tangible, passionate human love as a glimpse and a reflection of the divine.

LADY WISDOM: SIRACH AND THE WISDOM OF SOLOMON

Showing another facet of wisdom, the book of Sirach, written toward the beginning of the second century B.C.E., locates wisdom completely and perfectly in the Torah.[13] An opening poem affirms that wisdom is synonymous with "fear of the LORD," and much of the teaching of Sirach advocates the ethical norms consistent with the Torah statutes. These include, for example, filial duty (Sir 3:1–16), humility (Sir 3:17–24), generosity to the poor (Sir 4:1–10), honesty and sincerity (Sir 5:8–6:1), self-control (Sir 6:2–4), integrity in friendship (Sir 6:5–17), discretion in almsgiving (Sir 12:1–7), and the like. The wise person is the one who embraces this ethical path and who shuns the ways of the wicked and the foolish.

But perhaps the most striking feature of Sirach is its reflection on wisdom as a personified figure. In this, Sirach echoes a similar theme in the earlier chapters of the book of Proverbs, especially chapters 8–9, and one that will become the dominant theme of the Wisdom of Solomon. In these texts especially, Jews imagined wisdom in this personal way, as Woman Wisdom. Wisdom's origin and abode are with God:

> There is but one who is wise, greatly to be feared,
>   seated upon his throne—the Lord.
> It is he who created her [i.e., wisdom];
>   he saw her and took her measure;
>   he poured her out upon all his works,
> upon all the living according to his gift;
>   he lavished her upon those who love him. (Sir 1:9)

She is a creature of God and yet unlike any other because she surpasses all. Proverbs 8 hymns her praises and grandeur: "When [the

Lord] marked out the foundations of the earth, then I was beside him, like a master workman" (Prov 8:29–30). God sent Woman Wisdom into the world (Prov 1:20, 9:1–10), where she cries out to the foolish to come to her, "Come, eat of my bread and drink of the wine I have mixed" (Prov 9:5), "Come to me you who desire me, and eat your fill of my produce" (Sir 24:19). Sirach declares that God sent Woman Wisdom specifically to Israel: "So I was established in Zion . . . in Jerusalem was my dominion" (Sir 24:10–11). Imagining wisdom in this personified way, as God's cocreator and ambassador, came very close to affirming Woman Wisdom as herself divine, and yet, for Jewish monotheistic sensibilities, such a claim would have flirted with blasphemy.

And yet that is exactly what the text known as the Wisdom of Solomon has done. This is the latest text among the wisdom books and comes probably from the Jewish community in Alexandria around the middle of the second century B.C.E. In chapter 7 a long speech, put on the (fictional) mouth of "Solomon," praises the twenty-one attributes of Woman Wisdom (21 = 3 x 7). Both the numbers three and seven were considered complete or "perfect" numbers. Hence, Woman Wisdom is praised as the perfection of perfection: "There is in her a spirit that is intelligent, holy, unique, manifold, subtle, mobile, clear, unpolluted, distinct, invulnerable, loving the good, keen, irresistible, beneficent, humane, steadfast, sure, free from anxiety, all-powerful, overseeing all, and penetrating through all spirits that are intelligent, pure, and altogether subtle" (Wis 7:22–23). A few verses later we hear: "She is a breath of the power of God . . . a pure emanation of the glory of the Almighty . . . a reflection of eternal light, . . . an image of [God's] goodness" (Wis 7:25–26). These many adjectives speak about Woman Wisdom as almost equal with God. Moreover, the author affirms that creatures have access to Woman Wisdom, for "in every generation she passes into holy souls and makes them friends of God and prophets" (Wis 7:27). It will be important to keep this portrait of Woman Wisdom in mind when we turn, in chapter 10, to the person of Jesus. There we will see how Christian religious imagination returned to these texts about Wisdom in order to speak about Jesus.

THE SCHOOL OF PRAYER—PSALMS FOR ALL SEASONS

As we have seen through this long encounter with the books of the wisdom tradition, the covenant people searched for wisdom in many and varied ways. We could not conclude this survey without listening briefly to the voices of the Hebrew psalmists as they offer their conviction that the way of wisdom is finally the way of prayer.

Praise and petition poured out to God is a universal experience of the human heart. Capturing the sentiments of both the individual and the collective soul of its people, the Hebrew Psalter reflects Israel's faith, her longing for God, her identity as God's own people. The Psalter constitutes a whole "school of prayer," so to speak, not in the sense merely of a collection of prayers to be said but, rather, as a *lesson in how to pray*, as an illustration of the many motifs, aspirations, fears, and hopes that can be employed by a community of faith. A full spectrum of the human condition is covered in these prayers.

Like many of the prophetic and wisdom texts that we have discussed, the psalms are poetic speech. The psalmists express an enormous range of understandings of God, self, and community as they talk to God in language that employs dynamic and often extravagant imagery. And so, in the psalms "mountains skipped like rams" (Ps 114:4, 6), "meadows clothe themselves with flocks" (Ps 65:13), "the wicked man conceives evil, and is pregnant with mischief" (Ps 7:14), and God rides a cherub "on the wings of the wind" (Ps 18:10).

Many psalms reflect the dynamic liturgical encounter between YHWH and Israel in the setting of the Temple liturgy. This context means that the communal dimension of faith and prayer was essential and that the "I" of the psalms is never solely individual. Moreover, seen through the lens of the Psalter, liturgical expression was totally free and authentic. There were shouts of enthusiasm: "All you peoples, clap your hands. Acclaim God with shouts of JOY!" (Ps 47). There were cries of desperation: "Help YHWH! No one loyal is left, the faithful have vanished. . . . Friends tell lies to friends" (Ps 12). This is no tame book of antiseptic prayers; the psalms school us in the characteristics of authentic prayer. They are also subject to the prophetic critique of insincerity that we consider in the last chapter (Am 5:21–24; Isa 1:12–16; Ps 50:7–23). Without the integrity of a whole life that is in harmony with the Word, prayer will be to no avail.

The psalmists knew themselves as sinful persons. So there is no room for hypocrisy on the part of the one who reads and prays these psalms. The psalms are not an outlet for pious thoughts but, rather, an honest dialogue with God in which human meanness and spite will not be absent. Many are shocked by the violence and vengeance evident in the psalms. We have many examples of asking God to take vengeance, as, for example, in the prayer against the wicked: "God break their teeth, rip out the young lions' fangs" (Ps 58:7). To this we might say, Isn't it better to pray that *God* take vengeance than that the person take it in his or her own hands? Other examples horrify us with their violent images, such as the exiles' prayer against their captors: "Happy is the one who takes your little ones and dashes them against the rock!" (Ps 137:9).

These examples are the index of the intensity of the prayer itself, as well as of the sinful person who is praying. The marvel is that, for the Israelite, every human emotion could be brought to prayer. We can all recognize ourselves in the humanness of these psalms, as well as in the joy and celebration of the hymns of praise.

The psalms of lament are particularly instructive. Walter Brueggemann has written eloquently about "the costly loss of lament" in our day and the need to revive this mode of prayer in the Christian assembly.[14] The lament psalms deal with life in all its stark reality: hurt, betrayal, loneliness, disease, threat, anxiety, bewilderment, anger, hatred, and anguish. The astonishing thing is that Israelites brought all these painful experiences to God with their raw human emotion—they held *nothing* back. The psalmist stares God in the face "without blinking" and speaks to God with candor, so that the human struggle becomes an ever deepening relationship with God. We usually excise these offensive verses, but in doing so, we violate the integrity of the psalm and deprive it of the power to teach us and to bring us face to face with the violence in ourselves.

Psychology teaches us of the importance of healthy expressions of anger and the detrimental effects of repressed anger, which does not disappear but festers and finally explodes or slowly eats away at us, sapping us of energy and life. For Israel, the right to speak honestly with God was presumed. The prayers of lament gave form to the worst experiences of life and placed them in the presence of the One who alone could redress their suffering. The lament enabled one to articulate suffering and also to cope with it according to the resources of the community. One thing that the laments make clear is that faith and worship are shaped by life as it is.

CONCLUSION

The title of this chapter, "Wisdom Has Built Herself a House," is taken from the opening verse of Proverbs 9. I use it as a metaphor to describe the grandeur, the variety, and the comprehensive scope of Israel's wisdom teaching. And we have only touched the surface of this body of wisdom. The spirituality, therefore, of wisdom's way is as diverse as the texts we have surveyed. They span the gamut from the exalted praise of Woman Wisdom to the skeptical words of Qoheleth, from the homespun aphorisms of Proverbs to the philosophical disputations of Job. Biblical wisdom, however, is always a gift from God and not merely the product of our own strivings. It begins always from a posture of reverence and "fear of the LORD." God's wisdom is something we must seek tirelessly and for which we must earnestly pray. It is not synonymous with the wisdom of the world, not reducible to easy answers or fancy formulas. This kind of biblical wisdom is the antithesis of what the advertising world often tries to lure us into believing. It finds a home in questions as well as answers and is comfortable with both faith and doubt.

On a terribly disturbing day in June 1979, I learned that my father was dying with pancreatic cancer. The surgeon told me that there was nothing that he could do because the tumor had already invaded the portal vein and spread throughout the abdominal cavity. It was only a matter of a few months before death would come. As I waited for my father to return from the recovery room, I was terrified that I would have to be the one to give him this ominous news. What could I possibly say to him? How would the words come out? When I finally went into his room to talk with him, before I could speak a word he said, "Don't worry, I know." And then he added simply, "We have to play the hand we are dealt, Barbara." *There* was the voice of wisdom; *there* was the essence of faith. He was an avid bridge player and knew well the meaning of the proverb "to play the hand you are dealt." But in that simple proverbial one-liner (my father *loved* one-liners) he had captured the deepest wisdom of life and death—not with a pious formula but with the ordinary wisdom of life.

The wise ones in our midst know the truth about things and are not afraid to speak their truth to others. They refuse to deal in charades and obfuscation. There is a deep humility associated with biblical wisdom, the kind that Job embraced as he stood before the mysteries of the creator God. If we are truly wise, then we know ourselves for who we are before God. We neither inflate our goodness nor exaggerate our shortcomings; we are simply at home in the truth of who we are. Wisdom figures in every age build up the communal body because they are attentive to the God dimension of all life and nurture that presence in others. This is the kind of wisdom of a parent who knows when, out of love and care, to be fiercely demanding and when to give some slack so that a child may learn to grow into the freedom God has intended. A person with this kind of godly wisdom willingly takes risks in order to build bridges to others because he or she knows that we are really all one, part of a common humanity. In chapter 10 we will see how Jesus, too, embodied this type of wisdom as he challenged people, in his parables and sayings, to ponder the mystery of God's ways in our midst.

It is true that the blessing/wisdom traditions mentioned rarely if at all the mighty deeds of YHWH that we have come to call salvation history. But they know this saving and blessing God just as intently from their daily observation of the mysteries of life. These wisdom/blessing traditions place us in the midst of life lived to the full, and they invite us to find God right there. Indeed, in wisdom's house there are many places to dwell.

QUESTIONS FOR REFLECTION

1. Think about three or four wise people who have influenced you in your life—a grade school teacher, a pastor or friend, a grandparent or colleague—and identify what attributes you admired in them. How did they teach you wisdom?
2. Proverbial wisdom is part of every culture of the world. Which proverbs form part of your own wisdom about life, and how do they become revelatory of God for you?
3. In a profound way, suffering has the potential to teach us wisdom because it brings us face to face (as it did Job) with the unexplained mystery of life and death. How has this mystery touched your life and taught you about God?
4. Contrast the three most essential bits of "worldly wisdom" with the wisdom that comes from God. What does worldly wisdom teach us to value and acquire? How does the wisdom of God challenge those assumptions, and where, in your life, have you experienced these competing "wisdoms"?
5. The blessing/wisdom tradition teaches us to find God in the beauty of creation. Where, in nature, have you sensed God's presence being revealed to you?

9

CRISIS AND HOPE

For I am about to create new heavens and a new earth;
the former things shall not be remembered or come to mind.
But be glad and rejoice forever in what I am creating.

—Isaiah 65:17–18

In 587 B.C.E. the kingdom of Judah and the Davidic monarchy came to an end when the Babylonians destroyed Jerusalem. This catastrophe ushered in a centuries-long era that was simultaneously disheartening for Jews and theologically creative.[1] These two realities—loss of autonomy and eventually persecution and the creative growth of the Jewish tradition—are related. The calamity and the long years of struggle afterward instilled in the descendants of the ancient Israelites a desire to tell the story of their relationship with their God from its very beginnings. In the Babylonian exile, scribes began to collect, edit, compile, and supplement the various oral and written traditions of Israel into the grand narrative that eventually became their scriptures (and the Christian Old Testament). The great theme that runs through Israel's story is that the God who called first the world and then Israel into being is a God who never abandons what God has created. Through centuries of struggle, confusion, and profound human infidelity, God remained unwilling to abandon the covenant relationship with Israel.

This central affirmation of the Bible—that God is absolutely trustworthy and faithful—gave hope in time of loss and of severe crisis. But the traditions of the past were not simply conserved as a memory; they provided raw material for new visions of the future that grew out of the ancient stories and prophetic visions, now transformed in light of new realities. Through the long centuries under the rule of the Babylonians, the Persians, the Greeks, and the Romans, Jews drew strength from the scriptures by interpreting their current struggles through the lens of the past, and at the same time developed new visions of the future. These visions of the future would contribute significantly to the rich and complex matrix of Jewish expectations in the first century C.E., and they shed much light on how Jesus of Nazareth and the early church understood who he was and what he had come to do.

PROPHETIC HOPE FOR THE FUTURE

In ancient Israel, as in the rest of the ancient Near East, the gods were believed to be behind all human events, particularly those involving whole nations and peoples. The rise and fall of kingdoms was the result of divine decisions and actions.[2] Also in the ancient Near East, every nation worshipped its patron god or gods. In Israel, of course, that was YHWH. In such a world, the conquest or destruction of one kingdom was in reality the result of a battle between the patron gods of the vanquisher and the vanquished. When a kingdom fell, it could only mean one of two things: either the god of the defeated nation had been unable to protect it from enemies or the patron god had for some reason caused or allowed the disaster to happen. Israel maintained this same view of the relationship between human events and the divine world.

Thus it was that in the years leading up to the destruction of Jerusalem and the temple, Jeremiah warned that God would be bringing upon the people a great disaster through the Babylonians. God will not protect a people, he insisted, who do not honor him or live according to his commandments (Jer 7:9–10). For Jeremiah, the proper response to the threat of the Babylonians was not to resist them, assuming that God would protect them against their enemies, but to accept that the Babylonians were instruments of God's righteous punishment for gross and persistent covenant violation. Jeremiah's critique could at times be harsh, but the stakes were high. No one came under stronger condemnation than the Davidic kings, whose failure to uphold justice and ensure covenant fidelity was a serious abrogation of their sacred duty as representatives of God. Jeremiah was tasked with making God's judgment clear to them (Jer 22:1–5).

This critique and warning must be understood against the background of what is often called royal Judahite theology. Ancient Judahite tradition held that God had established the Davidic dynasty to act as God's representative, ensuring justice and proper religious observance, and to be the beneficiary of God's protection and blessing. The foundational narrative for this tradition is the famous scene in which David decides to build a temple—or house—for God in Jerusalem. God rejects this decision, saying that task would fall to David's son Solomon. Instead, God promised to build David a house, that is, a dynasty (2 Sam 7:12–16; see also Ps 89). There are two things worth noting about this promise. First, the promise is for an everlasting kingdom, a permanent dynasty. Second, the promise comes with no conditions. If the Davidic kings fail to live up to God's expectations, they will be punished "with blows inflicted by human beings" (this is, through what we would call historical means, 2 Sam 7:14). In other words, God will not ignore when the kings are unfaithful, but will never allow the dynasty to come to an end. This promise was the basis of the royal Judahite theology, which maintained that the Davidic monarchy was created, supported, and protected by God—forever.

But there are in the Bible other versions of this same promise, that insist that the everlasting Davidic dynasty is conditional, that God will only keep this promise if, in turn, the Davidic kings are loyal to the covenant (Ps 132:11–12; 1 Kgs 8:25). Jeremiah clearly agreed with this latter tradition, and considered the promise to David conditional upon observance of the Sinai covenant by David's descendants. In his denunciations of the Davidic kings of his time, the prophet affirmed that God could, and would, bring an end to the Davidic dynasty if the kings persisted in their infidelity and injustice (see, for example, Jer 22:30).

When Nebuchadnezzar finally did destroy Jerusalem and the temple in 587 B.C.E., he brought the Davidic monarchy to an end, and the conditional form of the promise to David lay at hand to explain how God could allow it to happen. Nevertheless, the unconditional version of the promise to David remained "on the books," and would contribute many centuries later to Jewish messianic expectations. (More on that later.)

Toward the end of the exilic period, the anonymous prophet scholars now call Second Isaiah proclaimed the good news that the faithful God had not completely abandoned Israel, but had forgiven them and was preparing to bring them back to the land in a new exodus (Isa 43:16–19). Jeremiah too, for all his prophecies of doom, knew that God's anger would not last forever. In a letter to the exiles in Babylon, he assured them that after a time God would bring them back home (Jer 29:10–14). Like Second Isaiah, Jeremiah foresaw a time when Jerusalem would be rebuilt and filled once again with abundance and the sound of joy (Jer 31:4–5). The prophet also proclaimed that God would transform the people themselves, making them more capable of being faithful to the covenant relationship (Jer 31:31–34).[3]

While Second Isaiah's vision of the restoration of Jerusalem and of Israel does not include a Davidic monarch, both Jeremiah and the prophet Ezekiel foresaw God's renewal of the Davidic line. Specifically referring to the Davidic covenant, God promised through Jeremiah to provide for his people a new Davidic king who, unlike previous kings, will act justly:

> The days are surely coming, says the LORD, when I will fulfill the promise I made to the house of Israel and the house of Judah. In those days and at that time I will cause a righteous Branch to spring up for David; and he shall execute justice and righteousness in the land. . . . For thus says the LORD: David shall never lack a man to sit on the throne of the house of Israel. (Jer 33:14–15, 17)

These passages (and we could add many more) represent prophetic hopes for the renewal after the period of judgment. God would return all of the people to a rebuilt Judah and Jerusalem. The city and the land would overflow with prosperous, safe people, presided over in Jerusalem by a Davidic king (according to some), and blessed by the presence of God in a rebuilt temple. When Cyrus of Persia defeated Babylon in 538 B.C.E. and allowed the exiles to return to their land, many of them must have had great expectations for a glorious restoration that would fully vindicate their faith in the God who had promised never to abandon Israel.

The reality turned out to be very different. The biblical texts from the Persian period (538–333 B.C.E.), as well as the archaeological record, indicate that the period after the exile was a time of great struggle and confusion. Almost nothing unfolded according to the plan set forth by the prophets. True, the temple did get rebuilt, but only after two decades and only after considerable debate, as the books of Haggai and Zechariah make clear. The former kingdom of Judah was now a small, poor, backwater province of the Persian Empire, and this may explain why many people decided to stay in Babylon rather than return to their ancestral lands. Those who did return immediately found themselves in conflict with locals who had long gotten used to having the place to themselves. For many decades Jerusalem remained sparsely populated and largely unrebuilt. Now a part of the Persian Empire, the former kingdom of Judah had little chance of emerging in these years as a restored monarchy under a new Davidic king. Even several decades after the restoration had begun, the people struggled not only to find their economic and agricultural footing, but also to find a way forward religiously. The books of Ezra and Nehemiah, which recount events from these early decades, suggest a number of struggles within the community regarding proper religious observance. Finally, these religious struggles and daily life itself would have made it clear that God's people were no better able to be completely faithful to the covenant now than they had been before the exile. Injustice, greed, and all the usual forms of human sin and failing still plagued God's people.

The fact that prophetic visions of a glorious restoration had not come to pass presented a problem for those who put their trust in God's promises and fidelity. What was one to make of the present situation, which looked so little like what God had promised through the prophets? What was God up to? The "cognitive dissonance" caused by the discrepancy between what God had promised and what God had actually done (or not done, to be exact) eventually led to a reconsideration of how to interpret the prophetic oracles of restoration. Over time, the oracles of restoration found throughout the prophetic writings came to be seen as descriptions, or at least intimations, of a definitive moment not in the immediate future but in some later time when God would bring about a complete change of circumstances not only for Israel but for the whole world. Eventually, the prophetic writings, as well as an absolute conviction that God was both powerful and faithful, led to the development of a complex of expectations and traditions that we call eschatology.

JEWISH ESCHATOLOGY

Eschatology is a broad concept. It comes from the Greek word *eschatos*, which refers to extremes of time, space, or quality: last, furthest, utmost, the ultimate. Eschatology is discourse about what will happen at "the end," what will be the "the ultimate thing." This thinking has taken many forms over the centuries and has given rise to a rich variety of concepts, scenarios, and texts, many of which we find in the Old Testament. Other examples of eschatological thinking can be found in Jewish (and then later, Christian) texts that seemed to have enjoyed popularity but which, nevertheless, never became accepted as canonical. These texts are our primary source for understanding the nature and development of Jewish eschatological thought, which has very deep roots but only begins to emerge clearly in the Persian period. In the rest of this chapter we will briefly examine some of the most significant forms and concepts of eschatological thought as they emerged in the centuries leading up to the first century C.E. During these years biblical traditions, historical events, and an unshakable belief in the justice and fidelity of God gave rise first to prophetic eschatology, then to apocalyptic and messianic eschatologies, as well as belief in the resurrection of the dead. All of these would have profound influence on later Christian thought beginning already in the time of Jesus of Nazareth.

Jewish eschatology in any period never comprised a clear set of doctrines. There was never *a* Jewish eschatology. Rather, eschatological thought was complex, varied, and evolving. In all it forms, Jewish eschatology took as its starting point the conviction that the way the world is now is not the way God ultimately wants it to be. The divine project, so to speak, is not finished. The world is filled with injustice, greed, war, and violence, and faithlessness. Jewish tradition held that such was not the will of God, and firm belief in divine justice led to the hope that one day God would intervene to set things right. Eschatological thought is oriented toward the future and looks forward to a day when God will decisively intervene in the world to change it for the better, bringing about an era of peace and abundance for God's people.[4] This is the basic idea lying behind all eschatological thought, even up to today. From this foundation, eschatology grew in a number of different directions, with different emphases, drawing on different elements of the Jewish tradition.

The earliest forms of eschatological thought can be found in the prophets, and so scholars usually refer to this complex of traditions and texts as prophetic eschatology. These texts look forward to the day when the God of Israel will bring about peace and abundance not just for Israel, but for the whole world, who will come to recognize the sovereignty of YHWH. A familiar example of prophetic eschatology is from Isaiah:

> In days to come
> > the mountain of the LORD's house
> shall be established as the highest of the mountains,
> > and shall be raised above the hills;
> all nations shall stream to it.
> > Many peoples will come and say,
> "Come, let us go up to the mountain of the LORD,
> > to the house of the God of Jacob;
> that he may teach us his ways
> > and that we may walk in his paths."
> For out of Zion shall go forth instruction,
> > and the word of the LORD from Jerusalem.
> He shall judge between the nations,
> > and shall arbitrate for many peoples;
> they shall beat their swords into plowshares,
> > and their spears into pruning hooks;
> nation shall not lift up sword against nation,
> > neither shall they learn war anymore. (Isa 2:2–4)

We see in this passage some key elements of prophetic eschatology. The oracle begins with the phrase, "in days to come," a formula that signals its future orientation, but leaves the time unspecified. The Hebrew actually can mean something like "in the last days," and when the Hebrew scriptures were translated into Greek in the third century B.C.E., this phrase was rendered using the adjective *eschatos*: "in the ultimate days." The prophet is speaking not just of a future time, but of an ultimate time. This is a vision of God's decisive action. This action is characterized by other key eschatological concepts. First, the sovereignty of the God of Israel will be recognized by all peoples. The idea that *universality* the mountain of God, the place where God's temple is set, will be established as the highest mountain is theological, not geological. Everyone in the world will recognize YHWH as the supreme God (if not the only God), whose mountain is therefore the highest. This will lead to a desire to learn from God and to submit all disputes to God's judgment. This recognition of God's sovereignty and authority will ultimately lead to the end of war. So we have here a vision of the future that is thoroughly eschatological. But notice that the vision is also historical. In days to come, God will act decisively to change the nature and course of human history, but that history will continue. This is a characteristic feature of prophetic eschatology that distinguishes it from later apocalyptic eschatology, which will envision an even more radical break between the present era and the ultimate reality.

In time, as many of the prophetic oracles remained unfulfilled, they would come to be seen in eschatological terms, rather than as God's immediate intentions during the early period of restoration. "One day" God's people will be able to live justly and faithfully according to the covenant. "One day" Jerusalem will be filled with abundance and joy. Eventually Jewish eschatology would look forward to an end not only to war but to all imperfections and sorrow in the world, including death itself:

> On this mountain the LORD of hosts will make for all peoples
> a feast of rich food, a feast of well-aged wines,
> of rich food filled with marrow, of well-aged wines strained clear.
> And he will destroy in this mountain
> the shroud that is cast over all peoples,
> the sheet that is spread over all nations;
> he will swallow up death forever. (Isa 25:6–8)

These and many other texts are peaceful examples of prophetic eschatology. But others, which arose out of a situation of defeat or oppression, look forward to the day when God will decisively destroy those who harm or oppress God's people. This expectation that God will establish his sovereignty and defeat all who harm God's people (however that is understood) is a regular feature of eschatology. This is especially true in a set of texts that scholars refer to as proto-apocalyptic.

Proto-apocalyptic texts, as the term suggests, contain many elements that will come to be regular features of fully apocalyptic texts and the worldview behind them. These elements include the idea that future peace will only come after a period of doom, characterized by a battle between God and hostile forces. This battle, which invariably ends with God's defeat of God's enemies, is often envisioned in cosmic terms, involving the entire earth in a catastrophic scenario. The language of proto-apocalyptic prophecy tends to be especially vivid, with images of cosmic battle leading to earth-wide destruction and evil enemies being vanquished and thrown into prisons or pits. It is an unattractive vision, to be sure, but one that arises out of a keen sense that the world has gone terribly wrong and that the forces of evil—which are often human, but increasingly take on nonhuman forms as well—are running rampant. The battle between God and these hostile forces must take place before God's reign can be firmly established and peace can prevail. The vision of the end of death and the feast on God's holy mountain that we read earlier comes immediately after a scene of God's defeat of enemies in an earth-shattering battle (Isa 24:1–23). In proto-apocalyptic texts the good can come only after the defeat of the bad. These images and language will eventually contribute to a later development in Jewish tradition, apocalyptic eschatology.

APOCALYPTIC ESCHATOLOGY

During the course of the centuries after the return from exile, Jewish eschatology became increasingly more dramatic in its expectations. In the Hellenistic period, especially under the persecutions of Antiochus IV Epiphanes and the subsequent reign of the Hasmoneans, the language and imagery we find in proto-apocalyptic texts like Isaiah 24–27, Zechariah 9–14, and the book of Joel would contribute to a worldview and form of literature that was fully apocalyptic.[5]

Life under the Persians may not have been wonderful, but it was relatively peaceful. The Persians seem to have shown relatively little interest in meddling in the affairs of their subjects, a situation that allowed Jews to develop their beliefs and practices according to their own lights. When Alexander the Great conquered Persia in 333 B.C.E., the Persian period of Jewish history gave way to the Hellenistic period, which was marked among other things by the strong influence of Greek culture on the peoples now under Greek rule. This influence would be welcomed by some Jews and resisted by others, and the difference would lead to serious conflicts between Hellenistic Jews and anti-Hellenistic Jews. But in the very early years of Greek rule, life went on in what was now called Judea much as it had under the Persians.

When Alexander died in 323 B.C.E., however, things became complicated. On his death, Alexander's empire was divided among his generals: Cassander, Lysimachus, Ptolemy I, and Seleucus. Judea lay on the border between the land under Ptolemaic control in the south (Egypt) and the land under Seleucid control in the north (Syria). Originally ruled by the Ptolemies, Judea was under Seleucid control by the end of the second century B.C.E. The Jews enjoyed generally good relations with the Seleucids for several years, until the reign of Antiochus IV Epiphanes.

In the fall of 169 B.C.E., as he was returning to Syria from a successful campaign against the Ptolemies in Egypt, Antiochus stopped in Jerusalem and decided to help himself to large sums of gold and silver from the temple treasury. Being the ruler of Judea, Antiochus would have considered this wealth effectively his to take as he wished, but for at least the anti-Hellenistic Jews this despoiling of the temple treasury was not only illegal but impious. The action did not set a good precedent.

The next year Antiochus engaged with the Egyptians in a second campaign, during which word reached Judea that he had been killed in battle. This rumor, which turned out to be false, prompted a rebellion by anti-Hellenistic Jews in Jerusalem, which Antiochus promptly quashed on his return home. The growing troubles between the anti-Hellenistic Jews and Antiochus came to a head when in 167 B.C.E. Antiochus sent his general Apollonius to Jerusalem to tear down the city walls and erect in their place a single fortified citadel. Shortly after this, another Seleucid official arrived with a decree forbidding all Jewish religious practices, including Sabbath observance and circumcision. Torah scrolls were burned and all sacrifices at the temple ended. The penalty for disobeying was death. To make things worse, Antiochus converted the temple of YHWH into a temple for Zeus Olympius, replacing the altar of sacrifice with a statue of the Greek god. Other statues of Greek gods were set up in the temple and throughout Jerusalem. The complex history of this period is recounted in 1 and 2 Maccabees.

The combination of internal disputes over the proper Jewish response to Greek culture and the external persecutions by Antiochus IV Epiphanes (and then, later, by the Romans) created among many Jews a strong sense of crisis and suffering. For them the world was an arena of dark forces, not just historical forces but also supernatural forces hostile to God and God's people. Whereas earlier generations had looked forward to Israel's restoration within a basically good world, now many Jews looked forward to deliverance from a thoroughly evil one. From the raw material of earlier biblical traditions and the experience of extreme suffering and crisis arose a new, more radical eschatological expectation, which today we call apocalypticism.

The word apocalyptic is from the Greek *apokalypsis*, which means "unveiling" or "revelation." It is the Greek name of the final book of the Christian Bible, the book of Revelation, or Apocalypse, to John. That book, along with the book of Daniel, are the only examples of the genre of literature called "apocalypses" in the Christian canon. But they are certainly not the only apocalypses that emerged from either the Jewish or Christian traditions. In fact, a substantial proportion of Jewish literature created between 300 B.C.E. and 200 C.E. was apocalyptic, and it is no accident that this period coincides with the ages of first Greek and then Roman domination of the Jewish world.[6] Apocalyptic literature is firmly rooted in earlier biblical traditions, images, and concepts, but transforms these in radical ways to bring a stronger, more vibrant message of hope to a world many Jews experienced as increasingly hostile and dark.

Apocalyptic literature or eschatology is the product of an apocalyptic worldview. This view had in common with earlier prophetic eschatology the conviction that the present age was imperfect and did not represent the ultimate will of God for Israel or for the world. Both eschatologies presume that God is ultimately in control of the world and of history and that this just and faithful God will one day set all things right. Both look forward to a day when God will establish sovereignty, conquer those who threaten or oppress God's people, and bring about a period of peace and prosperity.

But apocalyptic eschatology takes a more radical view of the fallen nature of this world, which it considers irredeemably corrupt. Whereas earlier tradition experienced oppression from human enemies, Jews who held to an apocalyptic worldview understood that human oppressors were really the agents of supernatural, demonic forces opposed to God and humans. For this reason apocalyptic literature, which is filled with angels and demons, shows a lively interest in the supernatural world, much more so than older Jewish texts.[7] Ultimately, it is the events of this supernatural world that explain human realities. The conflicts and persecutions of the present age reflect supernatural realities in which, for the time being, demonic forces hostile to God control the world.

History is the human sphere in which a great cosmic drama is being played out. But for apocalyptic writers the outcome of this drama is sure and already determined. A key feature of much apocalyptic literature is the idea that history is divided according to divine plan into periods. As each period succeeds the next, the cosmic drama unfolds until, in the final period, God will definitively conquer the demonic forces of evil that currently control the world. The final battle between good and evil will be fierce, and in the process this corrupt world will be destroyed in a great cataclysm. Many apocalypses, including the book of Revelation, give detailed accounts of this great and final battle.

While this all seems very grim, the point of apocalyptic literature is to give hope to the faithful by assuring them of two things. First, while history may be chaotic and the forces of evil and oppression may have the upper hand, this is only temporary. All is firmly and ultimately under God's control, and in the end God and the forces of good will prevail. Second, apocalyptic eschatology assures the faithful that they will have a share in the good world that will rise from the ashes of the present evil age. The sufferings of the present age, as a later writer would assure his readers, are nothing compared to the glory that will eventually be revealed for those who are faithful to God (see Rom 8:18). According to apocalyptic eschatology, this great battle would be accompanied by a final judgment, in which God would determine the fates of the faithful and the unfaithful, the just and wicked.

It is here, in the notion of the final judgment, that we find perhaps the most consequential development in Jewish thought in the Hellenistic period. Christians are often surprised to discover that for the most part the Old Testament has no notion of a meaningful afterlife and what scholars often call (rather clinically) postmortem judgment. The idea that the righteous will receive a reward and the wicked will suffer for their wickedness is a fairly common expectation throughout the entire Old Testament, but this is almost entirely understood in terms of present life on earth. When the prophets warn the people that they will suffer punishment for their covenant infidelity, they mean historically, at the hand of human instruments like the Babylonians.[8] Ancient Israelites did believe that after they died they would go to a place called *sheol*, but this was just a place of bland, shadowy existence. It was not a place of blessedness or punishment; it was neither heaven nor hell.

It is only in later literature, stemming from the Hellenistic period and under the influence of Greek thought, that Jewish texts begin to imagine a postmortem existence with any real meaning. In the book of Wisdom, which was written no more than a century before Christ, the righteous who suffer in this life are assured that after death their disembodied souls (a Greek concept) will live on with God (Wis 3:1; 5:15). The wicked, on the other hand, receive punishment. The point is to encourage the faithful in their times of trial.

Other texts from the Hellenistic and Roman periods reflect the idea that the wicked and the righteous will receive their respective rewards not in this world, but in the next after a final judgment. An influential text from about the third century B.C.E., *1 Enoch*, contains visions of a place where the souls of the wicked wait until the great judgment, at which time they will be sent to a final place of punishment (*1 Enoch* 22:1–14).[9] In this period we begin also to see language that suggests a belief in a type of resurrection, although it is not always clear whether or not it involves a body of some sort. Several psalms from a collection called the *Psalms of Solomon*, composed in the first century B.C.E., speak of the righteous "rising up" to everlasting life (see, for example, *PsSol* 3, 13, 14, 15).[10] This gift of eternal life to the righteous is always seen as the work of a faithful God who will never abandon those who do not abandon God. In the period of crisis and persecution, it becomes increasingly important to affirm that God is just and merciful, and since God can give life in the first place, it falls within the logic of Israel's traditions to now confess that God can bring the righteous back to life again. This affirmation is most eloquently stated in 2 Maccabees by the mother of seven sons who are being killed one by one for the refusal to break the laws of their ancestors. Exhorting one son to be courageous in the face of death, she assures him: "The Creator of the world, who shaped the beginning of humankind and devised the origin of all things, will in his mercy give life and breath back to you again, since you now forget yourselves for the sake of his laws" (2 Macc 7:23).

We see from these texts that the idea of an afterlife or a resurrection is not limited to apocalyptic texts, but it is always a key component of those texts, as in this passage from Daniel: "But at that time your people shall be delivered, everyone who is found written in the book. Many of those who sleep in the dust of the earth shall awake, some to everlasting life, and some to shame and everlasting contempt" (Dan 12:1–2).

This passage comes toward the end of the book of Daniel, and reflects the outcome of the great judgment that accompanies the final battle between the forces of God and righteousness and the human and supernatural forces of evil. The book of Daniel, specifically Daniel 7–12, is the only fully apocalyptic book in the Old Testament.[11] We have space here only to note a short section from the book that nevertheless exemplifies many of the elements of apocalyptic literature.

Like most apocalypses, Daniel begins with a dream or vision, this one in the first year of King Belshazzar of Babylon (Dan 7:1). Although the book of Daniel was actually written during the persecutions of Antiochus IV Epiphanes, it is set many centuries earlier, during the period of the Babylonian exile. Apocalyptic literature is typically set in ancient times and features someone from that time receiving visions of a far distant future, which is actually the writer's past and present. In the visions of the book, Daniel is shown things that, within the narrative, have not happened yet but which, from the perspective of the writer and the reader, have already happened and are currently happening. The intention is not to deceive the reader, but to emphasize that history plays out according to divinely ordained stages. The effect is to assure the reader that nothing happens by accident, but is all unfolding according to divine foreknowledge. Everything has meaning, and the past as well as the present and the future are ultimately in God's hands.

In his dream vision, Daniel sees four monstrous, hybrid beasts rise out of a tumultuous sea. Apocalyptic literature is highly symbolic, and the symbols used are drawn not only from earlier biblical texts but also from mythic elements of the wider ancient Near Eastern culture, which was shared by Israel. In both the Bible and the ancient Near East, stormy seas and the beasts that live in them (serpents, dragons, creatures called Leviathan or Rahab) represent chaos.[12] Chaos is the state of complete disorder that opposes and prevents life and flourishing. Several passages in the Old Testament feature God conquering chaotic waters and hostile monsters. These passages emphasize that the God of Israel conquers chaos—personal, social, or natural—to bring about creative order that will foster and sustain life. Often chaos images of water or monsters are applied to historical enemies of Israel as a way of representing their destructive character. Readers steeped in Israel's scriptures would have no trouble recognizing the four beasts coming out of the water as symbols of such forces of chaos. In this case, each beast represents a kingdom. The lion-beast represents Babylon, the bear-beast the Medes (the precursors to the Persians), the leopard-beast the Persians, and the fourth beast—typically described as a dragon—the Greeks. This beast is particularly vicious, "terrifying and dreadful and exceedingly strong," with iron teeth and ten horns (Dan 7:7). The horns are symbols for the successors of Alexander the Great, which now make room for a new horn, "with a mouth speaking arrogantly" (Dan 7:8). This horn represents Antiochus IV Epiphanes, who was persecuting the Jews at the time this portion of Daniel was written.

This opening scene of Daniel's vision envisions the historical succession of empires that had ruled Israel beginning with Babylon. Their portrayal as monsters coming out of the sea expresses symbolically their tendency to bring chaos—war, injustice, persecution—whatever harms God's people Israel and opposes God's will. The next scene offers hope that this chaotic situation will not endure forever.

As I watched, thrones were set in place,
  and an Ancient One took his throne,
his clothing was white as snow,
  and the hair on his head like pure wool. . . .
The court sat in judgment,
  and the books were opened.
I watched then because of the noise of the arrogant words that the horn was
speaking. And as I watched, the beast was put to death, and its body destroyed
and given over to be burned in fire. (Dan 7:9, 10–11)

The Ancient One seated on the throne is of course God. Although there
is no battle against the chaos beast, as in other biblical texts, God nevertheless conquers him in judgment and condemns him to be destroyed.
The vision expresses the hope that God will soon vindicate God's people and destroy the chaotic force that is Antiochus and even the entire
Greek Empire that spawned him. Apocalyptic literature, through its
sometimes bizarre and violent imagery, always depicts the present period as so corrupt, and God's people under such terrible persecution, that
only God—or an agent of God—can defeat the hostile forces that
threaten and harm God's people. The scene continues:

I saw one like a human being [literally: son of man]
  coming with the clouds of heaven.
And he came to the Ancient One
  and was presented before him.
To him was given dominion,
  and glory and kingship,
that all peoples, nations, and languages
  should serve him.
His dominion is an everlasting dominion
  that shall not pass away,
and his kingship is one
  that shall never be destroyed. (Dan 7:13–14)

The figure presented to God is described as "one like a son of man."
The idiom "son of man," or "son of humanity [adam]," is very common
in the Bible, and it means simply "human being." This individual is
therefore someone who looks like a human, but is not. Although the
identity of this figure is not certain, most scholars suggest it represents
an angelic being, probably Michael, who appears later in the book,
referred to as a "prince" and protector of God's people who battles
earthly princes opposed to them (Dan 10:13, 21; 12:1).[13] To describe
Michael as looking like a human is quite consistent with older biblical
texts in which angels or messengers of God are sometimes mistaken for
humans.[14] Later in Daniel, Michael will defeat the forces that oppose
God and God's people, and this vision provides a foretaste of that by

showing him as victorious and receiving dominion. Much of the rest of the book of Daniel is thus an expansion of the basic dynamic of this vision. In scene after vivid scene the battle between God (and his angelic agent) and the monstrous, chaotic powers that persecute God's people is played out until the inevitable end, when God is victorious. It is after this victory that, as we saw, "many of those who sleep in the dust of the earth shall awake" (Dan 12:2). Those who have suffered for their fidelity to God will be rewarded with everlasting life.

This is the message of hope that pervades the book of Daniel and all apocalytic literature. The world is, for now, under the control of violent, cruel forces that oppose God's people and bring persecution, injustice, and pain. But God has a plan and will not be thwarted. Apocalyptic literature often understands history according to periods, and inevitably sees the era in which the text was written as the final era, which will end with a great cosmic battle, the defeat of God's enemies, and the restoration of God's people. Those who have died for their fidelity will gain new life from the God of life, who does not forget or fail to reward the faithful. For all its violent, bizarre imagery, apocalyptic literature affirms a classic biblical claim: God is on the side of life. Because God is more powerful than any force that opposes life, in the end—despite how things look now—life will win out. What is called for in the meantime is fidelity to God and trust that history is firmly in God's hands.

MESSIANIC ESCHATOLOGY

As we have seen, all eschatological scenarios—whether prophetic or apocalyptic—look forward to the day when God will finally bring about a period of peace and prosperity, either in this world or in a world to come. In some eschatological scenarios, this new era is ushered in through a divinely appointed agent, called a "messiah."

The word messiah is derived from the Hebrew word *mashiach* (the final –ch is pronounced like the "ch" in Bach), which means "anointed" or, as a noun, "an anointed one." In ancient Israel, kings and high priests were anointed as part of their installation into their new role, and so it was customary to refer to a king as God's anointed. Although some individuals are referred to in the Old Testament as *mashiach*, they were not messiahs in the sense we mean that word today. When we use the word messiah, we mean an eschatological figure anointed by God to bring about deliverance and perhaps judgment.[15] Expectations of such a figure did not arise in the Jewish tradition until around the time of Antiochus IV Epiphanes and the Jewish Hasmonean rulers who established their kingdom after him. It is certainly true, though, that depictions and expectations of a messiah (or messiahs) in this later period are rooted in earlier texts, whether or not they feature the word *mashiach*. In other words, the concept of a "messiah" sent by God to deliver God's people and usher in the new age developed only in the Hellenistic period. But when it did, it derived its images and its authority from a number of earlier texts, which would be creatively appropriated and combined to give rise to this new, powerful expectation of God's work in the world.

Not all eschatological scenarios that emerged in the Hellenistic and Roman periods featured a messianic deliverer, and those that did were generally more interested in the resulting era of peace than in the messiah. It was the result of the work of the messiah, rather than the messiah himself, that was of greatest interest. When texts do talk about the messiah, they envision him in different ways. In some circles, the expected messiah was a priest, or an angel, or a prophet like Elijah. Sometimes, two messiahs were expected, a priest and a king.[16] Rather than explore the wide variety of messianic expectations we find in the texts from this period, here we will focus on two motifs that are important for understanding the New Testament, the expectation of a Davidic king and the figure of the Son of Man.

Although fewer than one might have expected, several eschatological texts mention a Davidic messiah, a descendant of David who would defeat God's enemies and bring about the era of peace, justice, and prosperity. This expectation is rooted in the passages we saw earlier that affirm God's choice of the Davidic line, one of whom would sit on the throne "forever." Although the destruction of Jerusalem in 586 B.C.E. brought an end to the Davidic monarchy, in the early postexilic period there appears to have been some hope that God would restore the monarchy in the person of a man named Zerubbabel, who features prominently in the books of Haggai and Zechariah. This never happened and, after Zerubbabel, expectations of a restored monarchy seem to have waned for a few centuries.

The impetus that reawakened hopes of a restored Davidic line was the rise of the Hasmonean dynasty in the wake of the persecutions of Antiochus IV Epiphanes.[17] The struggle for power, both against the Seleucids and within the Jewish community itself, ignited a nationalistic fervor that was only partially satisfied with the establishment of the Hasmonean kingdom. True, the Jews once again had an independent kingdom, but the Hasmoneans, while Jews, were not a Davidic line, nor were they popular with many Jews for political and religious reasons. The rise of a native but non-Davidic and unpopular monarchy, along with the growth of apocalyptic expectations in the face of foreign and domestic oppression, gave birth in some circles to the hope that when God did finally act, God would raise up a Davidic messiah—an eschatological deliverer—who would vanquish the powers of evil. This hope was rooted in the firm belief that God would never be unfaithful to God's promises, including the promise to David. Whereas Jeremiah had stressed the conditional version of that promise to explain the demise of the monarchy, now Jews drew on the unconditional form of the promise to argue that God would one day restore the Davidic kingship, which really would last "forever."

Several fragmentary texts from the Dead Sea Scrolls, which date from around the time of the Hasmoneans, reflect this expectation of a Davidic messiah. The group that produced the Dead Sea Scrolls, almost certainly the community at Qumran, held a decidedly apocalyptic worldview and looked forward to the day when God would destroy all the wicked and deliver the righteous members of the community from the evil age. In many of their texts the writers at Qumran interpreted prophetic passages to refer to their own time and found in them indications of how God planned to bring about the new age.

Whereas Isaiah had looked forward to a righteous Davidic ruler in his own time, or at least in the historical future, the community at Qumran saw the fulfillment of this expectation only at the end of the age in an apocalyptic battle waged by the Davidic messiah. Although other fragments from Qumran attest to different messianic expectations, these texts show clearly that some Jews expected God eventually to restore the "everlasting" Davidic dynasty and through the new Davidic king usher in the new era.[18] This interpretation rests on several beliefs: that scripture authoritatively revealed the will and intentions of God; that God was unfailingly faithful to divine promises; and that ancient prophecies, whatever they may have meant when they were first uttered, were ultimately pointing to the present circumstances of the interpreter. The same three assumptions also informed the way the writers of the New Testament read their scriptures in light of the Christ event.

Other texts from about the same period as the Dead Sea Scrolls attest to expectations of a Davidic messiah. In the *Psalms of Solomon* we find a psalm that refers to the promise made to David of an everlasting dynasty, which was nevertheless taken away because of the sins of the people and replaced with other rulers. The psalmist calls on God to raise up a new Davidic ruler to destroy the "unrighteous rulers" and restore a righteous kingdom.[19]

These texts represent the messianic expectations of at least some Jews in the decades leading up to the New Testament period, although it is impossible to tell how many held out hopes of a Davidic messiah by the first century C.E. Nevertheless, it is easy to see how these expectations are directly derived from the biblical tradition, which affirmed that God's choice of the Davidic dynasty was permanent and that a ruler would sit on the throne of David forever. Other older texts expressed hope that despite the unrighteous kings who had ruled through the ages, God would one day raise up a truly righteous Davidic ruler who would ensure justice, peace, and prosperity for God's people and—in some scenarios—for the whole world (for example, Isa 11:1–9). When the kingdom came to an end, these hopes lay dormant for centuries, until they were once again aroused by historical circumstances that awakened hope that the ever-faithful God would at last bring to pass all God had promised David and Israel.

Another significant way of thinking about the messiah was derived from Daniel's vision of the "one like a son of man." In the gospels, Jesus refers to himself very often as "the Son of Man," as if it were a title, and a messianic one at that. By the time of Jesus, the figure of "one like a son of man" from Daniel 7 had been reinterpreted and transformed into an expected messianic figure who would one day usher in God's reign. Although Jesus would clearly have been familiar with the Daniel text, his use of the title reflects this much more developed messianic eschatology, and his language regarding the Son of Man is best understood against this background.

The *Parables of Enoch* was an influential Jewish text from the Hellenistic period that gives us insight into this figure of the Son of Man as he was understood in the first century C.E. The *Parables* is a section of the larger *1 Enoch* that, although not ultimately accepted into the Jewish canon, nevertheless reflected important apocalyptic and messianic ideas that inform both Jewish and Christian thought in the Greek and Roman periods.

The *Parables* announced the coming judgment in which God would condemn the mighty rulers of the age and vindicate the righteous. The section depicts a series of journeys, in which Enoch visits the heavenly realms and learns from his angelic guide the meaning of what he sees and what will happen "in those days," at the end of the present era. The drama of the coming days includes many characters, including God (called the Lord of Spirits), good and bad angels, and righteous humans. A key figure is called at various times by four titles: the Chosen One, the Righteous One, the Anointed One (Messiah), and the Son of Man.

In the *Parables* the Son of Man, although not a Davidic king, is clearly a messianic figure who is the agent of God's judgment. He is exalted and transcendent, higher than the angels. Although he is an entirely new individual in the Jewish tradition (at least in the texts we have), he is actually a combination of biblical figures, including "one like a son of man" in Daniel 7, the Servant of the LORD in Second Isaiah, the Davidic kings in the psalms and elsewhere, and the personified Woman Wisdom from Proverbs 8 that we met in the previous chapter. He is a good example of the creative ability of the Jewish tradition at this time to draw various strands of scripture together into new expressions of ancient ideas to address the concerns of the times.

The Son of Man appears at key points in the *Parables*. A few examples of these passages give us an idea of the nature and role of this messianic figure. In a section clearly inspired by the scene in Daniel 7, Enoch sees "one who had a head of days" (another way of saying "Ancient of Days") and "another, whose face was like the appearance of a man" (*1 Enoch* 46:1). When Enoch asks his guiding angel about "that son of man" and what he had to do with the Head of Days, the angel responds:

> This is the son of man who has righteousness,
>   and righteousness dwells with him.
> And all the treasuries of what is hidden he will reveal;
>   for the Lord of Spirits has chosen him. . . .
> And this son of man whom you have seen—
>   he will raise the kings and mighty ones from their couches,
>   and the strong from their thrones. . . .
> He will overturn the kings from their thrones
>   and their kingdoms. (*1 Enoch* 46:3, 4, 5)

While the advent of the Son of Man will spell doom for the wicked, it will be a blessing for the righteous. In another vision inspired by both Woman Wisdom and the Servant of the LORD in Isaiah, Enoch sees the naming of the transcendent Son of Man:

> And in that hour the son of man was named in the
>   presence of the Lord of Spirits,
>   and his name, before the Head of Days.
> Even before the sun and the constellations were created,
>   before the stars of heaven were made,
>   his name was named before the Lord of Spirits.
> He will be a staff for the righteous,
>   that they may lean on him and not fall;
> And he will be the light of the nations,
>   and he will be a hope for those who grieve in their hearts. . . .
> For this reason he was chosen and hidden in his presence
>   before the world was created and forever. (*1 Enoch* 48:2–5, 6)

Like other apocalyptic works, the *Parables* expects an imminent final judgment in which the wicked and the righteous will receive their respective rewards after a resurrection. This event will be presided over by the Chosen One, also known as the Son of Man:

> In those days, the earth will restore what has been entrusted to it,
>> and Sheol will restore what it has received,
>> and destruction will restore what it owes.
> For in those days, my Chosen One will arise,
>> and choose the righteous and holy from among them,
>> for the day on which they will be saved has drawn near. (*1 Enoch* 51:1–2)

In the end, the messianic Son of Man will be enthroned in heaven with God and from his throne:

> And the Lord of Spirits seated the Chosen One upon the throne of glory
>> and he will judge all the works of the holy ones
>> in the heights of heaven,
>> and in the balance he will weigh their deeds. (*1 Enoch* 61:8)

The *Parables* gives us valuable insight into how the figure of the Son of Man developed from Daniel 7 into a heavenly Messiah, the Chosen and Righteous One, chosen by God to judge all peoples at the end of the age, when God would finally defeat all hostile forces, human and non-human, that threaten God's people and the whole earth. Although *1 Enoch* was not ultimately accepted as scripture, it was nevertheless well known by Jews in the time of Jesus.[20] It is clear that the figure of the Son of Man, along with the expectation of the Davidic messiah, heavily influenced both his and the early church's understanding of who Jesus was and what his coming meant. He was the Son of Man, chosen by God to bring about the new era of the reign of God, when all evil, including death, would be finally vanquished.

CONCLUSION

We have seen in this chapter how various strands of the biblical tradition were reappropriated, combined, and supplemented to create a new, yet ancient, message of hope for Jews in times of crisis and persecution. In the centuries between the Babylonian exile and the first century C.E., Jewish expectations developed considerably. Whereas originally the prophets had held out a vision of a renewed and restored land and people in this world, over time these ancient prophecies were seen as intimations of a far more radical change when God would not only restore Israel, but would defeat all the manifestations of chaos and evil that plagued not just Israel but the whole world. These expectations were especially important in times of persecution, when faithful Jews needed assurances that their fidelity and even martyrdom were seen and cherished by God, who would reward them, not in this life but in the next. The violent and bizarre images in apocalyptic literature were highly symbolic expressions of the foundational Jewish belief that God was resolutely opposed to any manifestation of chaos and evil in the world and would one day decisively defeat all that opposed life and the flourishing of creation. Many Jews also expected that God would accomplish this through an appointed agent, a messiah. Although there were many ideas about this messiah in circulation, a prominent expectation was that God would send a Davidic messiah to vanquish God's enemies and inaugurate a new era of peace and justice and safety for all. The Jewish world was alive with hope and expectation in the first century C.E. The stage was set for Jesus of Nazareth to come and announce that God's reign had begun.

QUESTIONS FOR REFLECTION

1. In times of crisis, ancient Jews looked to their religious traditions to make sense of the present and to find hope for the future. When you experience challenges or crises, what aspects of your religious tradition to you find most helpful for interpreting your life? How does your religious tradition offer you hope for the future?

2. Apocalyptic literature uses vivid symbolic images to give meaning to history and human experience. Do you have any symbols that allow you to do the same thing? Where do those symbols come from? How do they help you understand and express the meaning of your experiences?

3. Jewish and Christian eschatology is a response of hope based on trust that God is ultimately faithful, even when it seems otherwise. What are some of the challenges you face in trusting in the faithfulness of God? How do you strengthen your trust in God's fidelity?

4. Biblical eschatology assumes that history has a purpose and is moving in a specific direction under God's guidance. What difference do you think it makes to have this view of history? Do you share it? Why or why not?

5. Many people today share the ancient apocalyptic view that the present world is evil, and look forward to the day when God will bring it all to an end in a final, cataclysmic battle. What do you think of the apocalyptic perspective? What does it still have to offer people of faith today? What are its limitations, and why?

10

THAT MAN JESUS

Jesus asked them, "Who do people say that I am?"
Some say John the Baptist; others say Elijah,
others one of the prophets. "But you,
who do you say that I am?"

—Mark 8:27–29

We have followed the historical journey of God's covenant people
from the stories of their ancient ancestors in Genesis down to the tumultuous years of the second and first centuries B.C.E. For Christians the
culmination and decisive turn in that long journey will now come with
the advent of Jesus. As we move into this era, we must begin by sketch-
ing briefly the political and religious movements at the time of Jesus'
coming.

JEWS UNDER ROMAN RULE

In 63 B.C.E. the Roman general Pompey intervened in a dispute between
two Jewish high priest contenders and established Rome's control over
the eastern Mediterranean region and Palestine. Greek culture and
language continued to be a dominant factor in Roman Palestine, but
political control rested firmly in the hands of Rome and in those local
Jewish collaborators who supported the Roman officials. Included
among the latter were the members of the high priestly families and
Herodian rulers (Herod the Great [37–4 B.C.E.] and his descendants)
whom Rome "allowed" to have a certain degree of autonomy in domestic issues. These rulers were supported by a host of persons who were

lackeys and retainers: "Moreover, the power of rulers was exerted in very personal ways. The ancient Mediterranean was composed of 'face to face' societies at every level on the basis of personal contact. The emperor personally appointed prefects and procurators, and he held them accountable. . . . The Herodian client-kings and tetrarchs depended upon their families, clients, and spies to keep them abreast of their realms' activities."[1]

All through the decades of the first century, however, the ordinary, nonelite Jewish peasants chafed at the heavy burdens imposed on them by the ruling elite: from the emperor, to the local rulers and governors, to the colluding landed aristocracy of Palestine. The social and economic life of Palestine was defined by its highly stratified and agrarian character. No more than 5 percent of the populace constituted the "elite" (imperial family, soldiers, senators, rulers and local magistrates, high priestly families) who owned and controlled most of the land and wealth. About 80 to 90 percent of the populace made up the "nonelite" (artisans, small traders, peasants who worked the land, those engaged in the fishing business) whose livelihoods depended totally on the good wishes and patronage of the elite. Agricultural prosperity, moreover, was hard-won as the normal yield in Palestine was only "10 to 15 times the grain seed sown" compared with today's multiple of 40 with modern methods of farming and fertilizing.[2]

But by far the most difficult and oppressive factor in the Palestine of Jesus' day was the heavy taxation that doubly burdened the majority of the Jewish population. Every Jewish male was required to contribute to the support of the Temple in Jerusalem, with its elaborate rituals and sacrificial practices, its multitude of priestly and nonpriestly functionaries (the high priestly families, Levites, scribes and judges, money changers, singers, and gatekeepers), and its physical upkeep. Torah prescriptions (Deut 12, 14, 26:12–14; Lev 27:30–33) obliged the tithing of produce for the priestly families and required the "head tax" of one-half shekel per year for the upkeep of the Temple. These same Torah prescriptions governed the requirements regarding sacrificial animals and produce offered for sacrifice, with stipulations for the remainder of the animal or produce going to the priests. Some (like the Essenes at Qumran by the Dead Sea) criticized the affluence of Jerusalem's priestly aristocracy altogether and rejected their leadership and status, choosing instead to pursue a rigorous, Torah-observant ascetical life in the desert by the Dead Sea.

Furthermore, on top of the Jewish taxation policies, the Roman system of taxation added additional burdens: land taxes (1 percent of its value), a crop tax (as high as 12 percent), market taxes in cities, tolls on the transport of goods, port taxes for shipping, and the yearly head tax of one denarius.[3] The responsibility for collecting Rome's taxes fell to the local tax officers hired by Rome. These tax collectors paid their Roman employers a fixed amount and in return could levy exorbitant rates for their own profit. With this double tax burden, many peasants lost what little land they may have had, risked imprisonment, or fell prey to the swelling gangs of social bandits terrorizing the countryside.

As a result of this economic and political situation, the religious climate in Palestine in the first century was tense and at times desperate. Apocalyptic longings intensified for God to intervene in order to save and liberate ordinary Jewish peasants from their afflictions. Prophetic figures announcing the coming wrath of God against oppressors were common, but chief among them was one known in the New Testament as John the Baptist. Though John was himself a descendant of a rural priestly family, his message bore strong prophetic judgment against evildoers, denounced the excesses of Jerusalem's priestly aristocracy (Mt 3:7–10), and called for a baptism of repentance for all people and a life renewed in Torah observance and practices of justice for the poor, fasting, and prayer. John foresaw and preached one mightier than he (Mk 1:7–8) who would come after him and who would baptize not in water but with the Holy Spirit of God. It was into this climate of social-political and religious unrest that Jesus of Nazareth came.

ONE JESUS AND FOUR GOSPELS

Incarnation

> Long ago God spoke to our ancestors in many and various ways by the prophets, but in these last days he has spoken to us by a Son, whom he appointed heir of all things, through whom he also created the worlds. He is the reflection of God's glory and the exact imprint of God's very being. (Heb 1:1–3b)

So begins the New Testament document we call the "Letter to the Hebrews." This early Christian author, certainly not Paul himself but perhaps a disciple of Paul writing toward the end of the first century C.E., sums up our Christian conviction about Jesus as the incarnation of God. This *mystery* we call incarnation affirms two essential claims: (1) that God's very being is self-revelatory, that God continually reveals the divine Self to humankind; and (2) that humanity finds its final destiny and fulfillment, the ultimate goal of its self-transcendence, in God. The doctrine of the incarnation further claims that in Jesus, God's self-communication is irrevocably complete in a concrete, historical person, one who is like us in all things but sin and in whom we find the perfection of our humanity. As the Eastern Church put it: the divine became human so that the human might become divine. Therefore, for the Christian, knowing this man Jesus is an essential requirement for knowing God and for knowing ourselves and our own destiny.

Jesus, the Man from Nazareth

Each of the four gospels tells the story of the life and ministry of Jesus in its own unique way.[4] All four gospels, however, attempt to answer the same perplexing questions that the early followers of Jesus wrestled with for decades, questions like: Who *was* Jesus? What is the meaning of Jesus' life and, more importantly, of his death? How is Jesus related to the God of Israel? and How should Jesus' life and death change our human lives in the present and into the future? Each gospel presents its own answers to these questions, and each gives a different portrait of Jesus, highlighting different dimensions of his life, his teaching, and his mission. And for ourselves as contemporary Christians who seek to follow in this way of discipleship, each gospel story offers unique guidelines for our spiritual journey. Let us turn now to see these different faces of Jesus and their implications for our contemporary spiritual lives.

THE GOSPEL OF MARK: JESUS, THE CRUCIFIED MESSIAH

Most scholars agree that Mark is the earliest of the gospels, written probably during the turbulent years between 69 and 70 C.E. when the Roman legions were in the midst of putting down the first Jewish rebellion against Rome (66–70 C.E.).[5] The final demonstration of Roman power was to destroy completely the Temple in Jerusalem in the year 70 C.E. and to leave it in ruins. In the context of this unrest and turmoil, the essential question for Mark's community concerned the meaning of the call to discipleship in the midst of such suffering. And so the genius of Mark's gospel, and of the other gospels as well, is that it narrates the story of Jesus' life and death and at the same time *interprets* and comments on that story as the story unfolds. As the earliest gospel, Mark was the first to select and organize into a coherent narrative various pieces of the oral memory about Jesus that circulated in the Christian community for the first thirty or forty years after Jesus' death. Mark's story begins with the opening of the public ministry of Jesus and his baptism in the Jordan River by John the Baptist, and it ends with the women coming to the empty tomb and hearing the angel's message: "He is risen, he is not here!" In the course of the story we, as readers of the gospel, come to know this man Jesus as the Son of God, the Messiah and anointed one, and like the first hearers of the gospel, we too learn what it means to follow this crucified messiah.

For the author of Mark, the life of Jesus had to be set, first of all, in relationship to the story of the covenant community of ancient Israel. And so, as his story opens, we hear again the prophetic words of Second Isaiah (40:3) and of Malachi (3:1–2), who long before had prophesied a messenger to come who would prepare the way for the Lord's final and decisive coming. For Mark, therefore, John the Baptist is that messenger, who announces Jesus' coming after him and calls people to prepare with "a baptism of repentance for the forgiveness of sins" (Mk 1:4). Then, as if from nowhere, Jesus comes onto the stage of history from Nazareth in Galilee and receives the baptism of John. But at that first moment at the Jordan, the voice from heaven verified that this man— and this story—was to be no ordinary occurrence. As Mark narrates: "And just as he was coming up out of the water, he saw the heavens torn apart and the Spirit descending like a dove on him. And a voice came from heaven, 'You are my Son, the Beloved; with you I am well pleased'" (Mk 1:10–11). The divine voice confirms that this man Jesus is "Son" and "Beloved" of God, who, though tempted by Satan in the wilderness (Mk 1:12–13), remained there with the angels ministering to him.

The first words of Jesus in Mark announce a decisive moment and a new beginning: "The time is fulfilled, and the kingdom of God has come near; repent, and believe in the good news" (Mk 1:15). The *kairos*, God's appointed time, has come to its fulfillment in Jesus. The turning point in history has come; the new age foretold by the prophets has dawned. And so, Jesus challenges his hearers, as he does us, to believe this Good News about God's reign. As Mark's gospel continues to unfold, however, we learn that the one who proclaims this message is part and parcel of the fulfillment he announces. And with almost breathless pace, Mark sets out to narrate the words and deeds of this mighty one who "teaches with authority" (Mk 1:22), who heals and expels demons with a mysterious power, as the crowd wonders aloud: "What is this? A new teaching—with authority! He commands even the unclean spirits, and they obey him" (Mk 1:27). The disciples in the story, and we ourselves as modern readers, receive this strong challenge to believe, to believe in the one who announces this message and to follow in his way. The successive chapters of the first half of Mark's gospel, from this opening scene to the middle of chapter 8, invite us to see the mighty one at work: curing Simon's mother-in-law (Mk 1:31), cleansing the leper (Mk 1:40–42), healing the paralytic and extending to him forgiveness of sin (Mk 2:5–11), and challenging the religious leaders of his day (Mk 7:1–23). We also puzzle at Jesus, this devoutly religious Jew, consorting with sinners and tax collectors (Mk 2:15), taking questionable liberty with the sacred Sabbath regulations (Mk 2:23–28), and even healing a man with a withered hand in the synagogue in open violation of the Sabbath (Mk 3:1–6)!

Jesus' teaching, moreover, unsettles us with its riddles and parables. Just as the disciples in the story, we ourselves also look for clear answers and unequivocal direction for the way we must follow. But instead of clarity, we hear Jesus tell stories about sowers (Mk 4:1–9), and mustard seeds (Mk 4:31–32), and harvest times to come, and together with the crowds in the gospel story we, too, find ourselves asking, "What can all this mean?" Jesus, this strong one of God, is not confined or limited by the boundaries of his Jewish faith, neither by its ideas of what is holy nor by its geographic boundaries. Jesus ventures readily into Gentile regions and uses his power to free even the wild demoniac languishing in the tombs (Mk 5:1–20). His power reaches completely to the limits of life and death itself as he restores to life the daughter of Jairus (Mk 5:21–24, 35–43) and allows his power to heal the nameless woman's flow of blood (Mk 5:25–34).

Above all else, compassion seems to be the hallmark of this strong and holy man: compassion on the hungry crowds whom he fed and who "ate and were satisfied" (Mk 6:42, 8:1–10), compassion on all who were sick and possessed by evil demons, compassion even on the Syrophoenician woman who, after all, was an outsider and had no business making demands on him (Mk 7:24–30). As Mark tells his story, he seems to imply that through such encounters with those outside the boundaries of Judaism, Jesus himself grew in his awareness of the universal dimensions of God's reign and of the inclusion of all as recipients of God's promises. If the gospel were to stop here, in the middle of chapter 8, then we would be left with a portrait of Jesus as the mighty hero, the "divine man," the man of power able to overcome natural elements, demons, and every human opponent. But, as John Donahue, the contemporary Jesuit scripture scholar, has so perceptively observed:

> Mark's presentation of Jesus offers a progression in the creation and shattering of illusions. In the first part of the Gospel the reader identifies with a figure of power and renown. Jesus joins successful combat with demonic forces. He exercises power over death, sickness, and natural forces. He offers bread to the hungry and solace to

the bereaved. In the middle section the reader sees that this illusion is to be shattered. The figure of power is to be handed over to people who kill him. Yet, even this illusion is to be shattered, for the brokenness of the cross is itself broken by the message, "He is risen." And yet the final illusion is shattered. "Risen" does not mean a return in power and presence to the community. The community must continue to struggle with illusions (with false christs, false messiahs) until they finally "see" him (13:26; 16:7).[6]

The turning point of the gospel comes in the middle of Mark 8. As Jesus was with his disciples on the northern shore of the Sea of Galilee in the fishing village of Bethsaida, some people brought a blind man to him to be cured. Jesus made spittle and anointed his eyes and asked him, "Can you see anything?" (Mk 8:23). The man responded, "I can see people, but they look like trees walking" (Mk 8:24). And so Jesus repeated the treatment, and this time the man saw clearly. From there Jesus and the disciples continue on to the far north, to the region of Caesarea Philippi (the city built by Herod Philip, the son of Herod the Great), where he posed the question to his disciples: "Who do people say that I am?" (Mk 8:27). Peter, acting as spokesperson for the group, professes that Jesus is "the Messiah [the Christ]" (Mk 8:29), whereupon Jesus immediately instructed him about his coming suffering, rejection, and death. But Peter, again as spokesperson, rejected this announcement and received Jesus' strong rebuke: "Get behind me Satan! For you are setting your mind not on divine things but on human things" (Mk 8:33).

This sequence of stories—the blind man cured in two stages and Peter's failure to understand and accept the message about Jesus' suffering and death—is carefully placed by Mark. A second blind man, the blind beggar Bartimaeus near Jericho, will be cured later in Mark 10:46–52. But in between these two stories of blindness Mark has placed the concentration of teaching about the nature of discipleship of those who would be followers of the crucified messiah. The blindness that needs curing is, of course, the blindness of Peter and of the other disciples—including ourselves as readers—so that they (and we) might "see" that Jesus' power is a power revealed in weakness, that discipleship entails costs, and that true greatness is found only in those who become servants of all. We can see graphically the progressive development of this theme by looking at an overview of these chapters. The three announcements of the passion appear here, interspersed with Jesus' teaching about their "taking up the cross" (Mk 8:34), "true greatness" in service (Mk 9:34), and the "cost of discipleship" (Mk 10:35–45):

The Way of Discipleship (Mk 8:27–10:52)
BLIND MAN (trees walking . . .) (Mk 8:22–26)

1. Disciples' Eyes Opened (Mk 8:27–30)
2. *1st PASSION PREDICTION* (Mk 8:31–33)
3. Way of Discipleship (Mk 8:34–9:1)
4. Transfiguration (Mk 9:2–8)
5. Elijah and the Son of Humanity (Mk 9:9–13)
6. A Dumb Spirit Driven Out (Mk 9:14–29)
7. *2nd PASSION PREDICTION* (Mk 9:30–32)
8. True Greatness (Mk 9:33–37)
9. For or Against Jesus (Mk 9:38–41)
10. Saying about Life and Death (Mk 9:42–50)
11. Question on Divorce (Mk 10:1–12)
12. Jesus Blesses Children (Mk 10:13–16)
13. Rich Man Loses Eternal Life (Mk 10:17–31)
14. *3rd PASSION PREDICTION* (Mk 10:32–34)
15. Cost of Discipleship (Mk 10:35–45)

THE BLIND BARTIMAEUS (seeing clearly) (Mk 10:46–52)
"When they were approaching Jerusalem . . ." (Mk 11:1)

These central chapters are the turning point for the disciples and for the readers of Mark. As Jesus and the disciples journey from the extreme northern boundary of Israel southward toward Jerusalem and toward the inevitable fate awaiting Jesus there, Jesus attempts to heal their blindness and, analogously, our own as readers of the gospel. Especially poignant is the senseless question of the sons of Zebedee, James and John, who after all Jesus' teaching from Mark 8:31 to Mark 10:34 approach Jesus wanting to sit "one at the right and one at the left" (Mk 10:37) in his glory. Their question reveals the pathetic extent of their blindness and, by extension, mirrors our own. They were still lusting after power rather than embracing the service the gospel message requires. Jesus responded to them with the clearest denunciation of abusive power anywhere in the gospel: "You know that among the Gentiles those whom they recognize as their rulers lord it over them, and their great ones are tyrants over them. But it is not so among you; but whoever wishes to become great among you must be your servant, and whoever wishes to be first among you must be slave of all. For the Son of [Humanity] came not to be served but to serve, and to give his life as a ransom for many" (Mk 10:42–45).

As Jesus entered into Jerusalem to meet his fate, the story moves to its most solemn moment for which the whole gospel has prepared us. We are invited to look on this crucified one who has embraced the shame of the cross and relinquished power in exchange for an ignominious death, for giving his life as a ransom. We learn in this passion story that Jesus, although he prays in the garden that the cup might pass from him (Mk 14:36), remained faithful to his God until the end. In doing so, he shows us the way to fidelity and new life. And as all desert him except the few women "looking on from a distance" (Mk 15:40), we learn how fallible are these disciples who are so much like ourselves.[7] Only the Roman centurion, ironically, fully comprehended who this crucified, holy one was—"the Son of God" (Mk 15:39). The mystery of the empty tomb remains as the final word of this gospel. The despair of death in Mark's story is shattered by the message of the angel, "He is risen!" But, together with the women in the story, we are told that we must "go to Galilee," as the angel says. That is, we must go back to where the story began and listen again to its powerful message. And perhaps, if we do as the angel commands, our blindness, too, might be healed.

Mark's gospel story challenges its readers to embrace the cross as the way of discipleship today. It does not invite us to impose suffering and hardship *on others* in the name of some skewed piety or false sense of sanctity, but it does call on us freely to embrace the cross ourselves and to place *ourselves* in solidarity with all those who suffer. It asks us to renounce every form of domination and power, every kind of violence and abuse against others, all attempts to subjugate others denying them their dignity or to lord over them in the name of God. The message of Mark's gospel pronounces a scathing critique on all structures of oppressive power: economic, political, social, ecclesiastical, and personal. Instead, the Jesus of Mark's gospel is the holy and compassionate one whose heart is moved with pity on all who are in need and for whom he gave his life. This is the Jesus whom we seek to know and to follow on our journey of discipleship today.

THE GOSPEL OF MATTHEW—JESUS, SON OF GOD AND EMBODIMENT OF TORAH WISDOM

In the history of the Christian church, the gospel of Matthew has enjoyed a certain "pride of place," both in the canonical order of the gospels in the New Testament and in the liturgical prominence given to this story of Jesus. There is general agreement that this gospel text comes most likely from the early church in Antioch and was probably written around the year 85 C.E. as a further development—beyond Mark—of Christian reflection on the life and ministry of Jesus. In the composition of his gospel, the author used the Markan story and most probably another written source of Jesus' sayings commonly referred to as "Q."[8] In addition, we find other stories and traditions unique to Matthew that may have been the special treasure of the oral memory in the church of Antioch. If Mark's gospel teaches us about the radical necessity of suffering and the cost of discipleship for those who desire to follow Jesus, the crucified one, the gospel of Matthew develops the more elaborate norms of Christian living in the community of the church.

Matthew's gospel reveals a Christian community wrestling with its relationship to the community of post–70 C.E. Judaism, a Judaism that had nurtured its origins and been the matrix of its earliest development. A key statement in the gospel identifies this challenge that Matthew's church must have faced: "And [Jesus] said to them, 'Therefore every scribe who has been trained for the kingdom of heaven is like the master of a household who brings out of his treasure what is new and what is old'" (Mt 13:52). This gospel would never lightly discard the Mosaic Torah as "old," and so we hear Jesus say in Matthew emphatically, "Do not think that I have come to abolish the law or the prophets; I have come not to abolish but to fulfill" (Mt 5:17). The newness of Jesus' message, therefore, consists in new ways to interpret and to understand the old promises of God for a new time and for a wider Jewish *and Gentile* audience.

The church of Antioch, we assume, was just such a mixed Jewish and Gentile community living in the midst of one of the largest Hellenized, urban centers of the Roman world. This group of Christians saw in Jesus the definitive fulfillment of all the prophetic hopes of Israel and believed that his message was now to be shared with the whole world. Accordingly, we find in this gospel at least eleven formulaic quotations from the Old Testament claiming that Jesus is the fulfillment of the messianic hopes of the Jewish people.[9] And at the end of the gospel, the final command of Jesus to his disciples is, "Go!" and "make disciples of all nations, baptizing them . . . and teaching them" all that Jesus has commanded them (Mt 28:19–20).

Many texts of the gospel reveal the extreme degree of hostility that existed at this time between the fledgling Christian group and its Jewish "parent." During the final week before his death, for example, Jesus spoke a parable to the "chief priests and elders of the people" (Mt 21:23) while in the Temple precincts. As all parables do, this one challenges its hearers to think about things differently and to reassess familiar assumptions. The parable (Mt 21:33–41) describes a householder who planted a vineyard, hedged it all around, dug a wine press, built a tower, and let it out to tenants. At harvest time, the householder sent servants to collect the fruit, but the tenants beat one, stoned another, and killed a third. A second time with other servants the same fate awaited them. Finally, the householder sent his son, but the son, too, was killed by the tenants. The climactic saying that concludes the parable—"Therefore I tell you, the kingdom of God will be taken away from you and given to a people that produces the fruits of the kingdom" (Mt 21:43)—points to the conviction that "others" (presumably, Jesus' followers) have now inherited the "vineyard," the classic metaphor for Israel (see Isa 5). Matthew's gospel, furthermore, takes pains to distinguish between "their" synagogues and "my church" (Mt 16:18), and in this gospel Jesus levels biting criticism against the leadership of the synagogue community in his repeated catalog of woes: "Woe to you, scribes and Pharisees, hypocrites! Because you shut the kingdom of heaven against people" (Mt 23:13) and so on. A shrewd reader, however, will remember the earlier saying when Jesus' own followers were called hypocrites: "Why do you see the speck in your neighbor's eye, but do not notice the log in your own eye? . . . You hypocrite, first take the log out of your own eye, and then you will see clearly to take the speck out of your neighbor's eye" (Mt 7:3, 5). And remembering this admonition, we will recognize that the same warnings apply to all who would pretend to exclude others from the blessings of God.

When we explore the spiritual wisdom of Matthew's gospel we must begin with the Sermon on the Mount, the first of five great discourses in Matthew.[10] The setting of Jesus' teaching recalls Moses on the mountain of Sinai, and the teaching of a new law both repeats and interprets in new ways the words given to Israel centuries before. The sermon begins with the familiar beatitudes, those sayings of Jesus found in both Matthew and Luke (derived presumably from Q) that begin "Blessed is the one who . . ." or a variant thereof. These sayings pronounce a blessing for those who align themselves with God's eschatological promises of justice and blessing. They remind the disciples, and ourselves as readers of the gospel, that God's future promises a great reversal of fortunes for those who are poor, those who mourn, the meek, those who hunger and thirst, those who show mercy, and so forth. Matthew's version of the beatitudes generalizes and, some would say, "spiritualizes" the categories of people—"Blessed are the poor in *spirit*." But this tendency, as Raymond Collins argues, makes the beatitudes in Matthew more applicable for the ongoing life of the church: "Matthew's spiritualization of the traditional first and fourth beatitudes and his formulation of the fifth, sixth, and seventh, more active beatitudes, imparts to the entire collection the character of an ecclesial exhortation. Those who are praised in the Matthean beatitudes are those whose lives reflect authentic Christian existence from the viewpoint of continuing church life."[11]

Jesus' first sermon then continues with his affirmation of the enduring validity of the Torah—"Do not think that I have come to abolish" (Mt 5:17). But the Torah's enduring validity, for Matthew, depends on the new interpretation that Jesus' life and teaching give. Where the Torah had forbidden murder (Ex 20:13), Jesus now says, "But I say to you, that if you are angry with a brother you will be liable to judgment" (Mt 5:22). Here, and elsewhere (Mt 5:28, 34, 39, 44), Jesus seems to intensify the demands of the Torah and to go to the heart of the intent of the law as it was intended to guard the harmony and integrity of God's people. Jesus' call to discipleship in Matthew is synonymous with a life of attending to the person and words of Jesus but more importantly of *doing* what the Lord commands: "Not every one who says to me 'Lord, Lord,' will enter the kingdom of heaven, but only the one who does the will of my Father in heaven" (Mt 7:21). The *coherence* between word (profession of faith) and deed (righteous living) is essential, both as illustrated in the life of Jesus and as demanded of those who would be his disciples. This first sermon, given on the mount in Galilee, concludes with a summary statement by which Matthew calls our attention to the identity of Jesus, the authoritative teacher of Torah wisdom: "Now when Jesus had finished these things, the crowds were astonished at his teaching, for he taught them as one having authority, and not as their scribes" (Mt 7:28–29).

By way of summary, throughout the gospel of Matthew we might identify three major themes that constitute this gospel's spirituality: (1) a proclamation of Jesus as one who embodies the divine presence among us, (2) an acknowledgment of God's providential care for the world that will culminate in God's blessings on those who have been faithful in their living of righteousness, and (3) a focus on the spiritual formation of individuals and of the community called to be church. At a time when the early Christian community was still puzzling over how to speak of the relationship of the man Jesus to their God, YHWH, Matthew turns to the text of the prophet Isaiah (Isa 7:14) in order to understand Jesus' extraordinary birth. The words of Isaiah announced that the son to be born in his day (715–687 B.C.E.) would be called "Emmanuel"—"God with us" (Mt 1:23).[12]

But these words of Isaiah referring to Hezekiah's child were exactly what the Matthean community believed had happened with the coming of Jesus. This man Jesus was, mysteriously, a child of God, bound in filial relationship to God in a way that none other before had been. He was able to speak with the same authority as God, to heal with the same power as God, to extend God's forgiveness, and to proclaim God's promises to faithful people. He was, in short, hailed as Emmanuel—God with us. Jesus' presence was manifest, Matthew claims, in and for the life of the community, as Jesus reminds us, "For where two or three are gathered in my name, I am there among them" (Mt 18:20). The Jews of Jesus' day believed that when they gathered together to study Torah, God was in their midst. But Jesus now proclaimed that God was present whenever they gathered *in the name of Jesus*. His presence, moreover, as the Risen savior was to be an abiding, eternal presence, as the final words of Jesus in the gospel attest: "And remember, I am with you always, even to the end of the age" (Mt 28:20). A contemporary spirituality drawing on Matthew's story of Jesus, therefore, will draw deeply on this conviction of Jesus' identity as Emmanuel—God with us.

A second aspect of Matthew's spiritual wisdom concerns the certainty that God's providential care extends to all the world and to all the creatures of the world without exception. God's protective care guards, as Jesus says, the "birds of the air, . . . the lilies of the field, . . . the grass of the field" (Mt 6:26, 28, 30). Both the universal and the extensive compass of God's providence are integral to Matthew's understanding of the divine purpose and of God's presence in Jesus. Even in the infancy narrative the presence of the wise men from the East (unique to Matthew's story) presages the universal significance of this child. And all of the gospel passages that show Jesus extending the boundaries of those included in the promises of God reaffirm this central conviction that God's blessings belong to all: the Roman centurion (Mt 8:5), the synagogue ruler (Mt 9:18), tax collectors, and sinners (Mt 9:9–10, 11:19). But even Jesus seems to have grown in his understanding of the universal significance of his message. Twice the gospel records Jesus' words delimiting divine favor as intended only for the "lost sheep of the house of Israel" (Mt 10:5–6, 15:24), a reference to the hope of Israel to reunite the ten northern tribes that were dispersed by the Assyrians after the destruction of Samaria in 722 B.C.E. But such a limited vision was not to be God's intent in this new moment inaugurated by Jesus. In conversation with others like the Canaanite woman (Mt 15:21–28) who challenged Jesus and pleaded for healing for her daughter, Jesus himself seemed to learn that God's blessings are meant for all.

Third, the most developed aspect of Matthew's spiritual wisdom is its extended reflections on the essential elements of discipleship. Beginning with the emphasis in the Sermon on the Mount that intensified many aspects of the Torah teaching toward a "greater righteousness" than that of the scribes and Pharisees (Mt 5:20), Jesus instructed his disciples and the crowds about both hearing and doing his words. He emphasized the core values of Judaism—prayer, fasting, and almsgiving—but warned against performing these deeds of righteousness merely "for show" (Mt 6:1–9). Jesus' words stress the need for interiority, right motivation, and principled moral action as foundations of the spiritual life. In another passage we hear the parable of the "pearl of great price" (Mt 13:45–46), which underscores the need for single-minded commitment in the service of God that is willing "to sell all" in order to acquire that "pearl of great price." In this way, Matthew emphasizes the radical ethical demands and practical spirituality necessary for a follower of Jesus. When asked by John the Baptist's disciples, "Are you the one who is to come, or should we look for another?" (Mt 11:3), Jesus' reply implicitly points to the essential signs of holiness: "And Jesus answered them, 'Go and tell John what you hear and see: the blind receive their sight, the lame walk, lepers are cleansed, the deaf hear, the dead are raised up, and the poor have good news brought to them'" (Mt 11:4–5). Holiness, discipleship, and following in the way of Jesus should be evident in our deeds that bring life and hope to those in need.

A final dimension of Matthew's story of Jesus is the explicit teaching for "the church" (Mt 18). Earlier in the gospel, Jesus had acknowledged Peter's unique role of leadership in Matthew 16:18–19, with the bestowal of the "keys of the kingdom." But the longer discourse in chapter 18 addresses the whole circle of Jesus' followers as one people. Here, Jesus teaches us that we must have humility like that of a child (Mt 18:4). We must demonstrate staunch resistance to temptation (Mt 18:7–9). We must have persistence in seeking out the lost (Mt 18:10–14). We must commit ourselves as church to mutual, communal correction (Mt 18:15–20). And we must be ready to show an infinite (i.e., 70 x 7!) willingness to forgive. This, then, is the meaning of Jesus' life and death as Matthew's community came to understand it. The life, death, and resurrection of Jesus inaugurated this new time and this new way of living the Torah and of "making disciples" among all the nations (Mt 28:19). Living resolutely these same commandments today, contemporary Christians can be confident that by the witness of our lives we too are faithful to Matthew's vision of Jesus and of the church.

THE GOSPEL OF LUKE—JESUS, THE ENVOY AND PROPHET OF WISDOM

Turning to the third gospel, we find still a different perspective on the life and ministry of Jesus. Luke saw the story of Jesus as only the first part of a larger story that continued into the spread of the Christian message throughout the great urban centers of the Mediterranean world. His gospel comes from the same time period as the gospel of Matthew—that is, around the year 85 C.E.—and was written for a largely urban, Gentile audience. Luke's audience no doubt included some people of considerable wealth, given the attention to the problem of riches in the gospel, most notably in the story about the Rich Man and Lazarus (Lk 16:19–31). The very structure of Luke's gospel with its "companion volume"—the Acts of the Apostles—indicates that the author viewed the Christian movement as a phenomenon well established on the world stage. He was concerned to speak to the questions of the daily lives of Christians living in the second or third generation. For these, the intense apocalyptic expectation of an earlier generation had begun to diminish. In its place was the exhortation to live in the dailiness of Christian fidelity to the teachings and ministry of Jesus in the midst of the world. And so, for example, when Luke quotes Jesus' saying about taking up the cross (Mk 8:34; Mt 16:24) he adds the word *daily* to underscore the need for habitual fidelity in discipleship for the "long haul": "Then he said to them all, 'If any want to become my followers, let them deny themselves and take up their cross *daily* and follow me'" (Lk 9:23, emphasis added).

Luke writes for the community of his day in order to instruct them about the meaning and implications of the salvation from God effected in their midst through the life, death, and resurrection of Jesus. In the infancy narratives of Luke the repeated canticles of praise (Mary's Magnificat—Lk 1:46–55; Zechariah's Song—Lk 1:67–79; and Simeon's prayer—Lk 2:28–32) call attention to the marvelous work of God in our midst through the birth of Jesus. Zechariah's words capture the conviction of the whole gospel and of its sequel in the Acts of the Apostles:

Blessed be the Lord God of Israel,
    for he has looked favorably on his people and redeemed them.
He has raised up a mighty savior for us
    in the house of his servant David,
        as he spoke through the mouth of his holy prophets from of old,
        that we would be saved from our enemies and from the hand of all who
        hate us.
Thus he has shown the mercy promised to our ancestors,
    and has remembered his holy covenant,
        the oath that he swore to our ancestor Abraham, to grant us
that we, being rescued from the hands of our enemies,
        might serve him without fear,
in holiness and righteousness before him all our days. (Lk 1:68–75)

The implications for daily Christian life will be the subject of Luke's story of Jesus and of the early church.

Especially important throughout this entire two-part story of Luke–Acts is the role of the Spirit of God who directs, energizes, and guides all that happens. In the gospel it is Jesus who, like the prophets before him, embodied this Spirit of God perfectly and imparted the Spirit to the church in the great moment of Pentecost (Acts 2). Jesus was conceived through the mysterious power of the Holy Spirit (Lk 1:35), hailed by John the Baptist as the one who would "baptize you with the Holy Spirit and fire" (Lk 3:16), confirmed by the voice and presence of the Spirit at his baptism (Lk 3:22), and led by the Spirit into the wilderness where he prevailed against the temptations of the devil (Lk 4:13). Luke narrates the beginning of Jesus' public ministry in Galilee with these words: "Then Jesus, filled with the power of the Spirit, returned to Galilee" (Lk 4:14).

We might choose just two passages from Luke's story for special emphasis, as they illuminate in a special way Luke's teaching about the way of discipleship and provide spiritual guidance for following the Christian way today. The first passage describes Jesus' inaugural sermon in the synagogue of his hometown of Nazareth "where he had been brought up" (Lk 4:16). But Jesus resisted their familiar characterization of him as merely "Joseph's son" and began to read with authority from the scroll of the prophet Isaiah: "The Spirit of the Lord is upon me because he has anointed me to bring good news, . . . to proclaim release, . . . and recovery, . . . to let the oppressed go free, to proclaim the year of the Lord's favor" (Lk 4:18–19). He ended with the audacious claim: "Today this scripture has been fulfilled in your hearing" (Lk 4:21). This good news of release, healing, liberation, and blessing proclaimed by Jesus, even though it recalled the Old Testament traditions about the Jubilee Year (Lev 25), was not meant for Israel alone. And so Jesus makes this clear by citing the examples of the miracle of Elijah performed for the widow of Sidon (1 Kings 17:13–16) and Elisha's miracle of cleansing the Syrian leper (2 Kings 5:9–14). God's salvation, proclaimed and present now in Jesus, is meant for all as a message of healing, forgiveness, and salvation. As the rest of the gospel will make clear, in those we least expect, in tax collectors and sinners, even in the supreme outsider such as the despised Samaritan (Lk 10:29–37), the way of discipleship can be found. In this programmatic inaugural sermon, moreover, Jesus illustrates the prophetic character of the good news that must be preached and lived in the Christian mission.

For contemporary readers, the lessons of this Lukan passage are both timely and essential. This story invites us first of all to a spiritual discipline of listening and attending to the Spirit of God in our midst today through what Christian tradition calls discernment. Discernment is the wise discretion about, and the ability to choose among, the multi-

ple voices that we hear within and around us today, in order to identify
and to embrace the true voice of *God's Spirit*. This daily and careful
listening to the Spirit in our midst ought to be for every Christian an
essential call of discipleship today.[13] So, too, is renewed commitment to
the powerful prophetic word of God's healing and forgiveness extended
to all. In a world as broken and divided as our modern world is, this
summons stands at the heart of the gospel for today.

A second key passage in Luke comes at the end of the gospel. It is
the Resurrection story describing the two disciples on the road to Emmaus in Luke 24:13–35. As readers of the gospel we see Jesus, *the*
prophet of God and God's anointed one, teaching a message of salvation, healing the sick, extending forgiveness, seeking out the lost (Lk
15), and journeying resolutely on the way from Galilee (Lk 9:51) to
meet his fate in Jerusalem as the prophets before him had done. Along
this way, the disciples (and we, the readers of the gospel) have learned
that through Jesus God's reign *has come* into the midst of us (Lk 11:20)
and has been demonstrated most of all in Jesus' repeated and gracious
table fellowship even with tax collectors and sinners (Lk 5:29, 7:29,
7:34, 15:1). To his last breath, moreover, Jesus mediated to others forgiveness and reconciliation with God. As he hung on the cross, he
commended the "good thief" to God with a promise of paradise (Lk
23:39–43). Luke describes Jesus' death as the noble death of a righteous
and innocent man who surrendered his spirit to God with serene confidence in God's loving care (Lk 23:44–47).

In the aftermath of that noble but shameful death, Luke narrates the
story of the two disciples walking away from Jerusalem toward Emmaus. And as they made their sad journey a stranger walked alongside
them and began to talk to them, but they did not recognize who he was.
Their words to him capture so well the mood that must have been
shared by many other followers in those days after Jesus' death: "But we
had hoped that he was the one to redeem Israel" (Lk 24:21). And then,
as the two disciples continued their way toward Emmaus, the stranger
interpreted the scriptures to them with all the references "beginning
with Moses and all the prophets" that foretold the coming of the Messiah. As evening approached they prevailed upon the stranger to join
them at the inn. And in the midst of the meal as "he took bread, blessed
and broke it, and gave it to them" (Lk 30), suddenly they recognized
that it was Jesus—the Crucified One, now alive! And Luke tells us that
they recognized—only then—that their hearts had been burning all
along the way as he opened the scriptures to them and as he broke
bread with them. And with that, they raced back to Jerusalem to tell the
others.

This story of the two disciples on the way to Emmaus is the story of faith for each of us. And for the contemporary Christian the need to have our eyes opened to the presence of God in our midst is urgently apparent. The way to this revelation for the disciples, and for us, implies several elements. First, it is as *communities* of faith that we must ponder together the events of our lives, straining as these disciples did, to understand their meaning. These two disciples on the road can be seen as an image of the fledgling church struggling to make sense of Jesus' life and death and coming to faith in his resurrection. Second, it is in the sharing of the scripture that God's ways become revealed to us throughout our history as a community of faith. Searching the Scriptures, sharing the word, and steeping ourselves in the traditions of our ancestors opens us to God's ways. Third, in the sharing of table fellowship with the stranger and with anyone in need (as these two disciples did) the mystery of God's presence and the presence of the Risen Jesus becomes alive and we, too, "know him in the breaking of the bread" (Lk 24:35). Table fellowship shared is a sign of common purpose and common aspirations. As one contemporary Lukan scholar, Eugene LaVerdiere, says succinctly: "Those who open their table to the stranger and who take on the self-giving attitude of Jesus recognize the risen Lord and are reestablished in hope."[14] And this renewed hope becomes the energy, grounded in the Spirit's power, to live and in our day to proclaim the good news of God's blessings "to the ends of the earth" (Acts 1:8).

THE GOSPEL OF JOHN—JESUS, THE WISDOM OF GOD

The final portrait of Jesus, with its corresponding demands for the Christian life, is found in the gospel of John, or the "maverick gospel" as one scholar has appropriately called it.[15] Different in so many ways from the Synoptic gospels of Mark, Matthew, and Luke, John displays the ongoing reflection of Christians and their deepening understanding of who Jesus is. This latest gospel comes from the very end of the first century (ca. 90–95 C.E.) and exhibits the highest Christological claims of any document in the New Testament.[16] Central to John's understanding of Jesus is the certainty that Jesus is the one who "in the beginning was with God" (Jn 1:1). He is "the one sent from God," the "Word made flesh" (Jn 1:14), the "only begotten son" who rests eternally on the bosom of God and makes God known (Jn 1:18).[17] In this last verse of the prologue (Jn 1:18), the author chooses the Greek verb *exegeo*, meaning "to interpret, to exegete." Therefore, for this author, Jesus is to be understood as the exegesis of God. All that Jesus says and does in the gospel reveals to others something of the mystery and the glory of God. Another way to say this is that, in John, Jesus is the human face of God, the divine icon that draws our attention to words and deeds that reveal to us the mystery of God and challenge us to believe in the one whom God has sent.

In some ways the fourth gospel is the most difficult to understand, and the portrait of Jesus depicted there is the hardest to relate to for the modern reader. In John, Jesus seems to come into the world as a stranger from above. The gospel proclaims his divine origin from the first opening of the prologue, and throughout the gospel Jesus speaks and acts in ways that show his divine-like presence. He *knows* what people think and feel (Jn 1:48, 5:6, 6:6, 18:4, 19:28) and takes charge himself of every event in the course of the story, most notably in the arrest scene in the garden of Gethsemane (Jn 18:1–8).

Jesus speaks, in John, not with the familiar sayings and parables as in the Synoptics but with lengthy speeches and self-pronouncements about his identity and intimacy with God. In fact, he uses the same self-identification that Moses had heard so long ago in the voice from the burning bush of Exodus 3: "I AM. . . ." These "I Am" pronouncements in the gospel of John sometimes employ images or metaphors that help us to understand the mystery of Jesus' identity as bread of life (Jn 6:35, 51); light of the world (Jn 8:12, 9:5); gate (for the sheep) (Jn 10:7, 9); the good shepherd (Jn 10:11, 14); the resurrection and the life (Jn 11:25); the way, the truth, and the life (Jn 14:6); and the true vine (Jn 15:1, 5). These metaphors (water, bread, light, access door, shepherd, vine) convey different dimensions of human longing, and John's gospel wants to convince us that no matter what metaphor we use, Jesus is the fulfillment of our longings.

Everything Jesus says and does in the gospel of John is meant to show forth, to reveal, the human face of God. Whether we see Jesus talking with the Jewish leader Nicodemus about the necessity of being born "from above" (Jn 3:3), or conversing with the Samaritan women about his power to give "living water" (Jn 4:10), or healing the royal official's son (Jn 4:46–54), or forgiving the sin of the paralytic by the pool (Jn 5:1–14), or feeding the crowd with both bread *and his own words* (Jn 6:1–58), or giving sight to and eliciting faith in the man born blind (Jn 9:1–41), or even calling forth his friend Lazarus from the tomb—in each example from the first half of the gospel, these signs point to something beyond themselves. They reveal to us Jesus' intimacy with God and his share in the authority and power of God *for the life* of the world.

There is, however, a dark side of this gospel as well, one that has been a negative influence in the Christian church through the centuries. This darker side concerns the portrait of Jesus' hostile encounters with "the Jews" in the gospel story. The hostility builds especially from chapters 5–11 and culminates with John's description of the Jewish high priest Caiaphas as he prophesies that Jesus must die. The most bitter exchange between Jesus and the Jews happens in the long dialogue of chapter 8. There, after the Jews have challenged Jesus' claims to authority by appealing to their father Abraham, Jesus tells them that their true father is the devil (Jn 8:44) and trumps their claims with the final remark: "Before Abraham was, I am" (Jn 8:58). The hostility portrayed in these scenes is a painful part of the gospel, especially today when interreligious dialogue is such an important concern and respectful dialogue between Jews and Christians contributes to our mutual understanding and respect. Scenes like chapter 8 remind us, therefore, that the gospel writers reflected the real struggles of their own worlds as they tried to present the story of Jesus and its significance for them.

But one scene of the gospel, more than any other, shows the dramatic artistry of the Fourth Gospel and captures its unique portrait of Jesus.[18] It comes in the opening of chapter 13 and begins the second half of the gospel. Here the gospel story moves from the open proclamation of Jesus' word and action to the crowds and individuals he encountered throughout his public ministry to what will now be a private teaching, again in word *and* deed, to his inner circle of disciples gathered in the upper room. To fully appreciate the power of this scene the reader must be both drama critic and theologian, attentive as much to the dramatic details of the scene as to its theological content—for the latter depends on the former for its deepest meaning.

As the scene opens we hear no dialogue, but our attention is focused on the room where Jesus and his disciples are gathered. The narrator of the gospel slowly and deliberately begins to call our attention to the action that is about to begin: "Now before the festival of the Passover, Jesus knew that his hour had come to depart from this world and go to the Father. Having loved his own who were in the world, he loved them to the end" (Jn 13:1). With these solemn words, we learn that the end is near and that what Jesus is about to do is a demonstration of his love "to the end." Even more, his action will serve to interpret the meaning of his impending death. It is a serious and sacred moment. Mention of Judas' betrayal, and the "devil's" part in it, reminds us of the dark forces at work against him in the world. Nevertheless, in the midst of that ominous moment Jesus begins his action.

Again, without any dialogue or speech, the narrator begins, almost in slow motion, to tell the story: "Jesus, knowing that the Father had given all things into his hands, and that he had come from God and was going to God, got up from the table, took off his outer robe, and tied a towel around himself. Then he poured water into a basin and began to wash the disciples' feet and to wipe them with the towel that was tied around him" (Jn 13:3–5). The effect of this narrative technique is to slow the action down, to focus our attention, so that we may *see* and *ponder* each movement. I like to call this scene in John a "verbal icon" because the narrator paints a picture, like an exquisite Byzantine icon, that can be known only if we allow its power to seep into us by our fixed gaze and attention. This visual portrait of Jesus performing an act reserved for the lowliest of household slaves is a prophetic action, one that teaches us the meaning of Jesus' life and death as a profound act of love.

It is essential, moreover, to remember that this story in John comes exactly at that place in the narrative where the Synoptics tell us about Jesus' words over the bread and the cup in the institution of the Eucharist. John's gospel omits those important words but, instead, tells this story of the foot washing. Jesus, the one who throughout the first half of the gospel has revealed his divine status, his intimacy with God, and his God-given authority, out of love becomes the lowly servant. His action is meant to show us that the meaning of Jesus' life and death is to call us to be a human community where we are all foot washers.

No wonder Peter objects! This example of Jesus called Peter, as it calls each of us, to a radical conversion wherein we relinquish status and power (as Jesus did) *in love* and embrace a posture of service to one another. Just as the Synoptic institution narratives include a command by Jesus to "do this in memory of me" (1 Cor 11:24; Lk 22:19), so in John Jesus commanded his disciples to repeat the action he performed: "So if I, your Lord and Teacher, have washed your feet, you also ought to wash one another's feet. For I have set you an example, that you also should do as I have done to you" (Jn 13:14–15). For the Fourth Gospel this lesson is the key to understanding the meaning of Jesus' whole life and death and God's saving purpose for the world—namely, that we become for each other willing and eager foot washers, laying down our lives: "No one has greater love than this, to lay down one's life for one's friends" (Jn 15:13).

In John's story of Jesus we see the human face of God, and we learn to find God in the outpouring of love to one another. In this, we touch the depths of the Christian paradox that life comes through death, that only in giving ourselves will we come to possess our truest selves, that in extending forgiveness to others we ourselves receive, and finally, that we see the face of God when look into the face of another.

CONCLUSION

Each of the four gospels, as we have seen, tells the story of Jesus in a unique way, emphasizing different aspects of his life and ministry. While John's gospel makes the highest claims about Jesus' divine origins and his union and intimacy with God, all four gospels point us to Jesus' victory over the grave and his ultimate union with God beyond death. But it took the Christian church over four centuries to come to a detailed and philosophically grounded creedal formula of how to speak of Jesus' divine character and oneness with God. It was not until the Council of Chalcedon in 451 c.e. that Christians could for the first time define for themselves precisely (albeit still inadequately) the nature of Jesus as Son of God, his relationship with the Godhead, and how God's Spirit is present in our midst.

Once the divinity of Christ had been doctrinally affirmed it became harder and harder for Christians to see Jesus as truly human. Debates continued about the nature of the divine and human natures united in Christ. And knowing the historical Jesus continues to be an essential quest for the Christian. In our day a group of scholars has once again set about to determine with absolute scholarly precision the most accurate portrait of this historical Jesus. This group, called the Jesus Seminar, studies the gospel accounts to separate the historical core from the theological embellishments and accretions of ongoing Christian faith. But that endeavor can never be fully successful because the gospels themselves, our only data about Jesus, have already begun the process of theological reflection about the meaning of Jesus' life and death. And so, their stories are already interpreted stories.

Nevertheless, the gospels give us these portraits of Jesus, that man from Nazareth, who will become for every Christian the face of God for us. Discipleship, following in the way of Jesus, is the ultimate grounding and direction for our faith. Whether we turn to the Markan portrait of the suffering messiah, or Matthew's picture of Jesus as the teacher of Torah righteousness, or Luke's challenges to us to take up Jesus' mission to the Gentiles, from Jerusalem to the ends of the earth, in fidelity to the amazing power of the Spirit, or whether finally we are drawn to John's divine Jesus who shows us how to lay down our lives, as Christians we believe that all we can know about God is revealed to us in Jesus. Each of us, then, must answer Jesus' question, "Who do you say that I am?" (Mk 8:27). But we do so always as church, as members *together* of his body. Together Jesus invites us to become imitators of his example as people who follow in his way. This is a spiritual path that embraces all that the gospels teach us about Jesus. It is a way marked by forgiveness, a way of healing and compassion. Along this path we meet

God's demands for justice, for selfless service, and for love. And, like the two disciples on the road to Emmaus (Lk 24), as we walk along this way, we discover that the Jesus we seek to know is already there with us.

QUESTIONS FOR REFLECTION

1. Every Christian sooner or later needs to answer Jesus' question for her- or himself: Who do you say that I am? Who is Jesus for you? What aspects of his life, words, and deeds capture your imagination and speak to your heart? Why?

2. In what ways do you try to *imitate* Jesus? What does this invitation mean for you?

3. How in your life have you experienced the gospel paradox of life coming through death, of strength showing itself most clearly in weakness?

4. The need for infinite forgiveness (70 x 7!) is a teaching Jesus gives in the gospel of Matthew. Where have you experienced this forgiveness in your life either as the one who extended it to others or as the recipient of forgiveness yourself?

5. Luke's portrait of Jesus emphasizes Jesus at prayer and seeking solitude with God in the midst of his daily life. How do you pray? What methods or resources are most helpful to your life of prayer?

6. Read again the foot washing scene in John's gospel (Jn 13:1–17). How can this picture be a *verbal icon* of God for you? What does it prompt you to be and do in your life? Have you ever had your "feet washed" by another in the literal or the metaphorical sense? What happened to you because of this?

11

PAULINE SPIRITUALITY

For the message about the cross is foolishness
to those who are perishing, but to us who
are being saved it is the power of God.

—1 Corinthians 1:18

No study of biblical foundations of spirituality would be complete without attending to the writings of the apostle Paul. In fact, over half the documents of the New Testament (fourteen of the twenty-seven texts) were at one time claimed to have been written by Paul. Modern scholarship now carefully distinguishes among the various groups of letters. There are "genuine or undisputed" letters (those believed to be authentically written by the apostle Paul), there are "Deutero-Pauline" letters (those probably written by later disciples of Paul), and there are "pastoral" epistles (those letters coming from a later time and showing a greater development in church organization and theology). Hebrews is not a letter at all but probably an early Christian sermon or treatise. But the early church at one time or another accepted all these as Pauline letters. Table 11.1 gives the list of letters in each category.

This chapter focuses on the genuine Pauline letters in order to sketch Paul's own understanding of the Christian life and its developing theology. And in the next chapter, I shall make reference to the other, non-Pauline letters only as they differ significantly from Paul.

CHAPTER 11

Table 11.1. Pauline Letters

Undisputed	Deutero-Pauline	Pastorals	Certainly Not Pauline
1 Thessalonians	Colossians	1 Timothy	Hebrews
Galatians	Ephesians	2 Timothy	
1 and 2 Corinthians	2 Thessalonians	Titus	
Philippians			
Philemon			
Romans			

PAUL THE PASTOR AND PRACTICAL THEOLOGIAN

Before turning to the letters themselves, it is important to situate Paul in his world of first-century Hellenistic Judaism. Our knowledge of Paul's life comes to us primarily from his own letters and (used cautiously) from the Acts of the Apostles. Paul himself tells us that he was raised a strict law-observant Jew, "circumcised on the eighth day, a member of the people of Israel, of the tribe of Benjamin, a Hebrew born of Hebrews; as to the law, a Pharisee, as to zeal, a persecutor of the church, as to righteousness under the law, blameless" (Phil 3:5–6). Acts confirms this portrait of the Pharisaic Jew, Saul of Tarsus, when it narrates the death of the first Christian martyr, Stephen, and concludes with the remark: "They cast him out of the city and stoned him; and the witnesses laid down their garments at the feet of a young man named Saul" (Acts 7:58).

But this fervent Pharisee became one of the most well-known Christian apostles after his experience of the Risen Lord on the road to Damascus. Three times Acts narrates this extraordinary encounter (Acts 9:1–22, 22:4–16, 26:9–18), and in the letter to the Galatians Paul himself refers to this life-changing event. His own words are very restrained and not at all like the "Hollywood" version in the story of Acts. Paul says about himself only this:

> For I want you to know, brothers and sisters, that the gospel that was proclaimed by me is not of human origin; for I did not receive it from a human source, nor was I taught it, but I received it through a revelation of Jesus Christ.
> You have heard, no doubt, of my earlier life in Judaism. I was violently persecuting the church of God and was trying to destroy it. I advanced in Judaism beyond many among my people of the same age, for I was far more zealous for the traditions of my ancestors. But

when God, who had set me apart before I was born and called me through his grace, was pleased to reveal his Son to me, so that I might proclaim him among the Gentiles, I did not confer with any human being, nor did I go up to Jerusalem to those who were already apostles before me, but I went away at once into Arabia, and afterwards I returned to Damascus.

Then after three years I did go up to Jerusalem to visit Cephas and stayed with him fifteen days; but I did not see any other apostle except James the Lord's brother. In what I am writing to you, before God, I do not lie! (Gal 1:11–20)

We can never know what exactly happened to Paul on the road to Damascus that day any more than we can explain the extraordinary moments of God encounters in our own lives. But, in both cases, when God has touched a human being in a powerful way, her or his life can never be the same.

For Paul, this event meant a life dedicated to proclaiming the gospel among the gentiles, so convinced was he that Christ had commissioned him for this mission. From Damascus he found his way to the Christian community in Antioch and began a collaborative mission there with Barnabas (Acts 11:25–26; Gal 1:21–2:21) before beginning his own missionary travels throughout Asia Minor and the Aegean region. According to one reckoning, Paul traveled over 3,100 miles in the course of his missionary journeys proclaiming the gospel (nearly 1,800 miles by land and roughly 1,300 by sea) and founding communities of Christians everywhere he traveled.[1] By his own admission, these travels were marked by hardships of every kind over difficult terrain in the harshest of circumstances:

Three times I was beaten with rods. Once I received a stoning. Three times I was shipwrecked; for a night and a day I was adrift at sea; on frequent journeys, in danger from rivers, danger from bandits, danger from my own people, danger from Gentiles, danger in the city, danger in the wilderness, danger at sea, danger from false brothers and sisters; in toil and hardship, through many a sleepless night, hungry and thirsty, often without food, cold and naked. (2 Cor 11:25–27)

Reliable tradition tells us that Paul met a martyr's death in Rome at the end of the reign of Nero (ca. 67–68 C.E.) but not before he had founded communities of Christians throughout the Mediterranean. His travels and his letters were the means to nurture and connect these communities from the eastern region of Syria westward to Rome and possibly even as far west as Spain, if we can believe the remark from the text of 1 Clement, written probably near the end of the first century:

> Because of jealousy and strife Paul by his example pointed out the way to the prize for patient endurance. After he had been seven times in chains, had been driven into exile, had been stoned, and had preached in the East and in the West, he won the genuine glory for his faith, having taught righteousness to the whole world and having reached the farthest limits of the West [i.e., Spain]. Finally, when he had given his testimony before the rulers, he thus departed from the world and went to the holy place, having become an outstanding example of patient endurance. (1 Clem 5:5–7)

Paul's letters reveal a man who was absolutely convinced that the Risen Jesus had appeared to him on the Damascus road. Within the context of his Pharisaic and apocalyptic tradition, Paul understood that, if Jesus had died but was now alive, then the long-awaited end time had come. Unlike the Sadducees who denied the resurrection, the Jewish Pharisees waited eagerly for that time when God would raise the dead and all the righteous ones would receive their reward. If Paul had experienced the Risen Jesus on the road to Damascus, then the end time had arrived, and the Risen Christ was the proof: the "first fruits" (1 Cor 15:23; Rom 8:23), the down payment or "first installment" (2 Cor 1:22, 5:5), and the promise of more to come. This claim is the bedrock of Paul's faith. Paul was convinced that through the death and resurrection of Christ, God had ushered in the New Age and made possible a new relationship with God. The old way was finished; the stipulations of the Mosaic law were no longer necessary or effective. Righteousness before God had been gained for all, Jew and Greek (Gal 3:28; Rom 1:16, 2:9, 10:12) through Christ. And through the faith of Christ (Gal 2:15–16) Paul believed everyone had gained equal access to God's blessings and grace.

Paul's theological reflection and the practical theology that he articulates is not a careful systematic rendering of a new religious perspective. Paul's theology is ad hoc and practical, worked out in the day to day as he tried to respond to situations and circumstances in the various gentile churches he visited. The bottom line and starting point for Paul was his own profound experience of the Risen Christ. The meaning of this event he interpreted through the scriptures, and this gave him the conviction of a mystical union with Christ made possible through the outpouring of the Spirit, so that Paul can say, "For through the law I died to the law, so that I might live to God. I have been crucified with Christ; and it is no longer I who live, but it is Christ who lives in me.

And the life I now live in the flesh I live by faith in the Son of God, who loved me and gave himself for me" (Gal 2:19–20).

LIFE IN THE SPIRIT

In Pauline terms, therefore, Christian life is life in the Spirit. Romans 8 has been described as a sort of "précis" of Paul's teaching concerning the Spirit, and it is there we learn that "the law of the Spirit of life in Christ Jesus has set [us] free from the law of sin and of death" (Rom 8:2). The effect of Christ's death and resurrection, then, was to unleash God's Spirit in the community of believers. And all "who are led by the Spirit of God are children of God" (Rom 8:14). This is the dynamic Spirit at work among us: "When we cry, 'Abba! Father!' it is that very Spirit bearing witness with our spirit that we are children of God, and if children, then heirs, heirs of God and joint heirs with Christ—if, in fact, we suffer with him so that we may also be glorified with him" (Rom 8:15–17). The Spirit aids the Christian and even "intercedes for the saints according to the will of God" (Rom 8:27).

Paul maintains, as said above, that the Spirit comes to the Christian at baptism and is the "first fruits" (Rom 8:23) and the "down payment" (2 Cor 1:22) of the sure redemption to come. The Spirit is thus the gift for the time in between baptism and redemption—in between the "already" of Christ's resurrection and the "not yet" of our own promised eternal life with God. In addition, Paul emphasizes in 1 Corinthians especially that the Spirit is given to and for the community: "For in the one Spirit we were all baptized into one body—Jews or Greeks, slaves or free—and all were made to drink of the one Spirit" (1 Cor 12:13). The Spirit is the source of the hope among us (Rom 5:5) and the origin of our freedom (Gal 3:1–3). And so Paul can exhort Christians to "walk in the Spirit," that is, to live in a way that is attuned to the Spirit of God: "If we live by the Spirit, let us also be guided by the Spirit. Let us have not become conceited, competing against one another, envying one another" (Gal 5:25–26).

THE SPIRIT AND THE BODY OF CHRIST

In his arguments with the pneumatic enthusiasts in Corinth, Paul refined his teaching about the Spirit in a way that reclaimed its communal character and reasserted its purpose to build up and nurture the body.[2] Against those in Corinth who claimed superior status on the basis of their individual spiritual gifts, especially the gift of speaking in tongues, Paul would say emphatically: "To each is given the manifestation of the Spirit *for the common good*" (1 Cor 12:7). Paul recognized that the Spirit works in many and varied ways within the community bestowing gifts of all kinds: utterance, wisdom, knowledge, faith, healing, miracles, prophecy, discernment of spirits, and various kinds of tongues. The reality of Christian identity and the essence of the Christian life were, for Paul, to be "in Christ." By this he meant taking on a new corporate identity as part of the body of Christ, the visible manifestation of the Risen Christ in the world.

Paul borrowed a political metaphor that had been common in Greek political philosophy concerning the "body politic" to speak of the Christian community. The metaphor of the human body was particularly suited to his message that every part was essential for the whole and that all members of the body breathed the same Spirit as the vivifying source of life. And so he could borrow the extended metaphor of the "body parts" speaking to each other (1 Cor 12:14–26) to expose the foolishness of his Corinthian opponents who seemed to act in a way that presumed that spiritual gifts were solely for the individual's greater prestige and status. Nowhere is Paul's conviction more evident than in his treatment of the question of glossolalia, or speaking in tongues. Whenever he lists spiritual gifts, the gift of tongues is always the last to be mentioned (perhaps because it was the most prized by the so-called spiritual elitists in Corinth). But Paul's reasoning is consistent with his principle of the common good. Contrasting the relative value of prophecy and tongues, Paul does not mince words: "Those who speak in a tongue build up themselves, but those who prophesy build up the church. . . . One who prophesies is greater than the one who speaks in tongues, unless someone interprets, so that the church may be built up" (1 Cor 14:4–5).

This lesson for our own day is no less needed. Somehow, as Christians, we have often missed the main point—that Christian identity is a corporate identity and there is no such thing as "an *individual Christian*." Those words are an oxymoron. To be a Christian is to be a member of the body of Christ. Paul's insistence on the corporate character of the body and his exhortations to communal living are key to his preaching of the gospel and to the way he responded to almost every pastoral question. For example, when some Corinthians (presumably the elite because they were the only ones who could afford to eat meat) put the question to Paul about eating meat from the carcass of an animal that had been offered in sacrifice at a pagan temple, Paul's response again reflected his conviction that all should be done for the common good (1 Cor 8:4–13). The elite were saying that "an idol has no real existence" and therefore they felt free to eat this "idol meat" sold in the market-place. Paul agreed, in theory, with their *theological* claim: idols are nothing, and eating meat offered to idols is permitted. But his *pastoral* advice takes a very different turn:

> "Food will not bring us close to God." We are no worse off if we do not eat, and no better off if we do. But take care that this liberty of yours does not somehow become a stumbling block to the weak. . . . So by your knowledge those weak believers for whom Christ died are destroyed. But when you thus sin against members of your family, and wound their conscience when it is weak, you sin against Christ. Therefore, if food is a cause of their falling, I will never eat meat, so that I may not cause one of them to fall. (1 Cor 8:8–9, 11–13)

For Paul, therefore, the only *pastoral* criterion is the question: "Does the action build up the body, does it help and strengthen the community?" If yes, then it is permitted; if no, then no matter how theoretically or theologically correct it may be, it is not permitted if it gives offense to or injures others. How different this Pauline principle is from our contemporary insistence on individual rights and privileges to be safeguarded at all costs.

Another example of this fundamental Pauline ecclesiological principle is found in Paul's discussion of the celebration of the Lord's Supper in Corinth (1 Cor 11:17–34). In Paul's day, Christians gathered in the private homes of some of their wealthier members in order to share fellowship and prayer at a normal evening meal during which they would recall the words of Jesus at the supper before his death.[3] This sacred remembrance would make the meal not just an ordinary private meal (*idion deipnon*; 1 Cor 11:21) but the Lord's supper (*kuriakon deipnon*; 1 Cor 11:20).

The reports Paul had heard about what was happening in Corinth, moreover, distressed him. The leisured class among the Christian group arrived earlier than the others, began to eat choice food and to consume the finest drink (1 Cor 11:21). The nonelite Christians (slaves, freed persons, laborers, and artisans) arrived only after the day's labors and found that there was little or no food remaining, while the others were already sated and drunk (1 Cor 11:21). In the strongest of terms Paul condemned their actions and again laid down the principle of the common good: "Whoever, therefore, eats the bread or drinks the cup of the Lord in an unworthy manner will be answerable for the body and blood of the Lord. Examine yourselves, and only then eat of the bread and drink of the cup. For all who eat and drink without discerning the body, eat and drink judgment against themselves" (1 Cor 11:27–29). The key words are *discerning the body*.[4] Here, Paul put his finger on the essential requirement of Christian life: attentiveness to the needs of the Christian body. Only then, in Paul's judgment, can it be possible to eat the "Lord's Supper." The conduct at the supper in Corinth led to Paul's strong statement: "When you come together, it is not really to eat the Lord's Supper" (1 Cor 11:20).

Again, the lesson for contemporary Christian life is compelling. In fact, as we saw in an earlier chapter, Paul's words only echo the strong critique of the biblical prophets against "empty worship" that is devoid of righteousness and covenant justice. With that tradition in mind, we might ask ourselves how often we approach the sacraments examining ourselves on this question: "Am I truly discerning the body?" "Am I aware of and attending to the needs of the community?" "Am I really living as a member of the body of Christ?" Or have we fallen victim to the belief that our religious practice and devotion are a private matter, only between God and ourselves? If so, then Paul would have very strong words for us as well.

That is why so much of Paul's advice and exhortation urges the Christians of his day to live their lives in harmony and fellowship. In Romans, Paul again invoked the image of the body to remind Christians of their essential identity and obligation to one another: "For as in one body we have many members, and not all the members have the same function, so we, who are many, are one body in Christ, and individually we are members one of another" (Rom 12:4–5). He goes on to encourage the community to use the many different gifts they have received—prophecy, service, teaching, exhortation, and the like—and to use them freely with zeal and cheerfulness (Rom 12:6–8). Then, Paul calls Christians to lives of genuine love:

> Let love be genuine; hate what is evil, hold fast to what is good; love one another with mutual affection; outdo one another in showing honor. Do not lag in zeal, be ardent in spirit, serve the Lord. Rejoice in hope, be patient in suffering, persevere in prayer. Contribute to the needs of the saints; extend hospitality to strangers. Bless those who persecute you; bless and do not curse them. Rejoice with those who rejoice, weep with those who weep. Live in harmony with one another; do not be haughty, but associate with the lowly; do not claim to be wiser than you are. Do not repay anyone evil for evil, but take thought for what is noble in the sight of all. If it is possible, so far as it depends on you, live peaceably with all. (Rom 12:9–18)

Paul's words are as urgent and fitting today as they were for the Christians in Rome (ca. 60 C.E.) who first heard them.

THE FOLLY OF THE CROSS

Underlying all of Paul's exhortation about the community is a faith grounded in a theology of the cross. "The cross" meant for Paul the entire mystery of the death and resurrection of Christ through which God had brought us into the new possibility of life and righteousness. To the Corinthians, he preached his entire gospel as simply the "word of the cross": "For Christ did not send me to baptize but to proclaim the gospel, and not with eloquent wisdom, so that the cross of Christ might not be emptied of its power" (1 Cor 1:17). Paul's conviction was that worldly wisdom, eloquent speech, demonstrations of rhetorical power, philosophical display, and any other worldly signs of power (such as some of the elite in Corinth were no doubt claiming) count for nothing before God. And so he testified, "I decided to know nothing among you except Jesus Christ and him crucified" (1 Cor 2:2).

It seems that Paul's own personal weaknesses and limitations were apparent to all, and perhaps it is precisely this personal experience that gave Paul insight into the meaning of the suffering and death of Christ. In fact, Paul even quoted his detractors, whom Paul derided as "super apostles" (2 Cor 11:5, 12:11) and who said about him, "His letters are weighty and strong, but his bodily presence is weak, and his speech is contemptible" (2 Cor 10:10). And scholars continue to puzzle over Paul's reference to his "thorn in the flesh" (2 Cor 12:7), a source of humiliation and suffering for him that limited his apostolic effectiveness. Perhaps because of this, Paul had a deeper insight into the meaning of Jesus' suffering and death. In Philippians 2, Paul quotes an early Christian hymn that proclaimed Christ's death as a voluntary offering. Christ Jesus "emptied himself, taking the form of a slave" (Phil 2:7), to embrace fully the human condition in all its weakness and powerlessness. This act of obedience, even to death on a cross, was honored by God, who exalted Christ in glory. The pattern of this story—death, resurrection, and exaltation—therefore, became for Paul the example to be followed for all of the Christian life: "Let this same mind be in you that was in Christ Jesus" (Phil 2:5).

His own life reflected these sufferings, and his apostolic mission was marked by repeated hardships for the sake of the gospel:

> But we have this treasure in clay jars [or earthen vessels], so that it may be made clear that this extraordinary power belongs to God and does not come from us. We are afflicted in every way, but not crushed; perplexed, but not driven to despair; persecuted, but not forsaken; struck down, but not destroyed; always carrying in the body the death of Jesus, so that the life of Jesus may also be made visible

in our bodies. For while we live, we are always being given up to death for Jesus' sake, so that the life of Jesus may be made visible in our mortal flesh. (2 Cor 4:7–11)

To accept these sufferings was, for Paul, the necessary cost of disciple-ship and the proof that God's power at work in us was greater than any weakness or hardship, or suffering we might bear. And so Paul gives us the example of his own life as a pattern to imitate. Not that we should go in search of suffering, looking for the most difficult way, or the hardest task. No, our goal is to fix our gaze on obedience to God in Christ Jesus as Paul exhorts:

> Yet whatever gains I had, these I have come to regard as loss because of Christ. More than that, I regard everything as loss because of the surpassing value of knowing Christ Jesus my Lord. For his sake I have suffered the loss of all things, and I regard them as rubbish, in order that I may gain Christ and be found in him, not having a righteousness of my own that comes from the law, but one that comes through faith in Christ, the righteousness from God based on faith. I want to know Christ and the power of his resurrection and the sharing of his sufferings by becoming like him in his death, if somehow I may attain the resurrection from the dead. (Phil 3:7–11)

A FUTURE FULL OF HOPE

The ultimate goal of all striving will be this final redemption of our bodies and of the whole earth. And Paul is certain that God is at work within the very fabric of life, bringing the world toward this glorious end. Therefore, we have great cause for hope, even though as Paul admits, the "whole creation is groaning in travail" waiting for this fulfill-ment (Rom 8:22–25). Paul expected that the promised end time would come very soon, "like a thief in the night" (1 Thess 5:2), perhaps in his own lifetime. With the long interval that has elapsed since Paul's mes-sage was first heard, contemporary Christians face an even greater chal-lenge to keep hope alive through the turmoil and travail of our own modern times. Paul used the example of Abraham to convince believers that there are persuasive precedents of those who have "hoped against hope" (Rom 4:18) despite all evidence to the contrary. Similarly, that is still the challenge in our day when the world tilts precipitously toward catastrophe and we find ourselves straining, like Abraham, to "hope against hope."

CONCLUSION

The apostle Paul is a wonderful companion for us in our spiritual lives for many reasons, not the least of which is that he shared many of our same struggles and concerns. Paul is so *real*, so human, full of contradiction, arrogance, and self-doubt. But like Abraham, Moses, Jeremiah, and Job, Paul had an extraordinary experience of God that day on the road to Damascus. And it changed his life forever. For many of us today, perhaps, there has been a similar "Damascus Road" experience when we have come to know in a very personal way the power of God and the presence of Jesus in our lives. These "God moments," as contemporary author and editor Jeremy Langford aptly calls them, define our lives and become the grounding for all that we are and do.[5] For Paul, his experience of the Risen Jesus on the Damascus Road reordered his priorities, redirected his life's energy, and reaffirmed his faith in God's purposes for the world. Our God moments surely do the same.

"Life in the Spirit" is a fitting description of how Paul viewed Christian faith. By that he meant that all of life, the entire cosmos even, is animated by a power and energy beyond ourselves that comes from God, in Christ. This Spirit energizes us and compels us to spread the good news to others. This Spirit makes each of us a "new creation" (2 Cor 5:17) and invites us to walk in the way of responsible freedom. Paul enumerated the fruits of this Spirit as "love, joy, peace, patience, kindness, generosity, faithfulness, gentleness, and self-control" (Gal 5:22–23). This list is not merely a string of clichés but a reminder to us of "the heart of the matter" of what it means to be truly human and those qualities that we strive to attain, with God's help, throughout our lives.

Life in the Spirit is fundamentally and always *life together* in the Spirit. As we have seen, Paul is quick to disabuse us of our misguided notions of a "Jesus and me" spirituality. Instead, for Paul, building up the body, spending ourselves for the common good is the essential and nonnegotiable element of the Christian life. Paul reminds us also that, in Christ, God uses our weakness as strength. Whatever the "thorn" in our flesh (2 Cor 11:22–28), whatever the particular frailties that describe each of us as "earthen vessels" (2 Cor 4:7–12), we have been empowered with the life of Christ in us. And so, our lives lived in the Spirit, lived "in Christ," are lives of hope. As a final word, perhaps we too need to hear again Paul's comforting words to the Christian community in Rome: "For I am convinced that neither death, nor life, nor angels, nor rulers, nor things present, nor things to come, nor powers, nor height, nor depth, nor anything else in all creation, will be able to separate us from the love of God in Christ Jesus our Lord" (Rom 8:38–39).

QUESTIONS FOR REFLECTION

1. When, where, and how has God touched your life with experiences such as Paul's on the Damascus Road? What effect did these moments have on your life? What changes have they initiated in you?
2. What in your life do you "now consider loss" (Phil 3:7) in return for this new experience?
3. For Paul, faith in Christ meant an end to divisions and barriers between people, especially "Jew and Greek." Where do you need to be reconciled with others, other persons and other groups? How will you strive to extend reconciliation to them?
4. How might Paul's understanding of the Christian community as the body of Christ critique our contemporary understanding of church? What are the implications of this understanding for Christian life and discipleship?
5. Paul believed that Jesus' life and death brought freedom from the Mosaic law. *From* what and *for* what do you experience freedom in Christ? How does this freedom shape your life and daily actions?

12

A NEW HEAVEN AND A NEW EARTH

You see this city? Here God
dwells with us.

—Revelation 21:3 (Barbara Bowe's translation)

With this chapter, our biblical story finally comes full circle. As we
approach the end of this journey, however, it will be important to survey briefly some of the important developments that shaped the lives
and thinking of Christians as they moved toward the end of the first and
the beginning of the second century. In those years, the Christian communities included predominantly Gentiles living in urban centers
throughout the Mediterranean world. These Christians faced the increasingly difficult task of determining for themselves just how they
were to settle down and live in the Roman world and how they were to
interact with the non-Christian environments around them. The New
Testament provides a variety of answers, some 180 degrees different
from each other. But together these beliefs and strategies laid the
groundwork for Christian practice in the centuries that followed down
to our own time.

The year 70 C.E. marked a decisive watershed in the life of Palestine.
In that year the Roman legions under the command of Titus successful-
ly quelled the first Jewish revolt (66–70 C.E.). After winning decisive
battles in the Galilee region, the Romans laid siege to and finally captured the city of Jerusalem. And, with a vengeance still evident in the
fallen ashlars and burned-out houses excavated and visible in Jerusalem
today, they destroyed the city and its Temple and with it the normal
fabric of Jewish life in Judea. Many of the Christian apostles suffered
martyrs' deaths during this tumultuous decade as well. For example,

both Peter and Paul were martyred in Rome, probably during the last years of Nero's reign (ca. 67–68 C.E.). As I have noted, Mark's gospel was also written against the backdrop of this first Jewish revolt, and his emphasis on discipleship and on suffering reflects the challenges of this time. One smaller group among the Jewish Christians, the Ebionites, remained very close to the practices of Judaism. But in general these groups of Jewish Christians "rapidly became, if they were not already, a minority in the Christian movement, surviving longest in Transjordania and Syria. The mission to the Jews, which Paul already perceived to be largely a failure (Romans 9–11), had probably petered out by the end of the first century."[1] Especially in the gospels of Matthew and John we see evidence of the hostility emerging between the followers of Jesus and the mainstream Jewish community reconstituted under the leadership of the Pharisees after the destruction of the Temple. Although the definitive separation between the Jewish and the emerging Christian communities would come only by the late second (or some would even argue third) century, the two religious traditions, these "siblings," were beginning to part ways in the aftermath of the destruction of the Temple in the year 70 C.E.

VISIONARIES AND PRAGMATISTS—REVISITED

In our discussion in chapter 7 of Israel's postexilic period, we spoke of the struggle between two groups of people.[2] On the one hand, there were the prophetic visionaries, such as Third Isaiah and Zechariah, whose creative religious imagination envisioned a future time of God's inclusive blessings poured out on all. And on the other hand were the so-called pragmatists, the scribal leaders such as Ezra and Nehemiah who saw the future of the people linked to their strict living of Torah, their avoidance of intermarriage, and their more restrictive policies of Jewish communal solidarity in the midst of an alien world.

This distinction—that is, between the visionary and the pragmatic tendencies at work in the community—is evident in an analogous way in the late New Testament period as well. The expansive and visionary dimension of Christian reflection comes to the fore, for example, in the developing Christology of the late first century. The letter to the Colossians, most probably written by a disciple of Paul perhaps around 80 C.E., demonstrates this tendency in the hymn of praise to the cosmic Christ as "the image of the invisible God, the first born of all creation, for in him all things were created, in heaven and on earth. . . . For in him all the fullness of God was pleased to dwell and through [Christ] to reconcile to [God] all things, whether on earth or in heaven, making peace by the blood of his cross" (Col 1:15–16, 19–20, Barbara Bowe's translation). Continuing Paul's gospel of universal inclusion, the author of Colossians can say: "Here there cannot be Greek and Jew, circumcised and uncircumcised, barbarian, Scythian, slave, free, but Christ is all and in all" (Col 3:11, Barbara Bowe's translation). The letter to the Ephesians, likewise, echoes this expansive, cosmic perspective as part of the plan of God from all eternity: "For [God] has made known to us in all wisdom and insight the mystery of [the divine] will, according to [God's] purpose that [was] set forth in Christ as a plan for the fullness of time, to unite all things in [Christ], things in heaven and things on earth" (Eph 1:9–10, Barbara Bowe's translation). In this letter, the author sees the church as a universal phenomenon, as well:

> Because the Church is conceived here as being an integral part of the eternal plan and purpose of God, its existence transcends the boundaries of time as well as of space: believers were chosen for salvation "in the heavenly places . . . before the foundation of the world" (1:3–4), "destined" to be God's [children] and to receive the grace bestowed in Christ (1:5–6), "destined and appointed" to live for the praise of God (1:12), and "created in Christ Jesus for good works, which God prepared beforehand" (2:10).[3]

Even though in both these post-Pauline letters we find references to a specifically *Christian* self-consciousness, the cosmic perspectives they adopt locate the Christian life as a universal mystery within and at the heart of the world. The "participation of the gentiles in the promises of God is perceived to be a fundamental part of the divine 'plan' [*oikonomia*] to unite all things in him [Christ], things in heaven and things on earth" (Eph 1:10).[4] Likewise, the anonymous author of the treatise known as the "Letter to the Hebrews" presents a soaring and imaginative reflection on the exalted and eternal Son who as Christ is superior to all things. One commentator has even called the author of Hebrews "one of the most imaginative figures of the early Church."[5]

A more pragmatic perspective shows itself throughout in the so-called pastoral epistles, the letters to Timothy and Titus; in the regulatory exhortations of the "household codes" concerning the "appropriate" behavior of wives, slaves, and children (Col 3:18–4:1; Eph 5:21–6:9; 1 Pet 2:11–3:12; 1 Tim 2:8–15, 5:1–2, 6:1–2; Tit 2:1–10, 3:1); and in such things as the very practical ethical appeals of the letter of James (e.g., Jas 1:26–27). The pastorals, for example, concern themselves with setting boundaries that will delineate right action (orthopraxis) and right belief (orthodoxy). The uniformity of developing doctrine is a special concern in the pastorals, and so we hear the author of 1 Timothy say (taking on the persona of "Paul"): "I urge you, as I did when I was on my way to Macedonia, to remain in Ephesus so that you may instruct certain people not to teach any different doctrine, and not to occupy themselves with myths and endless genealogies that promote speculations rather than the divine training that is known by faith" (1 Tim 1:3–4). Likewise the preoccupation with "sound doctrine" is evident in 2 Timothy when the author warns: "For the time is coming when people will not put up with sound doctrine, but having itching ears, they will accumulate for themselves teachers to suit their own desires" (2 Tim 4:3; see also Tit 1:9, 2:1). Also, 1 Timothy has stern words for such false and lawless teachers:

> Whoever teaches otherwise and does not agree with the sound words of our Lord Jesus Christ and the teaching that is in accordance with godliness, is conceited, understanding nothing, and has a morbid craving for controversy and for disputes about words. From these come envy, dissension, slander, base suspicions, and wrangling among those who are depraved in mind and bereft of the truth, imagining that godliness is a means of gain. (1 Tim 6:3–5)

These pragmatic letters also lay down regulations and qualifications for Christian ministers: for bishops (1 Tim 3:1–7), for deacons (1 Tim 3:8–13), for the elders (1 Tim 5:17–22; Tit 1:5–7), and for the emerging order of widows in the Church (1 Tim 5:3–16). In addition, we find regulations for the conduct of worship (1 Tim 2:1–15) stipulating even the "proper" body posture: "I desire, then, that in every place the men should pray, lifting up holy hands without anger or argument; also that the women should dress themselves modestly and decently in suitable clothing, not with their hair braided, or with gold, pearls, or expensive clothes, but with good works, as is proper for women who profess reverence for God" (1 Tim 2:8–10). And, as most of these regulatory measures were largely in the hands of the male leadership, they proscribed certain behaviors for women that increasingly denied to them public leadership or ministerial roles in the Church, beyond those of the ecclesiastically controlled orders of "widow and deaconess." Modern tools of feminist criticism have tried to unmask these strategies of ecclesiastical control for women as certainly contrary to the gospel. And our reading, therefore, of texts like 1 Timothy 2:11—"Let a woman learn in silence with full submission"—needs to be informed by such critique.

It is true to say, perhaps, that in every age one could identify a similar debate between the voices of pragmatism, boundary maintenance, and social order, on the one hand, and the voices of prophetic visionaries, boundary breakers, and imaginative risk takers, on the other. The history of the Church, moreover, provides numerous examples of both these types of persons with their strategies and responses to the deeper questions of Christian life. And in our spiritual journeys, both as individuals and as the Church at large, we no doubt move back and forth between both of these poles, needing at times the clear guidance of creedal and dogmatic pronouncements and, at others, the courageous risk taking of the prophets and visionaries in our midst. Staying attentive to this creative tension, and keeping it alive, is essential and should be the serious commitment of every religious quest.

HOW ARE CHRISTIANS TO BE IN THE WORLD?

A final question facing the Christians of the late first century concerned how they should conduct themselves in the world. There is a hypothetical question that is often asked to generate reflection on a person's life and faith commitment today: "If you were put on trial for being a Christian, would there be enough evidence to convict you?" The question points to the serious dilemma that early Christians faced, and we face as well, in trying to determine how their *Christian* identity shaped and changed their being in the world. There have always been in the Church people who have chosen for religious reasons to withdraw from society, either as hermits or as members of monastic communities. But for the majority throughout the ages, Christian life has been lived in the midst of the world where we are. The first followers of Jesus, and the second and third generations of Christians of the first century, had many examples of a fully sectarian path they might have followed. The Jewish covenanters who went off to the shore of the Dead Sea to pursue a rigorously ascetical life and to guard intensely their ritual purity were only one example of ascetical groups that Christians might have imitated but did not.

Numerous New Testament texts give us glimpses of the different attitudes of early Christians toward their world and toward the social contexts in which they found themselves. Apocalyptic influences taught Christians that this world was soon passing away, and so Paul would exhort the Corinthians: "I mean, brothers and sisters, the appointed time has grown short; from now on, let even those who have wives be as though they had none, and those who mourn as though they were not mourning, and those who rejoice as though they were not rejoicing, and those who buy as though they had no possessions, and those who deal with the world as though they had no dealings with it. For the present form of this world is passing away" (1 Cor 7:29–31). He likewise reminded the Philippians that their "citizenship is in heaven" (Phil 3:20), and to the Thessalonians he assured that they would soon be with the Lord (1 Thess 4:13–18). But Paul's perspective is tempered by that of the gospels where Jesus seems to say that the place of encounter with God is available in this world and that, like the seed growing secretly, the reign of God is "in the midst" of us (Lk 11:20).

More than any other, John's gospel speaks directly to the question of Christian attitudes toward the world and comes closer than other texts to a fully sectarian outlook. In John's gospel, for example, Jesus solemnly warns his disciples at the supper: "If the world hates you, be aware that it hated me before it hated you. If you belonged to the world, the world would love you as its own. Because you do not belong to the world, but I have chosen you out of the world—therefore the world hates you" (Jn 15:18–19). Jesus then prays for the disciples, *not* that they be taken out of the world but that they be kept from the evil one: "They do not belong to the world, just as I do not belong to the world. Sanctify them in the truth; your word is truth. As you have sent me into the world, so I have sent them into the world" (Jn 17:16–18).

Here, exactly, is the Christian dilemma in every age: how to be *in* the world but not *of* it, not "conformed to this evil age" and its values, as Paul warned (Rom 1:18–32). In the later Christian texts of the New Testament we can see many examples of Christian accommodation to the larger Greco-Roman society in social patterns, ethical views, and political practice. Shall Christians pay taxes to the empire? Shall Christians serve in the military? Shall Christians allow divorce? These are only some of the obvious issues Christians wrestled with—then and now.

Two New Testament texts, in particular, illustrate opposite views on this larger question of the proper Christian attitude toward the world. The first is the letter known as 1 Peter, written probably toward the end of the first century by someone claiming to speak in the authority of the Petrine tradition. There we hear the author reinforce the special calling that Christians share by virtue of their baptism. But that special identity does not absolve them from embracing their citizenship in the world. And so the author can urge them:

> Conduct yourselves honorably among the Gentiles, so that, though they malign you as evildoers, they may see your honorable deeds and glorify God when he comes to judge. For the Lord's sake accept the authority of every human institution, whether of the emperor as supreme, or of governors, as sent by him to punish those who do wrong and to praise those who do right. For it is God's will that by

doing right you should silence the ignorance of the foolish. As servants of God, live as free people, yet do not use your freedom as a pretext for evil. Honor everyone. Love the family of believers. Fear God. Honor the emperor. (1 Pet 2:12–17)

By their "good conduct" others will see their faith and perhaps be converted to God. The tone of 1 Peter is conciliatory toward the secular world, even though the author is aware that Christians have suffered abuse and harassment (1 Pet 3:13–17). His advice urges Christians of his day to be fully participating citizens of their world, confident that by their actions God may be drawing others into the Christian body.

On the far opposite end of the spectrum of Christian viewpoints is the final text in the New Testament, the book of Revelation. Revelation was written also near the end of the first century by a prophetic seer named John who was a member of the Christian church in western Asia Minor, probably in Ephesus. His was the world of the eastern Roman Empire, in the province of Asia and in Ephesus, the fourth largest city of the Roman Empire where there was a flourishing cultic practice of emperor worship dedicated to Domitian (81–96 C.E.). The stone fragments (head and forearm) of a colossal cult statue of Domitian suggest that the standing statue of the emperor may have been as much as twenty-seven feet high (that is, almost five times life size).[6] It is no wonder that the author of Revelation saw the Roman world, and in particular the emperor himself, as the "beast" (Rev 13). Christians had suffered martyrdom for their belief in his day, perhaps for refusing to participate in the "cult of the beast."

In the Roman world, citizens were expected to offer their homage to the gods who protected and watched over the good of the empire. At their deaths, the deceased emperors would also be worshiped as gods. And Domitian, history tells us, fostered such worship in the eastern empire even during his lifetime.[7] To withhold one's sacrificial offering in the exercise of this civil religion was viewed as a subversive act because it angered the gods and threatened the peace and good order of the empire. And so, the author of Revelation comforts the Christians of his day urging them to stand fast against the threat of the "beast." They can do so, he argues, because Christ, the "Lamb that was slain for them," had already won the victory and now sits on the throne of God (Rev 5). Around the throne are the victorious martyrs, whose "robes have been washed white in the blood of the Lamb" (Rev 7:14).

The answer of the book of Revelation, therefore, to the question, "How are Christians to be in the world?" is simple and unequivocal: "Resist the beast!" The danger of this uncompromising viewpoint is patently obvious to anyone who has lived through the ordeal of David

Koresh and the Branch Davidians or any other similar confrontation.[8] What is important in both these viewpoints, one conciliatory and the other extremely hostile to the values of the world, is that the Bible has preserved both in our canonical scriptures. This may suggest to us that, as in the case of pragmatists and visionaries, there is partial wisdom to be found in each perspective and reason enough for self-examination on where we may stand today along this world-affirming or world-denying spectrum.

THE HEAVENLY CITY

The final word of communication in the entire Bible comes (perhaps appropriately) from the visionary imagination of the seer John. In the last two chapters of Revelation, John describes the new heaven and new earth and the descent of "the holy city, the new Jerusalem, coming down out of heaven from God" (Rev 21:2).[9] His vision borrows heavily from that other great visionary prophet of the exile (ca. 587 B.C.E.), Ezekiel, especially Ezekiel 47:1–12. There, Ezekiel had recounted a vision of the sacred river flowing out of the restored Temple in Jerusalem. Here in the book of Revelation, John develops and expands on Ezekiel's text. For John, the chasm between earth and heaven no longer separates humanity from the divine realm. By God's initiative the divine dwelling place is hereafter with humankind. The heavenly city descends, with all its radiance and beauty. And the divine voice proclaims: "Behold! The dwelling of God is with human beings. God will dwell with them, and they shall be God's people, and God himself will be with them; God will wipe away every tear from their eyes, and death shall be no more; neither shall there be mourning nor crying nor pain anymore, for the former things have passed away" (Rev 21:3–4, Barbara Bowe's translation).

Hidden in these beautiful words is even more than meets the eye. The "dwelling" of God here is, in Greek, the *skene*, the tent, a word that has profound and deep reverberations in both Jewish and Christian memory. It recalls the ancient wilderness wanderings at the very beginning of the biblical story when that first band of Hebrews crossed the barren desert and God's presence was "tenting" with them: "In Hebrew traditions the [tent of meeting was] an earthly representation of the heavenly abode of the deity, [and] served as an oracle tent where Yahweh appeared directly to his people."[10] The Israelite wisdom tradition had used this same language to describe personified Wisdom's dwelling on earth and "pitching her tent" (Sir 24:8) among the covenant people.

And the Gospel of John chose exactly these words to depict the human presence of Jesus, the "Word made flesh" who "pitched a tent among us" (Jn 1:14).

This vision of the heavenly city descending, therefore, declares that now God dwells in the midst of the human community, in the midst of all that symbolizes human culture, that is, the city, not in a temporary way but eternally—God in the midst of God's people. God's presence is to be a healing presence, giving life and satisfying the thirsty without payment (Rev 21:6), as the prophet had foretold long ago: "Ho, every one who thirsts, come to the waters; and you that have no money, come, buy and eat!" (Isa 55:1). The dimensions of this heavenly city, moreover, cannot be literal but must be symbolic, as they are drawn in grandiose proportion: "The city lies foursquare, its length the same as its breadth; and he measured the city with his rod, 12,000 stadia; its length and breadth and height are equal" (Rev 21:16, Barbara Bowe's translation). Using the standard modern equivalent, 12,000 stadia would equal 1,500 miles! This image, therefore, does not correspond to any known city but, rather, symbolizes the whole world as a "city," as the place of human civilization and culture, lavishly designed and beautifully adorned. Besides, God is the builder and designer of this city; it is the heavenly city, the holy city. This visionary image of Revelation contrasts dramatically with the story in Genesis 11 where humankind wanted to build a city that would reach up to the divine realm, so that they could "make a name for themselves" (Gen 11:4). This heavenly city descending will be God's city. And here, in this world city, God chooses to dwell.

It is significant that there will be no temple in this city, for "its temple is the Lord God Almighty and the Lamb" (Rev 21:22). This detail makes clear that, for the author of Revelation, sacred space is not restricted and localized in a building or in a particular portion of the city. The entire city (world?) is now the temple, the sacred place of God's presence. Nations, kings of the earth, all people shall enter into it freely, as its gates are never shut (Rev 21:25). But this city must remain a holy city, and "nothing unclean will enter it" (Rev 21:27). This expansive vision is careful to maintain the traditional care for ritual cleanness and to acknowledge that certain actions are incompatible with "holiness." Only those whose names have been written in the Lamb's book of life can, therefore, enter into this holy city (Rev 21:27). The inclusiveness of the vision does not cancel out the stern call for right action and for faithful witness.

As the vision continues in Revelation 22, the seer refines the description of the city with unmistakable allusions to the paradise motif drawn from the beginning chapters of Genesis: "Then the angel showed

me the river of the water of life . . . flowing from the throne of God and
of the Lamb through the middle of the street of the city. On either side
of the river is the tree of life" (Rev 22:1–2). [11] Earlier, in the letter to the
church in Ephesus, the author of Revelation designated the location of
the tree of life precisely "in the paradise of God" (Rev 2:7), and so here,
in the final vision of the heavenly city, the paradise motif is explicit. The
tree, moreover, produces lavish abundance: not one crop a year, or even
two growing seasons, but the tree of life in this new city will have
"twelve kinds of fruit, yielding its fruit each month" (Rev 22:2). The
leaves will be for "healing the nations" (Rev 22:2), and nothing accursed
shall detract from the glory of this city of God. And they will "see
[God's] face, and [God's] name [not that of the beast] will be on their
foreheads" (Rev 22:4). [12] With this description, the vision concludes:
"And night shall be no more; they need no light of lamp or sun, for the
Lord God will be their light, and they shall reign for ever and ever"
(Rev 22:5, Barbara Bowe's translation).

CONCLUSION

These final chapters of the book of Revelation, with their utopian vision
of the heavenly city descending, bring the biblical story at last full circle.
And as the story in Genesis began with the narration of the paradise
garden, so, too, Revelation closes with the garden revisited. But the
dream now is of the entire world as one great urban paradise garden
with God dwelling in the midst. This is a vision as much for the earth
itself as for all the creatures who inhabit God's creation. The evil ones
and evil itself will be conquered forever. Such is the persistent, relentless biblical hope for God's creation. But the tragic disparity between
this biblical vision and the reality of our broken world could not be
more apparent. If anything, the seer of Revelation with his vivid imagination and elaborate images points out to us just how far we stand from
this future promised by God.

How, then, does a text like the book of Revelation supply a foundation for our contemporary spirituality? It does so, I think (even with its
violent imagery and sometimes shocking depictions of the beast and the
fate of evildoers), by holding fast to a vision of a world where all have
access to a rich and abundant life and where God chooses to dwell in
our midst. The urgent refrain of its final verses, "Come, . . . Come, . . .
Come Lord Jesus!" (Rev 22:17–20), becomes the Christian prayer for
our time and for all time. And with the same urgency as the seer John
we must proclaim down the centuries our own "Amen!" Let it be so, let

this dream for our world become a reality in our day. And as we give voice to this prayer, we do so with the words of the prophet Habakkuk once again echoing in our ears:

> For there is still a vision for the appointed time;
> it speaks of the end, and does not lie.
> If it seems to tarry, wait for it;
> it will surely come, it will not delay. (Hab 2:3)

QUESTIONS FOR REFLECTION

1. For most of us, our lives as Christians are lived in the heart of the world. In what ways do you strive to be *in* the world but not *of* it? What worldly "beasts" do you struggle to resist?
2. What are the dangers for us of embracing an apocalyptic worldview? How does the message of Revelation influence us for the better and for the worse?
3. Contemporary politicians, taking their cue from Revelation, are fond of labeling other nations as the "Evil Empire." What are the effects on our world of this kind of language, and what other biblical wisdom might offer a different view?
4. The picture of the "heavenly city" at the end of Revelation mixes urban and rural images in its imaginary view. What virtues do you see in rural life or city life, and how can each of these settings nurture our Christian lives?
5. The Apollo astronauts have seen our planet from above as one beautiful and perfect sphere where life abounds and where there are no boundaries. The vision of the heavenly city descending in Revelation also sees the world as one great unity. What one thing do you feel called to do to bring us closer to this dream of unity?

CONCLUSION

Biblical Foundations of Spirituality

Your words were found and I ate them,
and your words became to me a joy
and the delight of my heart.

—Jeremiah 15:16

MAKING THE WORD OF GOD OUR OWN

One challenge now remains for those who desire to let these biblical texts become the guide and inspiration for their contemporary lives. We must continue to "eat these words."[1] This image that the prophet Jeremiah employs (compare Ezek 2:8, 3:3; Rev 10:9–10) points to the life-long task of steeping ourselves in the biblical Word, learning its wisdom, absorbing its images and metaphors, discerning its contours, and wrestling with its puzzles with all our mind and heart. This image of "eating the word" invites us to let the text confront us. If we do, the Word will sometimes comfort us, sometimes nourish us, but it will also challenge and disturb us. In the opening chapter of this book I spoke of "touching our fingers to the flame" of the sacred text as inspired Word of God. But Jeremiah suggests that even touching the flame is not enough. Merely to "touch" is not yet sufficient; no, we must "eat" in order to assimilate and make these words our own. "Eating" suggests that we taste and savor both the bitter and the sweet and learn from each the wisdom that it holds. Eating means that we ingest slowly, carefully turning over in our minds and hearts the words that we have "eaten." Eating the Word means that we dare to learn from the frightful "texts of terror" as well as from the words of comfort and joy.[2]

To engage the sacred scripture in this way demands of us that we use the tools and insights of modern exegesis, that is, "the discipline of attending to the text and listening to it rightly and well."[3] As we have seen, the levels of meaning in the words and traditions of scripture are never completely transparent; nor are they self-evident or limited to a single, obvious meaning. They require careful inquiry and serious thought. In short, if we want to deepen our grasp of the biblical foundations for our faith, exegetical insight is essential. Eugene Peterson has explained this best:

> Exegesis is the farthest thing from pedantry; exegesis is an act of love. It means loving the one who speaks the words enough to want to get the words right. Exegesis does not mean mastering the text, it means submitting to it; not taking charge of it and imposing my knowledge on it, but entering the world of the text and letting the text "read" me. Exegesis is an act of sustained humility. . . . Spirituality without exegesis becomes self-indulgent.[4]

TOWARD A RENEWED BIBLICAL SPIRITUALITY

How, then, shall we summarize the insights of this journey through the biblical story? Perhaps the best approach is to suggest some fundamental principles that have recurred again and again along the way. These principles have pointed out the path to understanding God in our midst today and have begun to show us how we might respond. First, a contemporary spirituality grounded in the biblical word will always bear witness to the unfathomable mystery at the heart of God. This "God beyond all names" is greater than all our attempts to name and understand the mystery, and, therefore, as creatures of God our proper response will always be awe and reverence. With Moses, we "take off our sandals" when on this holy ground in the theophanies, or God encounters, of our lives. Our feeble attempts to name and celebrate our experiences of God will imitate and draw on the richness and the variety of the biblical imagination, relishing in the myriad ways that God can be known and imaged in our day.

Second, a contemporary biblical spirituality will be marked by a profound sense of our own creatureliness, knowing who we are before God with our finitude and human limitations. We are indeed that "riddle" of which the British poet spoke and yet, as God's creation, invested with a dignity that no one can take from us. This birthright of our identity as creatures of God blesses us but also challenges us to live in such a way that we safeguard, for ourselves and more especially for others, this truth of who we are. There is no room for hubris, no room for "building towers to the sky in order to make a name for ourselves" (Gen 11:1–9). As human creatures we share equally the gifts and limitations of the human condition. Therefore, *every* person we encounter each day, *every* face we meet, should be a reminder to us of who we ourselves are and an invitation to reaffirm with them our *shared* dignity and humanity.

Third, a biblical spirituality in our day will find a more adequate balance in our understanding of God between the "saving and blessing" characteristics discussed in chapter 4. Never losing sight of our fundamental need for God's saving power in our lives, we will nonetheless affirm in new ways our God-given responsibility in the world as cocreators with God, as people who have been entrusted with the care of God's creation.

Fourth, our renewed spirituality today will draw on the central biblical metaphor of the Exodus event and bear witness to God's fundamental design and purpose for the world. The Exodus story illustrates that the biblical God "hears the cry of those in need" and is on the side of freedom from all that oppresses body or spirit and limits the capacity for the fullness of human life. And yet we saw, too, through the lens of that story, that those oppressive forces (symbolized by "Pharaoh") are both outside and within our very selves.

Fifth, the spirituality of the covenant vision will mark our consciousness at its core. This means that those core values that were ignored by the Israelite monarchs and proclaimed relentlessly by the prophets and by Jesus will be embraced with new vigor in our day: righteousness, justice, steadfast love for God and for the neighbor, compassion, faithfulness, and knowledge of God (as cited together especially in Hos 2:19–20). These are not just vague ideas or empty words; they are indicators of our lived faith. If embraced concretely they become the means toward building a more just world in our day. The fundamental insight of the covenant vision was at once a recognition of the holiness of God tabernacling in the midst of the people and the *corresponding requirement* for the people to "be holy, for I the Lord your God am holy" (Lev 19:2). And, as Vatican II reminded us, the call to holiness is not reserved only for some and not others. All God's people are called to live in holiness, that is, in fidelity to God's covenantal ways.

Sixth, a contemporary biblical spirituality will reclaim one of the central insights of the wisdom tradition, namely, that we encounter God not only in the dramatic moments but most of all in the dailiness of our lives. If so, then our worldview will be thoroughly sacramental and will recognize that we encounter God in every aspect of our ordinary lives. Our spirituality, consequently, will be always "on two feet," lived at the heart of the world where God is found. Surely the God of the Bible is a God engaged in the real world, in all the intrigue and foibles of human life, and right there God meets us each day.

Seventh, of course, for the Christian, Jesus the Christ is the perfect incarnation of God, the Word made flesh among us who, as the gospel of John asserts, is the very "exegesis" of God and the one through whom the Spirit has been poured out in the Church. Therefore, our Christian spirituality today will reaffirm the Trinitarian character of God. By that affirmation we confess that "we are created, called and sustained by God, and redeemed, re-created and made daughters and sons of God by Jesus, Word and Son, and renewed, empowered, and made participants in the divine life by the Spirit."[5] These affirmations guarantee that our God is not merely a distant, remote deity, or simply a companion who walks with us as one like ourselves, or only a vaguely defined spiritual presence—our Trinitarian God is all three: Creator, Redeemer, and Sanctifier.

Eighth, Jesus' proclamation of the Reign of God orients our spirituality toward a future promise that is still to be realized. With the proclamation of the reign or kingdom of God, Jesus echoed all that was said of the covenant vision with its demands of justice, righteousness, and steadfast love and extended its boundaries to include all those on the margins in his day. In the life of Jesus that promise of God's reign was marked and sealed by the Cross. If we are to live our spirituality today in fidelity to this message, then it therefore demands of us a radical obedience and the "laying down of our lives" in service of the neighbor. There is a cost to this discipleship as followers of Jesus, and, as Dietrich Bonhoeffer, the contemporary German Protestant theologian, once said, there is no such thing as "cheap grace." But if Jesus is our example, then the Christian spiritual life is fundamentally about our lives given in love.

Ninth, the apostle Paul reminded us that our Christian spirituality is life lived in the Body of Christ, in the concrete gathering of women and men who make up this body. It is to be therefore essentially communal and ecclesial, never simply a private matter. It is as Church that we hear the Word of God proclaimed with all its comfort and challenge. It is as Church that we gather together at the table to be fed by the one bread and the one cup. And it is as Church that we are sent forth "to serve the Lord and one another." Moreover, in this assembly, Paul reminded us, we have different charisms, but we all share the same Spirit for the common good. Finally, the last principle and characteristic of a contemporary spirituality drawn from our journey through the biblical tradition is the essential commitment to hope in a future that God will bring to birth. Whether this radical hope takes the form of a vision of a new heaven and a new earth or rests in a more mundane commitment to the here and now and the small incremental signs of new life among us, Christian spirituality is a spirituality of hope. Christian hope is not a Pollyanna wishful thinking but, rather, a deep confidence in God's promise of life for the world together with a commitment to work toward the fulfillment of that promise in cooperation with God. This hope is grounded in Jesus the Risen One and binds us to God and to one another in a radical trust.

The scripture itself should have the final word. We could choose no better text than the familiar lines from the prophet Micah.[6] In this text, Micah draws together the personal (humility), the interpersonal (gracious love), and the societal (just action) dimensions of our faith and spirituality. In a few words he sums up the components of an integrated biblical spirituality. And where the three dimensions intersect, there is God's final gift of *shalom*—life, peace, and prosperity for all: "This is what Yahweh asks of you, only this: that you act justly, that you love tenderly, that you walk humbly with your God" (Mic 6:8, Barbara Bowe's translation).

EPILOGUE

The Church That Sojourns

These are the last times. Therefore let us be reverent; let us fear the patience of God, lest it become a judgment against us. For let us either fear the wrath to come or love the grace that is present, one of the two; only let us be found in Christ Jesus, which leads to true life.

—Ignatius, To the Ephesians 11:1

At the conclusion of the Acts of the Apostles, the apostle Paul is preaching in Rome, where "he lived . . . two whole years at his own expense and welcomed all who came to him, proclaiming the kingdom of God and teaching about the Lord Jesus Christ with all boldness and without hindrance" (Acts 28:30–31). The author of Acts surely knew of Paul's martyrdom, but as part of his larger theological plan, he chose not to narrate it. The Gospel of Luke and Acts of the Apostles demonstrate that God is working through historical events in a linear, yet unfinished, manner. To emphasize this "orderly account," Luke arranges salvation history into three periods. [1]

First Period: The Law and Prophets, from Adam to John:

> The law and the prophets were in effect until John came, since then the good news of the kingdom of God is proclaimed and everyone tries to enter it by force. (Lk 16:16)

Second Period: Proclamation of the Kingdom by Jesus, from the descent of the Spirit on Jesus to the return of the Spirit to the Father on the cross:

and the Holy Spirit descended upon him in bodily form like a dove. And a voice came from heaven, "You are my Son, the Beloved; with you I am well pleased." (Lk 3:22)

Then Jesus, crying with a loud voice, said, "Father, into your hands I commend my spirit." Having said this, he breathed his last. (Lk 23:46)

Third Period: Proclamation of the Kingdom of God by the church, from the descent of the Spirit to the Parousia.

Clearly Luke envisioned this third period—the time of the church— as the one in which his community resided. Jesus is present through his Spirit within this church and will continue to do so until all flesh, particularly the Gentiles, come to faith.

Matthew's gospel closes with a similar trajectory:

And Jesus came and said to them, "All authority in heaven and on earth has been given to me. Go therefore and make disciples of all nations, baptizing them in the name of the Father and of the Son and of the Holy Spirit, and teaching them to obey everything that I have commanded you. And remember, I am with you always, to the end of the age." (Mt 28:18–20)

Likely written in the last quarter of the first century, the First Letter of Peter is addressed to a church that sojourns with a "living hope" toward the fullness of salvation.

To the exiles of the Dispersion in Pontus, Galatia, Cappadocia, Asia, and Bithynia, who have been chosen and destined by God the Father and sanctified by the Spirit to be obedient to Jesus Christ and to be sprinkled with his blood: May grace and peace be yours in abundance. Blessed be the God and Father of our Lord Jesus Christ! By his great mercy he has given us a new birth into a living hope through the resurrection of Jesus Christ from the dead, and into an inheritance that is imperishable, undefiled, and unfading, kept in heaven for you, who are being protected by the power of God through faith for a salvation ready to be revealed in the last time. (1 Pet 1:1–5)

Just as the Old Testament ends with the prophet Malachi announcing the coming day of the Lord (Mal 4:3–6a), the New Testament concludes with the Book of Revelation anticipating the consummation of God's reign with the creation of a new heaven and a new earth (Rev 21:1). Both testaments recognize that the actions of God are yet to be fully realized.

But the end of the Apostolic age—the period in which those com-missioned by Jesus continued his ministry of proclamation—did not see the anticipated Parousia, the second coming of Jesus. In effect, believ-ers today continue to live in Luke's third period of proclamation and are awaiting the fulfillment of the Matthean Jesus' charge to make disciples of all nations. *We* are the church that sojourns. "The delay of the Par-ousia, the return of Jesus Christ, acted as a force of decisive importance in the shaping of primitive Christian spirituality."[2] This delay and the waning of eschatological expectations forced early Christians to reexam-ine their beliefs and resulted in a variety of theological responses pre-served in our New Testament and other early Christian literature.

While Christians sang hymns, held liturgies, and engaged in pious acts of fasting and almsgiving, our only access to these practices and their spirituality is mediated through the texts these Christians saw fit to write and later generations preserved.[3] But not all of those early Chris-tian texts were to be included in the canon that became our Bible. Certainly "the biblical foundations of spirituality" properly end with the last book in the canon, but these lesser-known noncanonical texts give us insight into how our ancestors in the faith attempted to answer their emerging spiritual questions. In essence these writings provide glimpses into how Christian spirituality with its foundation in the Bible was first experienced. The ecumenical councils of the fourth and fifth centuries would hammer out the theological positions of the church, but until some manner of consensus was reached, Christians in various regions and influenced by different philosophical suppositions at-tempted to live and practice their faith guided by the scriptures, the Spirit, and an emerging ecclesial structure. The diversity of their devel-oping Christology is evident in the variety of texts they have left behind.

This Christian literature from the first two centuries can be variously categorized by genre, theological perspectives, and provenance.[4] In or-der to trace some of the spiritual trajectories emerging in this diverse period, we begin with a discussion on the establishment of the biblical canon and then explore examples of early Christian literature that re-flect differing responses to questions of Christology and praxis in the era immediately following the New Testament period. The collection known as the Apostolic Fathers bridges the Apostolic age and shows how the New Testament spirituality of witness and proclamation gave way to a spirituality of the meantime.

THE CURIOUS CASE OF THE CANON

The very title of our book, *Biblical Foundations of Spirituality*, pre-sumes the establishment of a *bible*, a set of scriptures believed to be authoritative for faith. Yet this collection of books did not receive its final form until the fourth century. Prior to that a variety of texts were read in the context of liturgy and considered "authoritative" by local communities. These texts varied greatly from region to region, so that some were virtually unknown outside their locale. The fourth-century church historian Eusebius of Caesarea records one such example. Sera-pion, the bishop of Antioch, had been asked whether the Gospel of Peter should be read publicly at the church in Rhossus. Evidently he initially assented. However, Serapion later deemed the work falsely attributed to Peter and heretical.

> We, my brothers, receive Peter and all the apostles as we receive Christ, but the writings falsely attributed we are experienced enough to reject, knowing that nothing of the sort has been handed down to us. When I visited you I assumed that you all clung to the true Faith; so without going through the "gospel" alleged by them to be Peter's, I said: "If this is the only thing that apparently puts childish notions into your heads, read it by all means." But as, from information received, I now know that their mind had been ensnared by some heresy, I will make every effort to visit you again; so expect me in the near future. . . . I have been able to go through the book and draw the conclusion that while most of it accorded with the authentic teaching of the Saviour, some passages were spurious additions. (*Hist. eccl.* 6.12.2)[5]

The theological authority of these texts appears to have derived from their use within the liturgy, hence the question to Serapion about the appropriateness of reading the Gospel of Peter. Eusebius acknowl-edged the popularity of some of these questionable writings:

> I have set down all the facts that have come to my knowledge regard-ing the apostles and the apostolic period; the sacred writings they have left us; the books which though disputed are nevertheless con-stantly used in very many churches; those that are unmistakably spu-rious and foreign to apostolic orthodoxy. (*Hist. eccl.* 3.31.6)

One of the questions confronting the late-second-century Christians concerned the suitability of the growing number of Christian texts to be read in the public assembly. This question led to the organization of "lists," first called canons, that included the title of the texts that were not necessarily "authoritative" doctrinally but were considered acceptable for public reading. Originally, the word "canon" came from *kanna* in Greek, a reed used as a measuring stick for building and construction, and later came to mean a rule or standard. The oldest such list is the Muratorian Canon, so called because it was discovered within an eighth-century manuscript by L. A. Muratori (1672–1750). The original was likely composed around 200 C.E. This list includes several texts not found in the canonical New Testament, such as the Apocalypse of Peter, "though some are not willing that the latter be read in church," and the Shepherd of Hermas. An explanatory note gives the reason for Hermas' inclusion:

> But Hermas wrote the Shepherd very recently, in our times, in the city of Rome, while Bishop Pius, his brother, was occupying the chair of the Church of the city of Rome. And therefore it ought indeed to be read, but cannot be read publicly to the people in church, either among the Prophets, whose number is complete, or among the Apostles, for it is after their time.[6]

The criteria used for determining the acceptability of the New Testament texts seem to have included apostolic origin (the text was associated with an apostle or someone from that age), the Catholic or universal dimension of the message, its liturgical use, and possessing content in accord with the basic rule of faith that summarized central Christian tenets. But church historian Harry Gamble suggests that, "What counted most was whether the church, in whole or large part, was accustomed to hearing the document read in the service of worship."[7]

The establishment of a canon coupled with the development of a rule of faith and emerging ecclesiastical structures resulted in the development of orthodoxy. Coming from the Greek *ortho* ("upright or straight," hence "correct") + *doxa* ("opinion"), the term came to refer to the "correct belief" about Christian creeds, practices, and ecclesial structures, and stood in opposition to heresy (from the Greek *hairesis*, meaning "choice," which came to mean a "party" or "sect"). "Christianity of the second century had developed an orthodoxy, but it was not yet the dominant, agreed-upon, or imperially supported form of Christianity."[8] While Irenaeus presented a picture of the church as uniformed from its inception, it would be more accurate to describe Christianity of the second century as "Christianities," holding diverse understandings of significant theological concepts.[9]

> The unifying factors that formed a pattern of emerging "orthodoxy" were first of all the emerging "New Testament canon" as the four Gospels and the letters of Paul gained authoritative stature and built

a common bond among Christians of different theological stripes across large geographic and cultural rifts. This emerging canon safeguarded not only unity but also a range of acceptable diversity centering on the identity of Jesus the human and the exalted Christ.[10]

While the canon may have aided in establishing Christian unity, a line had been drawn in the sand. Some early Christian texts would remain part of liturgical practice and spiritual reading. Others would be labeled "heretical" and nearly lost to history.

By the fourth century, the Christian church in both the East and the West had accepted a New Testament canon of twenty-seven books. The final form of the bible witnessed to the community's foundational beliefs concerning God's revelation in the past. As Dianne Bergant notes,

> These forms became the rule or standard for determining revelation within the believing community in the present and in the future. They also provided a means of achieving unity within the faith. Born of the community, they were instrumental in the rebirth of that community generation after generation.[11]

POSTCANONICAL WRITINGS

The need to determine the parameters of what could be considered authoritative in both scripture and practice attests to the variety and number of Christian texts emerging at the end of the first and into the second century. The oldest collection of writings considered orthodox in its theology but excluded from the final form of the canon is known in modern nomenclature as the Apostolic Fathers. Read through the lens of spirituality, these early Christian texts demonstrate continuity with the New Testament and express an emerging spirituality that is at once communal, ecclesial, and ethical. Written between the first and second centuries by leaders of the early Church, these documents did not originally circulate together. The fifteen documents by nine different authors encompass a variety of literary forms. Seven genuine letters were written by Ignatius, the bishop of Antioch, on his way to martyrdom in Rome. 1 Clement is a letter from the Roman church, which ancient tradition associated with Clement, about whom little is known.[12] Another leader, Polycarp of Smyrna, wrote a letter to the church at Philippi. Three others claim to be letters (2 Clement, Barnabas, and Diognetus) but in fact these treatises are more properly apologetic or sermonic in nature. The Didache, also known as the Teachings of the Twelve Apostles, is an early church manual, and the Shepherd of

Hermas is a Christian apocalypse. Though known by the early church, these documents were only rediscovered in the mid-seventeenth century.

> In many respects, [the Apostolic Fathers] parallel the literary forms and theological interests of New Testament documents. They address the immediate problems that arose in specific Christian communities, and at the same time, they reveal a pastoral sensitivity when their authors were forced to confront the broad issues of God's revelation to humanity as it intersected with the rise of the religious traditions of human faith. [13]

This flourishing of Christian literary efforts provides a glimpse into the practical and personal concerns of Christian communities. The different genres in which these texts were written demonstrate that post-apostolic communities needed to defend their faith (apologies), to "fill in the gaps" about the fate of the Apostles and the spread of the faith (gospels, acts), to sustain ecclesial connections over distances (epistles), to seek ongoing revelation (apocalypses) and to remember the witness of faith (martyrdom accounts). The following briefly explores examples of these genres in the post-apostolic literature.

It is not surprising that a religion rooted in the death of a crucified criminal would be viewed with suspicion by Roman authorities. Thus early Christian apologies attempted to respond to imperial concerns. An apology, from the Greek *apologia*, means a defense, and was a rhetorical treatise designed to refute charges against Christians on philosophical grounds. The three main charges that were variously presented appear to be accusations of atheism, immorality, and disloyalty. [14] In his "Apology," Tertullian (155–240 C.E.) sarcastically responded to the absurdity that Christians were the cause of natural disasters:

> If the Tiber rises to the city walls, if the Nile does not cover the flood-plains, if the heavens don't move or if the earth does, if there is a famine or a plague, the roar is at once: "The Christians to the lion!" Really! All of them to one lion? (*Apol.* 40.2)

The question remains as to how many of these early Christian apologies were actually presented to the imperial representatives to whom they were addressed. They may have served more like an open letter to the presiding official. Certainly these treatises served to inspire and encourage the community. We know the names and works of many of these second- to early-third-century apologists, including Quadratus (c. 125 C.E.), Aristides, Justin Martyr (100–160 C.E.), Aristo of Pella (c. 100–160 C.E.), Athenagoras (133–190 C.E.), Irenaeus of Lyons (135–202 C.E.), Melito of Sardis (died c. 180 c.e.), Tatian (c. 120–180 c.e.), Clement of Alexandria (c. 150–215 c.e.), and Tertullian (c. 155–230 c.e.).

Since an apology is forensic rhetoric,[15] and only those with a rhetorical education would likely have possessed the training and skills to prepare such a piece, we can surmise that our early Christian apologists were members of the Christian elite. The same cannot be determined of the authors of the noncanonical gospels and acts.

The noncanonical gospels only partially continued the biographical form found in the synoptic gospels, and some introduced ideas later to be considered heretical. Some of these texts were "gospels" in name only. The Gospel of Thomas possesses neither a narrative of the life of Jesus nor a Passion narrative, but rather is a collection of sayings attributed to Jesus. The Gospel of Peter contains only the narrative of the Passion and Resurrection. So the designation of "gospel" does not necessary indicate a strict adherence to all the expected elements of the genre. Some of these gospels would be designated as "gnostic," from the Greek *gnosis*, which means "knowledge." Gnosticism was a broad category of dualistic heretical thinking based on a complicated cosmology.

> Uneasiness about the physicality of the incarnation and resurrection lay behind some strands of Christian Gnosticism which maintained that Jesus' humanity and death were pedagogical devices, or even subterfuges, deliberately meant to obscure true teachings revealed only to Jesus's disciples and later to privileged initiates.[16]

Gnostics believed that they had been given secret knowledge and were destined for salvation. Those without such knowledge had no hope of salvation. In the dualistic world of Gnosticism, in which matter was evil and spirit good, Jesus could not have been truly human (matter), but only appeared to be so. Those who held that Jesus only "seemed to be human" were called Docetists, from the Greek *dokein*, "to seem or appear."

The Apocrypha Acts (apocrypha means hidden) at first glance seem to more clearly mirror the canonical Acts of the Apostles, which itself shares elements with ancient romance novels.[17] But scholars propose that these apocryphal acts are not simply a Christianizing of a Hellenistic novel, but appear to be collections of separately circulated material (personal legends, local tales) placed into a narrative framework focusing on the "acts" or praxis of particular apostles.[18] These acts record the travels of the apostles as they set out to preach the gospel to their allotted areas. The narratives are complete with talking animals, miraculous occurrences, and exotic locations, so that it becomes difficult to assess whether a historical foundation undergirds these stories or if they were simply meant to entertain. An interesting proposal is that the authors of the major Apocryphal Acts were groups of women "who practiced sexual continence, as an expression of their emancipation and their resistance to the patriarchal order in marriage, the family, in society and in the state."[19] While these acts likely were originally disseminated separately, the Acts of Andrew, Acts of John, Acts of Paul, Acts of Peter, and Acts of Thomas were brought together and circulated in the west in a single manuscript by the Manicheans, a second-century heretical group.

Of the twenty-seven books of the New Testament, twenty-one are designated "letters" and comprise nearly a third of the New Testament text. The letters are generally collected into two groups: Pauline literature and Catholic epistles. The sheer number of canonical letters confirms the prevalence of this form, though many of these so-called letters were never meant to be sent. Not surprisingly the postcanonical literature follows suit and makes frequent use of the epistolary format. Among the collection known as the Apostolic Fathers, the letter form is the most common genre. The seven letters of Ignatius, the Letter associated with Clement, an early leader of Rome, and a letter by the bishop Polycarp may have all been genuine letters. Second Clement, the Letter of Barnabas, and Letter to Diognetus utilize the epistolary format, but 2 Clement and Barnabas are likely sermons while Diognetus is an apology.

Another text included in the Apostolic Fathers is the Shepherd of Hermas, and like the Book of Revelation, it is considered Christian apocalyptic literature. The term apocalypse is derived from the Greek and means an "uncovering" or "revealing," hence "revelation." "In apocalyptic literature, scenes of heaven and hell, often depicted in lurid detail, are full of poetic imagery borrowed from the scriptures, and intended to disturb, persuade, and encourage those in danger of apostasy."[20]

Threats from civil authorities, social pressure, and familial resistance led some believers to renounce Christianity and become apostates, while others offered the ultimate witness to their faith: martyrdom (from the Greek *martus*, "a witness"). Accounts of martyrdom served to inspire Christians who saw the paschal mystery born out in the heroic death of the martyr. "Surviving 'Acts' of martyrs range from highly literary creations to laconic recounting of the most basic facts, which can be even more powerful than the dramatized accounts."[21] The source of information for some martyr acts may derive from official Roman trials of Christians and eyewitness accounts. Christians would expand these documents to include the last days and heroic death of believers. These acts served to "encourage Christians who might suffer persecution themselves with the example of sisters and brothers who through the power of the Spirit had triumphed in the contest with Satan (to whom the persecution is attributed: the mob and the Roman authorities appear to be no more than the devil's pawns)."[22] The oldest written martyr account outside of the New Testament is found in a letter from the church at Smyrna to the church at Philomelium, which reports the martyrdom of Polycarp, the 86-year-old bishop of Smyrna. While Eusebius dates his death at 167 C.E., scholars suggest 150 to 160 is a more probable range.

The variety of genres found in noncanonical literature witnesses to the interests and concerns among early Christians. As Helen Rhee suggests, these genres may point to a diversity of relationships among various Christian groups, civil authorities, and emerging orthodoxy.

> The Apologies essentially sought to present Christianity in harmony with Greco-Roman civilization and were endorsed by the later orthodox tradition; the Apocryphal Acts represented Christianity as the antithesis of the established Greco-Roman society and were rejected by the orthodox church; the Martyr Acts, inherently counter-cultural by genre, also portrayed Christianity in resistance to the established authorities of the Empire but were warmly embraced by the orthodox tradition.[23]

Early Christian literature demonstrates the complicated relationship between cultural location and developing orthodox. These various texts speak to the emerging theological questions at the end of the Apostolic age, and reveal how communities struggled to live their faith in an increasingly hostile environment.

SPIRITUALITIES IN THE MEANTIME

The late first- and early second-century Christian communities took to heart the exhortation of 1 Peter 3:

> In your hearts sanctify Christ as Lord. Always be ready to make your defense to anyone who demands from you an accounting for the hope that is in you, yet do it with gentleness and reverence. (1 Pet 3:15–16)

The author of 1 Peter envisions a law court in which Christians must defend their faith in Christ's return, and be able to account for their continued hope in the coming fullness of salvation so long delayed.

"The exiles of the Dispersion" (1 Pet 1:1), to whom Peter writes, are called upon to believe and to defend that belief, even in the face of trials. This defense of the faith took on different meanings in the Apostolic Fathers as writers attempted to interpret and integrate their experiences of separation from Judaism, sporadic regional persecutions, and a growing membership—all in the midst of waning eschatological expectation.

The provenances for the diverse texts that comprise the Apostolic Fathers include Egypt, Palestine, Antioch on the Orontes, western Anatolia, and Rome. Not surprisingly, these are the very locales of the earliest Christian communities. Though local customs and cultures would be evident in their writings, in general they reflect the common worldview of Greco-Roman society. In his study of the material, Clayton Jefford notes that despite their diversity the Apostolic Fathers do share similar theological assumptions about the future of the church, the nature of God, how to live as a Christian, and a struggle for self-definition.[24] These commonalties would be experienced in a spirituality that expressed itself in Eucharistic community, righteous living and, on occasion, martyrdom.

The Future of the Church

The Letter of Barnabas, the Didache, the Letters of Ignatius, and the Shepherd of Hermas demonstrate some of the apocalyptic expectancy that marked Paul's Letters, but in general the Apostolic Fathers accepted that Christ's expected return had been delayed.[25] This acceptance led to a recognition that the community needed to envision a way of being in the meantime. Who would lead the community? How would members relate to each other? What constituted appropriate worship and liturgy? How would the community and its leadership deal with problems both internally and externally?

While all the Apostolic Fathers essentially address these questions, the Didache does so most directly. Considered to be a church manual, the work sets out how those preparing for baptism are to live the faith.[26] Its full title is "The Teachings (*didache* in Greek) of the Twelve Apostles," indicating that its authority if not its content is derived from apostolic teaching. Dated to 110–120 C.E., the Didache appears to be a second-century redaction of an earlier first-century text. The initial six chapters comprise a tractate on the "Two Ways," which describe the way of life and the way of death, chiefly citing the Old Testament. The material likely derives from Jewish moral teaching that had been adapted for Christian use. The next section describes liturgy (7–10) and appropriate church order (11–15). These sections set out instructions on baptism, worship, Eucharist, and the treatment of wandering prophets and apostles. The work closes with an eschatological conclusion. "The Didachist is concerned primarily with the standardization of religious traditions within the community and the relationship of these traditions to correct teaching and community practices."[27]

To that end, the Didache admonishes:

> See that no one leads you astray from this way of the teaching, for such a person teaches you without regard for God. For if you are able to bear the whole yoke of the Lord, you will be perfect. But if you are not able, then do what you can. (Did. 6.1–2)[28]

The Nature of God

The Christological controversies and Trinitarian questions that led to the councils of the fourth and fifth centuries seem of little concern in the Apostolic Fathers. At first rooted in the Jewish religious framework, the concept of monotheism colored how God was understood. With the inclusion of a growing number of non-Jewish Christians, other philosophical conceptions and cosmologies would shade the understanding of God's nature. The Apostolic Fathers witness to a variety of theological perspectives on the identity of the Godhead. For example, the Didache does not distinguish between faith in God and faith in Jesus, whereas 2 Clement describes a clear distinction: "To the only God, invisible, the Father of truth, who sent to us the Savior and Founder of immortality, through whom he also revealed to us the truth and the heavenly life, to him be the glory forever and ever. Amen" (2 Clem 20.5).

The Shepherd of Hermas gives a primary role to the Spirit. "The preexistent holy spirit, which created the whole creation, God caused to live in the flesh that he wished. This flesh, therefore, in which the holy spirit lived, served the spirit well, living in holiness and purity, without defiling the spirit in any way" (Her. 59.5). Hermas' odd Christology has not gone unnoticed.

> The theology of the Church must have been very elastic at a time when such a book could enjoy popularity and implicit, if not explicit, ecclesiastical sanction, for its Christology does not seem to square with any of the Christologies of the New Testament, or with those of contemporary theologians whose occasional documents have reached us. The Shepherd speaks of a Son of God; but this Son of God is distinguished from Jesus.[29]

But as Carolyn Osiek has argued, a systematic Christology was not the author's concern. Rather, a greater focus is placed on the role and functioning of the Spirit. "The Spirit of God is in Hermas the prevailing, polymorphous presence, personified to an unusual degree. Pneumatology is more prominent than christology."[30]

How to Live as a Christian

Though theological questions about the nature of God and emerging Christological perspectives are evident in the post-apostolic writings, the delay of the Parousia had a more direct impact on the daily life of the Christian. Jesus had been preparing his followers for the imminent coming of the Kingdom. To that end, he had issued strong ethical requirements for those who would enter this kingdom. "For I tell you, unless your righteousness exceeds that of the scribes and Pharisees, you will never enter the kingdom of heaven" (Mt 5:20). But with the delay of his return and the consummation of God's kingdom, did Jesus expect human beings to love their enemies (Mt 5:43–48 / Lk 6:27–28) and act on that love perpetually? Whatever the original intent of the gospel's ethical commands by the close of the first century, the Parousia's late arrival forced a reevaluation. Paul had encouraged Christian participation in society (Rom 13 and later echoed in Tit 3:1), but what is a Christian to do when forced to offer sacrifice? The Apostolic Fathers attempt to interpret the mandates of Jesus within their own social context.

The Didache lists the appropriate behaviors expected of a Christian with a strong admonition to not "be double-minded" (Did. 2.4). Jeffrey McCurry translates Didache 1.3 thus, "And you, love those who hate you; indeed you will even have no enemy."[31] The ethical demands of the gospel remain in effect, and in fact, as McCurry proposes, the Didache is enhancing them.

> In facing the question of how to love one's enemies, the Didache does not change the answer to a question we think we already know; rather it changes the question itself: "How do I envision myself and the other who would harm me?" The Didache wants to train readers in the art of perception, an art of seeing like Jesus. Indeed the Didache offers a way of loving one's enemies by offering a pattern of vision in which the Christian's way of seeing is so transformed that she cannot see the enemy as an enemy any longer.[32]

If the Didache is any indication, the ethical demands issued by Jesus continued to direct the expectations of behavior among the growing numbers of Christians.

The seven letters of Ignatius of Antioch focus on ecclesial structure so as to maintain proper order, right belief, and unity. Ignatius encouraged respecting the authority of the council of presbyters and bishop, so that "in your unanimity and harmonious love Jesus Christ is sung" (Ign. *Eph.* 4.1). But Ignatius is also concerned about how one lives the faith (Ign. *Pol.* 4.1–3). He argued against a group of Christians who taught "strange doctrines" (Ign. *Pol.* 3.1), likely Docetists who did not believe in the humanity of Jesus. The threat of Docetism may be the reason that Ignatius' letters contain several early creedal statements, primarily focusing on the humanity of Jesus. For example, in his letter to the Ephesians, Ignatius states:

> There is only one physician, who is both flesh and spirit, born and unborn, God in man, true life in death, both from Mary and from God, first subject to suffering and then beyond it, Jesus Christ our Lord. (Ign. *Eph.* 7.2)

Ignatius accuses these Docetists of misleading believers, and as a result they were not caring for those in need.

> Now note well those who hold heretical opinions about the grace of Jesus Christ that came to us; note how contrary they are to the mind of God. They have no concern for love, none for the widow, none for the orphan, none for the oppressed, none for the prisoner or the one released, none for the hungry or thirsty. (Ign. *Smyrn.* 6.2)

Ignatius penned his letters as he was being taken to Rome for martyrdom, a martyrdom that he pleaded with the believers not to prevent (Ign. *Rom.* 7) for along the way, "now at last I am beginning to be a disciple" (Ign. *Rom.* 5.3).

Martyrdom versus apostasy became the new measurement for the moral life at the close of the first century. Ignatius' death at the hands of imperial authorities is presumed but not narrated. But the martyrdom of Polycarp, the 86-year-old bishop of Smyrna, is recounted in detail. Dated to the mid-second century, the Martyrdom is presented in the form of a letter from the church at Smyrna to the church in Philomelium "and to all the communities of the holy and catholic church sojourning in every place." Brought before the proconsul, Polycarp is encouraged to respect his age and swear by the genius of Caesar, and say, "Away with the atheists!" (Mart. Pol. 9.2). Polycarp responds, "If you vainly suppose that I will swear by the genius of Caesar, as you request, and pretend not to know who I am, listen carefully, I am a Christian" (Mart. Pol.).

Christian Self-Identification

From our twenty-first-century perspective, Polycarp's declaration, "I am a Christian," evokes a definition informed by two millennia of theological reflection. But by the end of the second century, what it meant to be "Christian" or even the use of that term was far from settled.

The importance of self-definition likely came to the fore with orthodox Christianity's eventual departure from the synagogue. The separation from Judaism was a complicated process that occurred at different times across different regions. As the Jewish Christian gospels suggest, not all Christians forsook their Jewish roots. The Acts of the Apostles and the Letter to Galatians indicate that the Jerusalem Church under the direction of James held to a more Jewish perspective with regard to upholding covenant requirements. But eventually, Christianity was seen as a distinct religion, no longer able to enjoy the imperial protections afforded Judaism.

During the time between its separation from Judaism and its triumphal emergence as a state-sanctioned religion, what was the entity that would be called Christianity? Or more importantly, to what did its practitioners think they belonged?

The earliest nomenclature appears to be Paul's *ekklesia*, found in 1 Thess 1:1, utilized by Matthew (16:18; 18:17) and perpetuated by Luke in Acts of the Apostles (5:11; 8:1, 3; 9:31; 11:22, etc., though Luke seems to prefer people of "the Way" as a corporate description, 9:2; 18:25–26; 19:9, 23; 22:4; 24:14, 22). By the turn of the century, this *ekklesia* has a formal structure, as seems to be indicated by Acts 14:23, where the churches appoint elders at Antioch Pisidia, and in Acts 15:4, where the *ekklesia*, apostles, and elders gather to meet Paul in Jerusalem. The Didache refers to the early communities as *ekklesia* (4.14; 9.4; 10.5; 11.11). The letters of Ignatius, the Letter of Polycarp to the Philippians, and 1 Clement recognize these structures and encourage respect of authority.

The actual term *christianos* is only found three times in the New Testament canon (Acts 11:26, 26:28; and 1 Pet 4:16), but is more widely used in the Apostolic Fathers. Because the name in the early years did not imply the institutional aspect that is today associated with it, many scholars now prefer to use "Christ followers." In the letter to the Philadelphians, Ignatius suggested that it was better to hear about Christianity (*christianismos*) from one who is circumcised than about Judaism from one who is not (Ign. *Eph.* 11.2). Ignatius identifies himself as a *christianos* (Ign. *Rom.* 3.2). But one should not settle for simply calling oneself a "Christian." He writes, "It is right, therefore, that we not just be called Christians, but that we actually be Christians" (Ign. *Magn.* 4.1). As a Christian, one is devoted to God (Ign. *Pol.* 7.3). However, the term *ekkeslia* appears much more frequently in the Letters of Ignatius, where he is referring to a corporate body.

The earliest nonreligious allusion to those who would become Christians is found in Tacitus. The *Annals* record the trial in 57 C.E. of Pomponia Graecina, the wife of Plautius. She is found innocent of belonging to an alien superstition (*superstitionis externae rea*), which was thought to be Christianity (*Ann.* 33.32).[33] The first explicit mention is found in *Annals* 15.44 where Nero blamed the *Christianos* for the fire in Rome. Suetonius also called the members of the early church *Christiani* (*Nero* 15) as did Pliny in his letters to Trajan (*Ep.* 10.96, 97).

By the mid-second century, the followers of Jesus Christ were called Christians by their supporters and by their detractors. Though the term began as a derogatory slur, it was quickly adopted and promoted. Along with an accepted terminology, various statements of creed were forged so that by the mid-second century, Christians not only shared a name but a common understanding of belief, at least regionally. It would be the tasks of the ecumenical councils of the fourth and fifth century to come to agreement as to what the universal church held in common.

CONCLUSION

The spiritualities emerging from the New Testament hold in tension the experience of the Resurrection with the horror of the Passion. In the New Testament texts, Jesus is presented as the Christ, whose Resurrection inaugurated the eschatological age. "The decisive battle against the powers of evil had been won and the final destiny of the world, a destiny of unceasing and abundant life (Jn 10:10), of light (Mt 4:16), of justice (2 Pet 3:13), and of joy (Lk 2:10) had been granted to humanity and the entire creation in the person of the risen Christ."[34] This profound act of God's resurrection of Jesus confirmed for his followers that the reign of God had begun and the Day of the Lord was imminent (Mt 25:13). In response, apostles and disciples were compelled to proclaim the good news (1 Cor 9:16).

But Christian spirituality is also rooted in the cross, the symbol of disappointment and death. Contrary to all expectations, the long-awaited messiah became the suffering Son of Man. "Christian spirituality was based on accepting as one's own the very scandal of the crucified Son of man, an acceptance that could lead to martyrdom. It was not, therefore, an easy and uncostly spirituality."[35]

One could not live as a Christian without holding in tension the joy of the Resurrection and the ever-present reality of the cross. But for early-second-century Christians, as evident in their literature, the waning of eschatological urgency and the delay of Jesus' return, coupled with civil conflict, forced a revisioning of expectations. Questions of identity, relationship to Judaism and its scriptures, appropriate response to the civil authorities, community organization, and the nature of God are reflected in the texts of early Christianity. What becomes apparent is that despite generic differences, regional variances, and theological perspectives, the literature of second-century Christianity presents a spirituality that is at its heart communal.

> Unlike other nonbiblical forms of spirituality, which could be understood individualistically, Christian spirituality was ecclesial in its nature. The church was not a means by which one would become spiritual in the sense that it provided the necessary instruction, worship, grace, and so on. The church was a set of relationships, which provide one with a new identity.[36]

Bonnie Thurston further defines early Christian spirituality in terms of qualities.

> Insofar as it has an "affective" quality, spirituality encompasses not only the will that decides to respond, but also the emotions. Insofar as it seeks to integrate faith and action, spirituality has an ethical component. Insofar as it is done in the company of others, it is communal.[37]

These qualities of the affective, ethical, and communal come to signify emerging Christian spirituality in the second century, a spirituality of the meantime.

QUESTIONS FOR REFLECTION

1. Jesus' disciples believed that his return was imminent. Now two thousand years later, we still await the Parousia. How might our lives be lived differently if we revived an "eschatological urgency"?

2. The biblical canon emerged in response to questions of orthodoxy. In the end, some early Christian texts were left on the cutting floor. What might we gain by reading the "extra-canonical" texts?

3. Early Christian literature appears in a variety of genres (apologies, gospels, acts, epistles, apocalypses, martyrdom accounts). If you were writing an account of your own faith journey, which genre would you find most suitable?

4. Both Ignatius and Polycarp faced their martyrdoms courageously, trusting that God would sustain them. How have you experienced a testing of your faith? What sustains you in those moments?

5. The literature known as the Apostolic Fathers addresses the theological questions and concerns of second-century Christians. What are the theological questions and concerns of our day and age and how might we address them?

NOTES

INTRODUCTION

1. I know of no work on the revelatory character of the Bible that surpasses in clarity and accessibility Sandra M. Schneiders, *The Revelatory Text: Interpreting the New Testament as Sacred Scripture*, 2nd ed. (Collegeville, MN: Liturgical Press, 1999). See also the Pontifical Biblical Commission, *The Interpretation of the Bible in the Church* (Boston: Pauline Books and Media, 1993).

2. Schneiders, *The Revelatory Text*, 41–42.

3. Karl Marx, *A Contribution to the Critique of Hegel's Philosophy of Right* (1844), preface.

I. WHAT IS SPIRITUALITY?

1. Lawrence S. Cunningham and Keith J. Egan, *Christian Spirituality: Themes from the Tradition* (New York: Paulist, 1996), 22–27.

2. Joann Wolski Conn, ed., *Women's Spirituality: Resources for Christian Development* (New York: Paulist, 1986), 3.

3. John Macquarrie, *Paths in Spirituality*, 2nd ed. (Harrisburg, PA: Morehouse, 1992), 40.

4. Edward Kinerk, S.J., "Toward a Method for the Study of Spirituality," *Review for Religious* 40, no. 1 (1981): 6.

5. Sandra M. Schneiders, "Spirituality in the Academy," *Theological Studies* 50, no. 3 (1989): 684.

6. Sandra M. Schneiders, "Theology and Spirituality: Strangers, Rivals, or Partners?" *Horizons* 13, no. 2 (1986): 264.

7. Quoted by Philip F. Sheldrake, *Images of Holiness: Explorations in Contemporary Spirituality* (Notre Dame, IN: Ave Maria, 1988), 2.

8. By using the traditional terminology for God, I choose convenience of expression over other concerns. At the same time, I fully agree with those who reject this word or who choose to spell it in its hyphenated form "G-d" as a way to demonstrate both its inadequacy and its sometimes idolatrous use. Chapter 2 discusses in more detail the problem of language for God and suggests criteria for discerning the adequacy of our God language and images.

9. See Joann Wolski Conn, "Toward Spiritual Maturity," in *Freeing Theology: The Essentials of Theology in Feminist Perspective*, ed. Catherine Mowry LaCugna (San Francisco: HarperCollins, 1993), 237.

10. Michael Downey, "Jean Vanier: Recovering the Heart," *Spirituality Today* 38 (1986): 339–40.

11. Historically, Christian tradition has embodied a unique claim to a fullness of divine revelation in Christ, once and for all. But see the recent critique of this perspective in Paul F. Knitter, *No Other Name?* (Maryknoll, NY: Orbis, 1985). See also Michael Amaladoss, S.J., "The Pluralism of Religions and the Significance of Christ," in *Asian Faces of Jesus*, ed. R. S. Sugirtharajah (Maryknoll, NY: Orbis, 1993), 85–103; and Diana L. Eck, *Encountering God: A Spiritual Journey from Bozeman to Banaras* (Boston: Beacon Press, 1993), especially chap. 7, "Is Our God Listening?"

12. "Hermeneutics of suspicion" is a phrase used to describe the interpreter's acknowledgment of ideological and perspectival distortions present, both consciously and unconsciously, in any text. In the field of history, for example, this suspicion takes the form of a recognition that all history is written from the perspective of its "winners" and cannot therefore but distort the loser's legitimate claims.

13. Alice Walker, *The Color Purple* (New York: Washington Square Press, 1982), 176–77.

14. Annice Callahan, R.S.C.J., "The Relationship between Spirituality and Theology," *Horizons* 16, no. 2 (1989): 268. On this important relationship, see also Schneiders, "Theology and Spirituality"; and Philip F. Sheldrake, "Some Continuing Questions: The Relationship between Spirituality and Theology," *Christian Spirituality Bulletin* 2, no. 1 (1994): 15–17.

15. William H. Shannon, "Contemplation, Contemplative Prayer," in *The New Dictionary of Catholic Spirituality*, ed. Michael Downey (Collegeville, MN: Liturgical Press, 1993), 209–14.

16. Sallie McFague, *The Body of God: An Ecological Theology* (Minneapolis: Fortress, 1993).

2. GOD BEYOND ALL NAMES

1. Quoted in Alister E. McGrath, *Christian Spirituality: An Introduction* (Oxford: Blackwell, 1999), 118.

2. *De Divinibus Niminibus* 1, 2, quoted in Elizabeth A. Johnson, *She Who Is: The Mystery of God in Feminist Theological Discourse* (New York: Crossroad, 1992), 115.

3. William L. Holladay, *Long Ago God Spoke: How Christians May Hear the Old Testament Today* (Minneapolis: Fortress, 1995), 23.

4. Walter Brueggemann, "The Book of Exodus," in *The New Interpreters' Bible*, vol. 1 (Nashville: Abingdon, 1994), 842.

5. Phyllis Trible, "God, Nature of, in the OT," in *Interpreters' Dictionary of the Bible Supplement* (Nashville: Abingdon, 1976), 368.

3. THE RIDDLE OF THE WORLD

1. Alexander Pope, "The Riddle of the World," in *The Golden Treasury of the Best Songs and Lyrical Poems*, ed. and rev. F. T. Palgrave and Oscar Williams (New York: Mentor Books, 1961), 266–67.

2. Richard P. McBrien, *Catholicism*, rev. ed. (New York: HarperCollins, 1994), 121–22.

3. McBrien, *Catholicism*, 122.

4. McBrien, *Catholicism*, 122.

5. The references to "Priestly" and "Yahwist" accounts refer to the traditional (though much debated) scholarly claim that there are four distinct narrative strands in the books of the Pentateuch: the "Yahwist" (ca. tenth century B.C.E.), the "Elhoist" (ca. ninth to eighth century B.C.E.), the "Priestly" (edited in the exile in the sixth century B.C.E.), and the "Deuteronomistic" (edited also during the exile and afterward). These narrative traditions took shape in different social-historical contexts in Israel's past and show, therefore, different interests and theological emphases.

6. Phyllis A. Bird, "'Male and Female He Created Them': Gen 1:27b in the Context of the Priestly Account of Creation," *Harvard Theological Review* 74, no. 2 (1981): 135.

7. The term *adam* is not a proper name but a term designating the human species as a whole, distinct from all the other creatures God made on the sixth day. In the second creation account (Gen 2:4b–3:24) the Yahwist writer connects the term *adam* with the related word *adamah*, the ground/earth, implying that the meaning of *adam* is best rendered as "the earth creature."

8. For a full discussion of this distinction, see Bird, "'Male and Female He Created Them,'" 158–59.

9. See the wonderful exposition of this text under the chapter heading "A Love Story Gone Awry," in Phyllis Trible, *God and the Rhetoric of Sexuality* (Philadelphia: Fortress, 1978), 72–143. Much of what follows is indebted to Trible's skillful analysis.

10. This Hebrew term *ezer* is not at all meant to signal a subordinate, inferior "other." For example, *ezer* is elsewhere used to name God's own active companionship to Israel (Deut 33:7, 26, 29; Ex 18:4; Ps 33:20, 115:9–11, 121:2, 124:8, 146:5).

11. Bird, "'Male and Female He Created Them,'" 158.

12. Trible, *God and the Rhetoric of Sexuality*, chap. 4.

4. THE GOD OF BLESSING AND SALVATION

1. See especially, José M. de Mesa and Lode Wostyn (Council of International Children's Ministries), *Doing Theology: Basic Realities and Processes* (Quezon City, the Philippines: CSP Books, 1982).

2. On this distinction, see Michael D. Guinan, *To Be Human before God: Insights from Biblical Spirituality* (Collegeville, MN: Liturgical Press, 1994), especially chap. 3, "Am I Saved or Am I Blessed?" 27–45. Two articles by Walter Brueggemann ("Trajectories in Old Testament Literature and the Sociology of Ancient Israel," *Journal of Biblical Literature* 98 [1979]: 161–85; and "A Convergence in Recent Old Testament Theologies," *Journal for the Study of the Old Testament* 18 [1980]: 2–18) have been pivotal in understanding these "trajectories." The writings especially of Claus Westermann have reclaimed the importance of "blessing theology": see *Blessing in the Bible and the Life of the Church* (Philadelphia: Fortress, 1978), *Elements of Old Testament Theology* (Atlanta: John Knox, 1982), and *What Does the Old Testament Say about God?* (Atlanta: John Knox, 1979), 25–52.

3. For the comparative comments that follow, I am indebted throughout to Guinan, *To Be Human before God*, 27–45.

4. I will not attempt to deal here with the important and critical questions of the historicity (or lack thereof) of the Exodus–Sinai traditions. My concern is with the biblical story as *story* and with the recognition that, when Israel began to tell the story of its faith, *this* is the story it told.

5. Guinan, *To Be Human before God*, 40.

6. Guinan, *To Be Human before God*, 40–41.

7. Westermann, *Elements of Old Testament Theology*, 106.

5. I HAVE HEARD THEIR CRY

1. An older generation remembers Cecil B. DeMille's film *The Ten Commandments* with Charlton Heston as Moses; younger generations know better the animated film *The Prince of Egypt*. In both, the Exodus drama with its climactic moment of the sea parting is an unforgettable spectacle.

2. The biblical site of Midian is the region to the east of the Sinai Peninsula, in what today is Saudi Arabia. Horeb is the name by which the Elhoist tradition identifies the holy mountain of God, elsewhere called "Sinai." Traditionally, this mountain is identified with Jebel Musa in the southern tip of the Sinai Peninsula.

3. Some other examples of theophanies include the appearances of God to Noah (Gen 6:13–21), Abraham (Gen 12:1–3, 15:1–21, 17:1–22), Jacob (Gen 28:10–18, 32:23–30), Moses at Sinai (Ex 19:16–25, 33:18–23), Jeremiah (Jer 1:4–10), and Paul (Acts 9:1–6), to name but a few.

4. Walter Brueggemann, "The Exodus Narrative as Israel's Articulation of Faith Development," in *Hope within History* (Atlanta: John Knox, 1987), 7–26.

5. The climax and culmination of this tradition will, of course, come in the New Testament, with its claims that Jesus, son of Mary and God's own Son, accomplishes this salvific work as no other before or since.

6. Brueggemann, "The Exodus Narrative as Israel's Articulation of Faith Development," 13–14.

7. The role and leadership of Miriam in the wilderness traditions are significant, not just here but elsewhere in the narrative (1 Chr 6:3; Deut 24:8–9; Ex 15:20–21; Mic 6:4; Num 12:1–15; 20:1, 26:59). See, on this theme, Phyllis Trible, "Bringing Miriam out of the Shadows," *Bible Review* 5, no. 1 (1989): 14–25, 34.

6. ROYAL POWER AND
THE COVENANT DREAM

1. The Hebrew text is better translated "Reed" Sea than Red Sea.

2. See Ex 13:21, 22, 24; Num 14:14. These same wilderness traditions are recalled in the postexilic period in Neh 9:12, 19.

3. Walter Brueggemann, "The Exodus Narrative as Israel's Articulation of Faith Development," in *Hope within History* (Atlanta: John Knox, 1987), 24–25.

4. As mentioned in the last chapter, there is no archaeological evidence whatsoever to document and validate the events narrated in the Exodus story. Archaeology can document the violent destruction by fire of some Canaanite cites at the time proposed for Israel's emergence. See especially George E. Mendenhall, *The Tenth Generation: The Origins of the Biblical Tradition* (Baltimore: Johns Hopkins University Press, 1973). It was Norman Gottwald (*The Tribes of Yahweh: A Sociology of the Religion of Liberated Israel 1250–1050 B.C.E.* [Maryknoll, NY: Orbis, 1979]) who developed Mendenhall's theories into a thesis of the "peasant revolt" in Canaan.

5. George E. Mendenhall, "The Monarchy," *Interpretation* 29 (1975): 157.

6. The Philistines were most probably migratory "sea peoples" who came from the Aegean islands to the coast of Palestine in the twelfth century B.C.E. after the downfall of the Mycenaean and Minoan civilizations. They possessed superior military power and had refined the skill of forging iron implements before the Israelites. The story of their great "giant," Goliath (1 Sam 17:1–58), illustrates well the mythic proportions with which the Bible views them.

7. PROPHETIC SPIRITUALITY

1. On the social function of prophecy in ancient Israel, see especially Robert R. Wilson, *Prophecy and Society in Ancient Israel* (Philadelphia: Fortress, 1980).

2. See the now classic study of Walter Brueggemann, *The Prophetic Imagination* (Philadelphia: Fortress, 1978).

3. Brueggemann, *The Prophetic Imagination*, 44–80.

4. Abraham J. Heschel, *The Prophets* (New York: Harper and Row, 1962), 3–26.

5. For all that follows, I rely closely on Heschel, *The Prophets*, 3–26.

6. Heschel, *The Prophets*, 4.

7. Heschel, *The Prophets*, 7, 9.

8. Tekoa was a small Judean town just south of Jerusalem, between Jerusalem and Bethlehem.

9. Bashan is the region to the east of the Sea of Galilee.

10. "Joseph" here refers to the Northern Kingdom as a whole. The ancestor Joseph received the tribal lands in Samaria that were incorporated into the Northern Kingdom.

11. Admah and Zeboim were ancient cities destroyed with Sodom and Gomorrah.

12. This oracle probably comes from the year 701 B.C.E. when, under King Hezekiah, the Assyrian ruler Sennacherib invaded Judah, leaving her in a state of vassalage.

13. Many think that Isaiah saw in the birth of the new king Hezekiah (727–698 B.C.E.) the possibility of a renewed and purified monarchy. This and other "messianic" prophecies from Isaiah became for Christians many centuries later the texts they turned to in order to interpret and describe Jesus' life and ministry.

14. Chaldea was the region in the southern Mesopotamian valley that became the center of the Babylonian Empire. The "land of the Chaldeans" is, therefore, Babylon. The Chebar is a tributary canal that flowed into the Euphrates near ancient Babylon and Nippur.

15. The claims to reappropriation of ancestral properties by the returning exiles, however, would cause fierce animosities and further hostility once they returned to the land of Palestine in 538 B.C.E.

16. Once a student who was unfamiliar with the Bible, upon hearing these words, exclaimed, "I thought Handel wrote it!" referring to the composer's famous work, *Messiah*.

8. WISDOM HAS BUILT HERSELF A HOUSE

1. The full list of "wisdom psalms" includes by most reckonings Ps 1, 37, 49, 73, 91, 112, 119, 127, 128, 133, 139.

2. Kathleen M. O'Connor, *The Wisdom Literature*, Message of Biblical Spirituality 5 (Collegeville, MN: Liturgical Press, 1988), 16.

3. Walter M. Abbott, S.J., ed., *The Documents of Vatican II* (Chicago: Follett, 1966), 199–200.

4. The following enumeration of characteristics follows closely that of Lawrence Boadt, *Reading the Old Testament: An Introduction* (New York: Paulist, 1984), 472–73.

5. O'Connor, *The Wisdom Literature*, 19.

6. This uses *fear* in the sense of religious awe and wonder before the magnificence of God.

7. Boadt, *Reading the Old Testament*, 474.

8. Here *satan* is a member of the divine council, not yet the personification of evil that he comes to be in the later tradition.

9. See Eccl 1:14, 1:17, 2:11, 2:17, 2:26, 4:4, 4:6, 4:16, 6:9.

10. See, for example, Dianne Bergant, *Israel's Wisdom Literature: A Liberation-Critical Reading* (Minneapolis: Fortress, 1997); and Robert Gordis, *The Song of Songs and Lamentations* (New York: KTAV, 1974).

11. Bergant, *Israel's Wisdom Literature*, 132.

12. The image of "hoops of steel" as the bond between those who love comes from a line in William Shakespeare's *Hamlet*, act 1, scene 3. Emlie Griffin (*Clinging: The Experience of Prayer* [San Francisco: Harper and Row, 1984], 36–43) regards this image as a fundamental description of the bond between those who love God and others.

13. Sirach is known also by its Latin title—Ecclesiasticus—or its Hebrew title—the Wisdom of Jesus Ben Sira.

14. Walter Brueggemann, "The Costly Loss of Lament," *Journal for the Study of the Old Testament* 36 (1986): 57–71.

9. CRISIS AND HOPE

1. The word "Jews" is derived from the Hebrew *yehudim* ("Judahites"), which appears first in the postexilic books of Ezra, Nehemiah, Daniel, and Esther. It was only during the years after the exile, in what is called the Second Temple Period, that the ancient texts, practices, and beliefs of Israel developed into the distinctive religious traditions, practices, and institutions eventually called Judaism, whose adherents are properly called Jews. This is why scholars generally use the terms "Israelites" and "Israelite religion" when referring to the preexilic period and "Judaism" and "Jews" when referring to the postexilic period. See Steven D. Fraade, s.v., "Judaism (Palestinian)," in *Anchor Bible Dictionary*, vol. 3 (New York: Doubleday, 1992), 1054–1061.

2. This does not mean that the ancients denied human causality. They were not blind to the normal political or economic reasons behind certain events. But they understood the gods to be their protectors and benefactors, as well as enforcers of divinely ordained institutions such as the monarchy. Therefore when a significant event occurred, they would seek the divine reality behind it. A good example of this "dual causality" is the story of the destruction of the Northern Kingdom of Israel by the Assyrians in 722 B.C.E. The biblical account tells us that King Hoshea conspired against Assyria and refused to pay his annual tribute, and so the king of Assyria retaliated (2 Kgs 17:4–5). But the

biblical authors affirm that the *real* reason behind the fall of the kingdom was because it had been consistently unfaithful to YHWH, who thus ordered its destruction using the human instrument of the Assyrian army (2 Kgs 17:7–23).

3. Ezekiel also looked forward to a renewal of God's people after the exile: "I will take you from the nations and gather you from all the countries, and bring you into your own land. I will sprinkle clean water upon you, and you shall be clean from all your uncleannesses, and from all your idols I will cleanse you. A new heart I will give you, and a new spirit I will put within you; and I will remove from your body the heart of stone and give you a heart of flesh. I will put my spirit within you and make you follow my statutes and be careful to observe my ordinances. Then you shall live in the land that I gave to your ancestors; and you shall be my people, and I will be your God" (Ezek 36:24–28).

4. George W. E. Nickelsburg describes eschatology as the expectation of "a decisive break between the present troubled time—an end to that time—and the beginning of a new age in which God's intentions at creation will be realized and God's sovereignty will extend over all humanity finally and forever" (*Ancient Judaism and Christian Origins: Diversity, Continuity, and Transformation* [Minneapolis: Fortress, 2003], 122).

5. The Hasmonean dynasty was established by the Maccabees, an anti-Hellenistic family that fought against Antiochus IV Epiphanes and the Seleucids until they were able to attain the throne and establish a dynasty that reigned from 140 B.C.E. to 37 B.C.E. The Hasmoneans, while Jewish, were not in the Davidic line.

6. For a fuller review of Jewish apocalyptic literature, see the standard work of John J. Collins, *The Apocalyptic Imagination: An Introduction to Jewish Apocalyptic Literature*, 3rd ed. (Grand Rapids, MI: Eerdmans, 2016). For an excellent and thorough exploration of the history of the Hellenistic and Roman periods and the great variety of Jewish works produced in those years, not all of which were eschatological or apocalyptic, see George W. E. Nickelsburg, *Jewish Literature between the Bible and the Mishnah*, 2nd ed. (Minneapolis: Fortress, 2005).

7. Angels or messengers from God appear from time to time in the Bible, but in earlier texts they play minor roles and are not named. In later literature, such as Tobit and Daniel, angels become key figures with names and significant roles (Raphael in Tobit, Michael in Daniel). Demons are virtually nonexistent in pre-Hellenistic biblical texts. The *satan* who appears in Job and Zechariah is a member of God's heavenly court who, while unpleasant and even cruel, is nevertheless not conceived of as demonic. It is only later that this figure develops into Satan, the Prince of Evil. Apocalyptic literature is populated with angelic and demonic figures (often spoken of as fallen angels), which is a good indication of the stress such literature placed on the supernatural realities thought to be behind the distressing events on earth.

8. The idea that the good receive good things and the wicked bad things is called retribution, and it strongly informs the worldview of much of the Bible. The book of Proverbs, a repository of traditional wisdom sayings, is filled with

examples of this perspective: "The LORD does not let the righteous go hungry, but he thwarts the craving of the wicked" (Prov 10:3). Here, as in most of the Old Testament, the assumption is that retribution happens in this life, not in an afterlife. This raised problems, however, because experience showed that often the righteous suffered and the wicked prospered. Ecclesiastes and Job, in different ways, address this conundrum. The problem became particularly acute when Jews suffered horrible deaths because of their fidelity to God and their religious tradition. It was during this time that we begin to see the development of the concept of retribution not in this life, but in the next.

9. The work called *1 Enoch* is a collection of apocalyptic texts composed over a long period, from around 300 B.C.E. to the first century C.E. For a recent introduction and translation of *1 Enoch*, see George W. E. Nickelsburg and James C. VanderKam, *1 Enoch: A New Translation* (Minneapolis: Fortress, 2004). Citations of *1 Enoch* in this chapter are from this translation.

10. For a discussion of the "Psalms of Solomon," see Nickelsburg, *Jewish Literature between the Bible and the Mishnah*, 238–47.

11. Most scholars accept Collins' definition of an "apocalypse" as "a genre of revelatory literature with a narrative framework, in which a revelation is mediated by an otherworldly being to a human recipient, disclosing a transcendent reality which is both temporal, insofar as it envisages eschatological salvation, and spatial insofar as it involves another, supernatural world" (*Apocalyptic Imagination*, 5). In the Bible, only Daniel and Revelation fit this definition. Nevertheless, elsewhere in both testaments can be found elements typical in apocalyptic works.

12. See, for example, Ps 74:12–14; Ps 89:12–13; Job 26:12–13; Isa 27:1.

13. For a discussion of this passage, see Collins, *Apocalyptic Imagination*, 98–104. See also Frederick J. Murphy, *Apocalypticism in the Bible and Its World: A Comprehensive Introduction* (Grand Rapids, MI: Baker, 2012), 79–83.

14. For example, the visitors to Abraham and Sarah in Gen 18:1–33 and Joshua's encounter with the angelic commander of the army of the LORD in Josh 5:13–15.

15. Joseph A. Fitzmyer defines a "messiah" as "an eschatological figure, an anointed human agent of God, who was to be sent by Him as a deliverer and was awaited in the end time" (*The One Who Is to Come* [Grand Rapids, MI: Eerdmans, 2007], 1). Not every depiction of a messianic figure from the Hellenistic and Roman periods conceived of him as human, however, so this definition may be slightly too narrow.

16. For more discussion of the variety of ways the messiah (or messiahs) was conceived, see Fitzmyer, *The One Who Is to Come*, 82–133, and John J. Collins, *The Scepter and the Star: Messianism in Light of the Dead Sea Scrolls*, 2nd ed. (Grand Rapids, MI: Eerdmans, 2010).

17. Collins, *The Scepter and the Star*, 50.

18. Qumran texts: 4Q161 and 4Q174.

19. *Psalms of Solomon* 17. A modern translation of the *Psalms of Solomon* can be found in Albert Pietersma and Benjamin G. Wright, eds., *New English Translation of the Septuagint* (New York: Oxford University Press, 2007).

20. It is even cited in Jude 14–15, which suggests that it was considered authoritative by at least some Jews. *First Enoch* is part of the canon of the Ethiopian Orthodox Church today.

10. THAT MAN JESUS

1. K. C. Hanson and Douglas E. Oakman, *Palestine in the Time of Jesus: Social Structures and Social Conflicts* (Minneapolis: Fortress, 1998), 70.

2. Hanson and Oakman, *Palestine in the Time of Jesus*, 104–5.

3. On these questions of taxes and the economy of Palestine, see Marcus J. Borg, *Jesus, a New Vision: Spirit, Culture, and the Life of Discipleship* (San Francisco: HarperCollins, 1991), 83–86; Douglas E. Oakman, *Jesus and the Economic Questions of His Day* (Lewiston, NY: Edwin Mellen Press, 1986); and Hanson and Oakman, *Palestine in the Time of Jesus*, 99–129.

4. The classic study of this theme is that of Helmut Koester, "One Jesus and Four Primitive Gospels," *Harvard Theological Review* 61 (1968).

5. The customary names of the gospel writers, Matthew, Mark, Luke, and John, will be used here even though, in fact, we know virtually nothing about who these writers actually were.

6. John R. Donahue, S.J., "Jesus as the Parable of God in the Gospel of Mark," *Interpretation* 32 (1978): 385.

7. See Elizabeth Struthers Malbon, "Fallible Followers: Women and Men in the Gospel of Mark," *Semeia* 28 (1983): 29–48.

8. The designation "Q" (for the German word *Quelle*—source) is a scholarly abbreviation for a hypothetical collection of Jesus' sayings presumed to have been used by both Matthew and Luke in the writing of their gospels.

9. See Mt 1:22–23, 2:5–6, 2:15, 2:17–18, 2:23, 4:14–16, 8:17, 12:17–21, 13:35, 21:4–5, 27:9–10.

10. The literary structure of Matthew's gospel is carefully organized around five parts or "books," each having a narrative and a discourse section: book 1, 3:1–7:29; book 2, 8:1–11:1; book 3, 11:2–13:52; book 4, 13:53–18:35; book 5, 19:1–25:46. The prologue, or Infancy Narratives (Mt 1–2), provides the initial context, and the gospel concludes with the story of the Passion and Resurrection of Jesus (Mt 26–28).

11. Raymond F. Collins, s.v., "Beatitudes," *Anchor Bible Dictionary*, vol. 1 (New York: Doubleday, 1992), 630.

12. In Isaiah's day the sign was probably referring to the birth of the child to King Hezekiah, signaling a new beginning of a reign of justice and peace.

13. The "Spiritual Exercises" of Ignatius Loyola, for example, give elaborate reflection on how one discerns the Spirit, and they provide detailed rules for recognizing the movement of the Spirit of God in both the individual and the community.

14. Eugene LaVerdiere, S.S.S., *Luke* (Wilmington, DE: Michael Glazier, 1980), 287–88.

15. Robert Kysar, *John: The Maverick Gospel* (Atlanta: John Knox, 1976).

16. To speak of "high" and "low" Christology is to describe the very exalted, divine (high) or the ordinary, human (low) characteristics of Jesus and his relationship to the God of Israel.

17. There are forty-two references to Jesus as the one sent from God in the gospel of John, and the great prayer of Jesus in John 17 culminates with a prayer that the world may come to believe that God has sent Jesus: "As you, Father, are in me and I am in you, may they also be in us, so that the world may believe that you have sent me" (Jn 17:21).

18. Barbara E. Bowe, "John 13 and Christian Service: A Study in Christian Spirituality," *The Bible Today* 32, no. 4 (1994): 223–27.

11. PAULINE SPIRITUALITY

1. Jerome Murphy-O'Connor, O.P., "On the Road and on the Sea with St. Paul: Traveling Conditions in the First Century," *Bible Review 1*, no. 2 (Summer 1985): 38–47.

2. See F. W. Horn, s.v., "Holy Spirit," *Anchor Bible Dictionary*, vol. 3 (New York: Doubleday, 1992), 260–80.

3. Dennis E. Smith and Hal Taussig, *Many Tables: The Eucharist in the New Testament and Liturgy* (Philadelphia: Trinity Press International, 1990).

4. A good indicator of the shift in Catholic thinking on the meaning of this verse can be illustrated by the two editions of *The Jerusalem Bible* (1966) and *The New Jerusalem Bible* (revised with notes in 1990). In the first edition, the notes comment that to "discern the Body" referred to an awareness of Christ's sacramental presence at the communal meal. In the revised edition, the notes explain that to "discern the body" is to be cognizant of the needs of the community.

5. Jeremy Langford, *God Moments: Why Faith Really Matters to a New Generation* (Maryknoll, NY: Orbis, 2001).

12. A NEW HEAVEN AND A NEW EARTH

1. Stephen G. Wilson, s.v., "Jewish–Christians Relations 70–170 C.E.," *Anchor Bible Dictionary*, vol. 3, 834–39.

2. See Paul D. Hanson (*The Dawn of Apocalyptic* [Philadelphia: Fortress, 1975]), who uses these helpful characterizations of "visionaries and pragmatists."

3. Victor Paul Furnish, s.v., "Ephesians, Epistle to the," *Anchor Bible Dictionary*, vol. 2, 535–42.

4. Furnish, "Ephesians," 535.

5. Harold W. Attridge, s.v., "Hebrews, Epistle to the," *Anchor Bible Dictionary*, vol. 3, 105.

6. Some also propose that the fragments might be from a statue of Titus (79–81 C.E.). For this view, see Steven J. Friesen, *Imperial Cults and the Apocalypse of John: Reading Revelation in the Ruins* (London: Oxford University Press, 2001).

7. Suetonius, *The Life of Domitian*, trans. J. C. Rolfe (New York: Macmillan, 1914), 7–14.

8. The Branch Davidian sect, with roots in the Seventh Day Adventist movement, was an intensely apocalyptic group awaiting the end time while holed up in a farmhouse near Waco, Texas. On April 19, 1993, U.S. federal marshals raided the complex and precipitated a conflagration in which eighty-six members of the Branch Davidian sect died.

9. See especially Barbara Rossing, *The Choice between Two Cities: Whore, Bride, and the Empire in the Apocalypse*, Harvard Theological Studies 48 (Valley Forge, PA: Trinity Press International, 1999).

10. E. Theodore Mullen Jr., s.v., "Divine Assembly," *Anchor Bible Dictionary*, vol. 2, 217.

11. See the description in Gen 2:9. There are also clear echoes here in Revelation of the vision of the waters streaming from the Temple in Ezek 47:1–12 and in Zech 14:8.

12. Contrast, of course, the many references that prohibit face-to-face contact with God or restrict that privilege only to certain individuals: Deut 5:4, 34:10; Ex 3:6, 32:30, 33:11, 34:29; Gen 33:10, 48:11; Num 12:8, 14:14. See also the description in Rev 13:16 of those who worship the beast about whom it was said that they were marked "on the right hand or the forehead" with the name of the beast.

CONCLUSION

1. On this metaphor, see Eugene H. Peterson, "Eat This Book: The Holy Community at Table with the Holy Scripture," *Theology Today* 56, no. 1 (1999): 5–17.

2. I borrow again the phrase of Phyllis Trible, *Texts of Terror: Literary-Feminist Readings of Biblical Narratives* (Philadelphia: Fortress, 1984).

3. Peterson, "Eat This Book," 8.

4. Peterson, "Eat This Book," 10–11.

5. Richard P. McBrien, "Criteria for Christian Spirituality," in *Ministry: A Theologcial-pastoral Handbook* (San Francisco: Harper and Row, 1987).

6. See the very insightful discussion of this passage and its implications for spirituality in Donal Dorr, *Integral Spirituality: Resources for Community, Peace, Justice, and the Earth* (Maryknoll, NY: Orbis, 1990), 1–5, to which I owe this final word.

EPILOGUE

1. Hans Conzelmann, *The Theology of St. Luke*, trans. Geoffrey Buswell (New York: Harper & Row, 1961), 16–17.

2. John D. Zizioulas, "Primitive Christianity: The Original Spirituality," *Church* 3.3 (1987): 11.

3. Early Christianity did not produce distinctive or identifiable material culture until the third century when catacomb art began to depict biblical scenes. See Larry W. Hurtado, *The Earliest Christian Artifacts: Manuscripts and Christian Origins* (Grand Rapids, MI: Eerdmans, 2006). Likely the oldest identified "church" structure is the *domus ecclesiae* found at Dura-Europos on the Euphrates River in present-day Syria. See L. Michael White, *The Social Origins of Christian Architecture*, vol. 2, *Texts and Monuments for the Christian Domus Ecclesiae in Its Environment* (Valley Forge, PA: Trinity Press International, 1997).

4. Helpful introductions to the literature of this period include Helen Rhee, *Early Christian Literature: Christ and Culture in the Second and Third Centuries* (New York: Routledge, 2005); Clayton N. Jefford, *Reading the Apostolic Fathers: A Student's Introduction*, 2nd. ed. (Grand Rapids, MI: Baker, 2012); and Fred Lapham, *An Introduction to the New Testament Apocrypha* (London: T & T Clark, 2003).

5. Eusebius, *The History of the Church from Christ to Constantine*, trans. G. A. Williamson (New York: Penguin Books, 1965), 190.

6. Translation of Muratorian Canon 73 by Bruce M. Metzger, *The Canon of the New Testament* (Oxford: Oxford University Press, 1997), 307.

7. Harry Y. Gamble, *Books and Readers in the Early Church: A History of Early Christian Texts* (New Haven, CT: Yale University Press, 1995), 216.

8. Nicola Denzey Lewis, *Introduction to "Gnosticism"* (Oxford: Oxford University Press, 2013), 20.

9. For a more detailed discussion, see Bart D. Ehrman, *Lost Christianities: The Battles for Scripture and the Faiths We Never Knew* (New York: Oxford University Press, 2003).

10. Rhee, *Early Christian Literature*, 11–12.

11. Dianne Bergant, "Introduction to the Bible," in *The Collegeville Bible Commentary*, ed. Dianne Bergant and Robert Karris (Collegeville, MN: Liturgical Press, 1989), 3–34; here 10.

12. "There is no indication from the text of 1 Clement . . . that a monarchical episcopacy was in place in Rome, or that Clement was *the* bishop" (Barbara Ellen Bowe, *A Church in Crisis: Ecclesiology and Paraenesis in Clement of Rome*, Harvard Dissertations in Religion [Minneapolis: Fortress, 1988], 1–3).

13. Jefford, *Apostolic Fathers*, xxii.

14. Philip Francis Esler, ed., *The Early Christian World*, vol. 2 (London: Routledge, 2000), 158–63.

15. Aristotle outlined three species of rhetoric: juridical or forensic, deliberative, and epideictic. Forensic rhetoric belongs to the law court, where orators argue about something that has occurred. The audience acts as a jury deter-

mining which party has best stated its case. Political speeches are an example of deliberative rhetoric, in which an orator attempts to encourage or discourage a particular action. Epideictic rhetoric hopes to enhance knowledge and understanding through praise or blame. Eulogies are often considered epideictic (*Rhet.* 1.3).

16. Columba Stewart, "Christian Spirituality during the Roman Empire (100–600)," in *Blackwell Companion to Christian Spirituality*, ed. Arthur Holder (Oxford: Blackwell, 2005), 73–89, here 73.

17. For more information on the genre of the apocryphal acts, see: Ronald F. Hock, J. Bradley Chance, and Judith Perkins, *Ancient Fiction and Early Christian Narrative*. SBL SymS 6 (Atlanta, GA: Scholars Press, 1998), and Hans-Josef Klauck, *The Apocryphal Acts of the Apostles* (Waco, TX: Baylor University Press, 2008).

18. Wilhelm Schneemelcher and R. McL. Wilson, eds., *New Testament Apocrypha,* vol. 2. (Louisville, KY: Westminster John Knox Press, 1992), 76–83.

19. Schneemelcher and Wilson, *New Testament Apocrypha,* 81.

20. Lapham, *An Introduction to the New Testament Apocrypha,* 18.

21. Stewart, "Christian Spirituality during the Roman Empire," 83.

22. Richard Norris, "Apocryphal Writings and Acts of the Martyrs," in *The Cambridge History of Early Christian Literature*, ed. F. Young et al. (Cambridge: Cambridge University Press, 2005), 35.

23. Rhee, *Early Christian Literature,* 4.

24. Jefford, *Apostolic Fathers,* xxiv–xxvi.

25. Jefford, *Apostolic Fathers,* xxiv.

26. For a thorough analysis of the Didache, see Kurt Niederwimmer, *The Didache*, Hermeneia (Minneapolis: Fortress, 1998).

27. Jefford, *Apostolic Fathers,* 33.

28. Michael W. Holmes, *The Apostolic Fathers: Greek Texts and English Translation*, 3rd ed. (Grand Rapids, MI: Baker, 2007), 353. All subsequent quotations from *The Apostolic Fathers* are taken from Holmes' translation.

29. Arthur Denner Howell-Smith, *Jesus Not a Myth* (London: Watts, 1942), 120–21.

30. Carolyn Osiek, *The Shepherd of Hermas*, Hermeneia (Minneapolis: Fortress, 1999), 36.

31. Jeffrey McCurry, "'Indeed You Will Have No Enemy': A Spirituality of Moral Vision in the Didache," *Spiritus* 7 (2007): 193–202, here 195.

32. McCurry, "'Indeed You Will Have No Enemy'," 197.

33. T. D. Barnes, "Legislation Against the Christians," *Journal of Roman Studies* 58 (1968): 32–58.

34. Zizioulas, "Primitive Christianity," 11.

35. Zizioulas, "Primitive Christianity," 11.

36. Zizioulas, "Primitive Christianity," 13.

37. Bonnie Thurston, "The New Testament in Christian Spirituality," in *Blackwell Companion to Christian Spirituality*, ed. Arthur Holder (Oxford: Blackwell, 2005), 55–70, here 58.

GLOSSARY

androcentric a male-centered perspective in which the male norm and the human norm are collapsed and become identical.

apartheid the name given to the system of absolute racial separation between blacks and whites in South Africa that officially came to an end in May 1994 with the election victory of the first black president, Nelson Mandela.

apocalyptic (Greek: *apokalypsis* or "uncovering, revelation") refers to a complex of worldviews and literature marked by an expectation of an imminent end of the present world as a result of a final battle between the forces of good and evil, to be followed by a great judgment and eternal happiness for the righteous, eternal punishment or extinction for the wicked.

apocryphal (Greek: "hidden") is the term used to describe noncanonical gospels and acts written in the second to sixth centuries.

apodictic law laws formulated in an absolute and universal sense, such as the Ten Commandments: "Thou shall not . . ." or "Thou shall. . . ."

apology (Greek: *apologia* or "defense") a verbal defense of one's conduct.

apophatic spirituality (Greek: "without images") affirms the absolute unknowability of God and seeks union with God through silence, negation, and surrender to the unknown.

Apostolic Fathers the oldest collection of writings considered orthodox but excluded from the New Testament canon. These fifteen documents by nine different authors encompass a variety of genres and reflect the concerns of second-century Christian communities.

apostolic spirituality denotes an active way of discipleship, a following in the footsteps of Jesus, in which believers participate in and further his saving mission.

Ark of the Covenant a portable rectangular "chest" in which the tablets of the covenant received by Moses were kept. The ark was carried with the Israelites in the wilderness and into the promised land.

Babylonian exile the period from 597 to 538 B.C.E. when the Babylonian armies under Nebuchadnezzar, having conquered Palestine, destroyed Jerusalem (587) and carried off many of its people to exile in Babylon.

Bible (Greek and Latin: *biblia* or "books") designates the Old or First Testament sacred to Jews and the New or Second Testament, a collection of Christian writings. Together these books make up the Bible for Christians. Two versions of the Old Testament circulated among Jews, the Hebrew original and a Greek translation (forty-six books) that contained additional books (such as the Wisdom of Solomon) highly regarded by Greek-speaking Jews. The New Testament (twenty-seven books) includes gospels, letters, and other types of early Christian writings.

biblical anthropology the Bible's collective wisdom and perspective on what it means to be human: our origin and destiny and our purpose in living within the human community.

biblical spirituality a way of life and faith inspired by the biblical writings and their multifaceted vision about the nature of God, human creatures, the world, and our ultimate destiny.

blessing theology a name given to the overarching biblical perspective that stresses God's bestowal of blessings on all creation at every moment and the innate goodness of humankind. Emphasis in this perspective is given to order and harmony in creation and to the royal authority on earth.

Canaan, Canaanite name in the Old Testament for the land of Palestine on the eastern shore of the Mediterranean Sea whose inhabitants were called "Canaanites."

canon, canonical (Greek: *kanon* or "measuring rod") a term to designate those sacred writings from Jewish and Christian authors deemed by the community of faithful to be officially authoritative and normative for faith.

Christology, Christological a theological discipline that studies the understanding and nature of Christ, his divinity and humanity, and his saving action in human redemption.

contemplative refers to that transforming and unitive movement, in love, toward the mystery of God. It involves a person's desire or longing for God, together with the realization that God lives in all created things, and it implies the corresponding effort to make oneself present to and aware of this presence of God through stillness and silence.

covenant theology a term describing Israelites' claim that God entered into a binding agreement (expressed and reiterated through Abraham, Noah, Moses, David, etc.) with them as a people that established both divine promises and their corresponding responsibilities for holiness and right living.

Decalogue, Ten Commandments the set of ten moral laws written on stone tablets believed to have been given by God to Moses on Sinai (Ex 20:1–17; repeated in Deut 5:6–21).

desert monastics men and women who, in the spirit of the Hebrew prophet Elijah, went into the desert regions to pursue an ascetical life of prayer and penitence either as solitary hermits or as members of communal groups.

diaspora (Greek: literally, "scattering") refers to the movement of Jewish people from their biblical home in Palestine to live throughout the known world. This movement happened especially after the Assyrian destruction of Samaria (721 B.C.E.) and then again after Jerusalem was destroyed by the Babylonians (587 B.C.E.).

Didache (Greek: "teaching") the shortened title for "The Teachings of the Twelve Apostles," an early church manual likely written at the end of the first century or the beginning of the second.

Docetism (Greek: *dokein* or "to seem or appear") a heresy that held Jesus Christ was not truly human but only appeared to be so.

Eastern and Western Christianity terms to designate divisions stemming from the origins of Christianity in the Roman Empire. The eastern regions centered in Antioch, Alexandria, Jerusalem, and Constantinople, whereas the origins of the western churches were in Italy, Spain, Gaul, and Africa. Theological controversies (especially at the Council of Chalcedon [451 C.E.] and the Great Western Schism of 1054) further divided the Christian world into East and West.

Ebionites (Hebrew: literally, "the poor") refers to a group of Jewish Christians perhaps originating in Jerusalem who, though they accepted Jesus, remained very close to the practices of Judaism.

ecological spirituality a contemporary dimension of spirituality that affirms the unity and harmony of all created things and stresses the need for protection of and care for the environment as a responsibility of faith.

Elohist writer an anonymous author responsible for one of the strands of tradition in the Pentateuch, probably originating from the northern tribes and showing favor for God's name as Elohim.

eschatology (Greek: *eschatos* or "last, ultimate") refers to a belief that one day the present, imperfect age will come to an end, God will transform the world in accord with God's vision for creation, and God's sovereignty over all of humanity will finally and forever be confirmed.

exodus (Greek: a "going out") a term that refers to the story in the book of Exodus describing the escape from Egypt of a small band of Hebrew slaves under the leadership of Moses, Aaron, and Miriam and their journey to the land of Canaan.

faith a dynamic term describing the quality of trust, reliance on, and fidelity to God or Christ.

Gnosticism (Greek: *gnosis* or "knowledge") a broad category of dualistic thinking that held that matter was evil while the spirit was good. Gnostics believed they had been given secret "knowledge" and were destined for salvation. Those without such knowledge had no hope of salvation.

Hellenization, Hellenism the influence and adoption of Greek culture from Greece eastward to the Indus Valley of India after the conquests of Alexander the Great (333–330 B.C.E.). This influence persisted throughout the Roman period down to the time of Constantine (i.e., 333 B.C.E.–ca. 312 C.E.).

heresy/heretic (Greek *hairesis* or "choice" which came to mean a "party" or "sect"). A term used to describe those whose Christian beliefs and practices diverged from emerging orthodoxy. See **Docetism** and **Gnosticism**.

hermetical or monastic tradition (Greek: *eremos* or "desert") refers to the tradition and writings of the men and women who went into the desert in search of an ascetical life of prayer.

Holy of Holies denotes the inner sanctum, the most holy place of the Temple in Jerusalem where the Ark of the Covenant was enshrined and the invisible presence of YHWH was thought to dwell.

Jewish Christians term designating those Christians who were converts from Judaism but who remained in thought and practice very close to the traditions of Judaism.

kataphatic a spiritual tradition that affirms that God the Creator can be known, by way of analogy, through images, symbols, and concepts drawn from human experience in the created world.

messiah (Hebrew: *mashiach* or "anointed;" Greek: *christos*) an eschatological figure "anointed" by God as agent of the new age and deliverer of God's people.

metaphor, metaphorical the application of a word or phrase to an object or concept that it does not literally denote in order to suggest a comparison.

orthodoxy (Greek: *ortho* or "upright or straight," hence "correct" + *doxa* or "opinion." The term came to refer to the "correct belief" about Christian creeds, practices, and ecclesial structures, and stood in opposition to heresy (from the Greek *hairesis* meaning "a personal choice or opinion").

Parousia (Greek: the state of being present). In early Christianity, believers awaited Jesus' "second coming," which would signal the end of the age and the consummation of the reign of God.

patriarchy, patriarchal a male pyramid of graded subordination of females to males and the whole structure of "father-ruled society."

patristic writers (Latin: *patres* or "fathers") Christian authors writing from the end of the first century C.E. to the eighth century C.E. who shaped the development of theology and doctrine.

Pentateuch (Greek: "five scrolls") the first five books of the Bible: Genesis, Exodus, Leviticus, Numbers, and Deuteronomy.

postmodernism name given to the contemporary worldview that is characterized by fragmentation, by a belief that everything we claim to "know" is partial and perspectival; hence relativism is universal, and there is no overarching grand story that unites all the disparate elements.

praxis (Greek: literally, "practice, action") refers to one's deeds or actions.

preexilic, postexilic terms designating the relationship of an event or a movement as either before or after the Babylonian exile (597–538 B.C.E.).

priestly writer the supposed author of the latest strand of tradition in the Pentateuch or a member of the priestly class in Judaism concerned especially with ritual or cultic matters, genealogical tables, and legal traditions of all kinds.

Promised land refers to the land believed to be promised by God to Abraham (Gen 12:1–9) referred to elsewhere by its name of Canaan.

prophet one who claims to possess the spirit of God and who proclaims God's words of both hope and challenge to the people.

royal Judahite theology the claim that God had chosen David and his successors to rule over God's people "forever." In preexilic

times the Davidic kings ruled over the Southern Kingdom of
Judah.

sacrament (Latin: *sacramentum* or "sign") a sacred word or action
that communicates the divine presence and paschal mystery of
Christ's death and resurrection.

saving theology the dominant biblical tradition that stresses God's
mighty acts of rescue and liberation for humankind, beginning
from the Exodus event as the defining paradigm.

Semitic according to Genesis 10:21–31, the peoples descended
from Noah's son Shem. More generally today it refers to the
linguistic group including Akkadian, Aramaic, Hebrew, and Arabic.

spirituality our everyday, lived experience of faith including our
beliefs, prayers, liturgical expressions, and good works of righteousness.

Synoptic gospels (Greek: "with one eye") the gospels of Matthew,
Mark, and Luke that share much common tradition and follow
for the most part the narrative sequence established by Mark.

Temple the sacred building housing the Ark of the Covenant and
center for sacrificial worship first built under Solomon circa 950
B.C.E., destroyed and then rebuilt circa 515 B.C.E., and finally re-
modeled by Herod the Great from circa 20 B.C.E. to 60 C.E. before
it was finally destroyed by the Romans in 70 C.E.

tetragrammaton (YHWH) a term designating the four Hebrew
consonants of the divine name given to Moses by the voice from
the burning bush in Exodus 3.

theophany (Greek: an "appearance of a god") designates the many
biblical accounts (e.g., Gen 32:26–32) of God appearing in various ways to humans.

Ugaritic language spoken by the inhabitants of the Canaanite city of
Ugarit (Arabic: Ras Shamra) in modern Syria where cuneiform
tablets were found that shed light on the early settlement of the
Israelites in Canaan.

Vatican II the twenty-first ecumenical council in the history of the
Church, convened by Pope John XXIII on October 9, 1962, and
closed by Pope Paul VI on December 8, 1965. It set the agenda
for Church reform for the past forty years and into the future.

Yahwist the anonymous author of one of the strands of tradition in
the Pentateuch that reflects especially the theology of the Southern Kingdom of Judah with its emphasis on the Davidic covenant.

BIBLIOGRAPHY

GENERAL WORKS

Abbott, Walter M., S.J., ed. *The Documents of Vatican II*. Chicago: Follett, 1966.

Alexander, J. "What Do Recent Writers Mean by Spirituality?" *Spirituality Today* 32 (1980): 247–56.

Amaladoss, Michael, S.J. "The Pluralism of Religions and the Significance of Christ." In *Asian Faces of Jesus*, edited by R. S. Sugirtharajah, 85–103. Maryknoll, NY: Orbis, 1993.

Balthasar, Hans Urs von. "The Gospel as Norm and Test of All Spirituality in the Church." *Concilium* 9 (1965): 14–17.

Barnes, T. D. "Legislation Against the Christians." *Journal of Roman Studies* 58 (1968): 32–58.

Baur, F. *Life in Abundance: A Contemporary Spirituality*. New York: Paulist, 1983.

Bergant, Dianne. "Introduction to the Bible." In *The Collegeville Bible Commentary*, edited by Dianne Bergant and Robert Karris, 3–34. Collegeville, MN: Liturgical Press, 1989.

———. *The World Is a Prayerful Place: Spirituality and Life*. Collegeville, MN: Liturgical Press, 1991.

Billy, Dennis J., C.S.S.R., and Donna Lynn Orsuto, eds. *Spirituality and Morality: Integrating Prayer and Action*. New York: Paulist, 1996.

Bruteau, Beatrice. "Eucharistic Ecology and Ecological Spirituality." *Cross Currents* 40 (1990–1991): 499–514.

Burton-Christie, Douglas. *The Word in the Desert: Scripture and the Quest for Holiness in Early Christian Monasticism*. New York: Oxford University Press, 1993.

Callahan, Annice, R.S.C.J. "The Relationship between Spirituality and Theology." *Horizons* 16, no. 2 (1989): 266–74.

Carter, Harold. *The Prayer Tradition of Black People*. Valley Forge, PA: Judson Press, 1976.

Casey, Michael. *The Undivided Heart*. Petersham, MA: St. Bede's Publications, 1994.

Cherian, C. M. "Now My Eyes See Thee: The Bible as a Record of Religious Experience." *Review for Religious* 32, no. 4 (1973): 1002–11.

Collins, Adela Y. "An Inclusive Biblical Anthropology." *Theology Today* 34 (1978): 358–69.

Conn, Joann Wolski. "Toward Spiritual Maturity." In *Freeing Theology: The Essentials of Theology in Feminist Perspective*, edited by Catherine Mowry LaCugna, 235–59. San Francisco: HarperCollins, 1993.

Conn, Joann Wolski, ed. *Women's Spirituality: Resources for Christian Development*. New York: Paulist, 1986.

Cunningham, Lawrence S., and Keith J. Egan. *Christian Spirituality: Themes from the Tradition*. New York: Paulist, 1996.

de Mesa, José M., and Lode Wostyn. *Doing Theology: Basic Realities and Processes*. Quezon City, Philippines: CSP Books, 1982.

Doohan, Leonard. "Scripture and Contemporary Spirituality." *Spirituality Today* 42 (1990): 62–74.

Dorr, Donal. *Spirituality and Justice*. Maryknoll, NY: Orbis, 1984.

————. *Integral Spirituality: Resources for Community, Peace, Justice, and the Earth*. Maryknoll, NY: Orbis, 1990.

Downey, Michael. "Jean Vanier: Recovering the Heart." *Spirituality Today* 38 (1986): 339–40.

————. "Understanding Christian Spirituality: Dress Rehearsal for a Method." *Spirituality Today* 43 (1991): 273–77.

————. *Understanding Christian Spirituality*. New York: Paulist, 1997.

Dreyer, Elizabeth. *Earth Crammed with Heaven: A Spirituality of Everyday Life*. New York: Paulist, 1994.

Eck, Diana L. *Encountering God: A Spiritual Journey from Bozeman to Banaras*. Boston: Beacon Press, 1993.

Fischer, Kathleen. "Come to the Banquet: Women's Prayer and Spirituality Today." *Praying* 77 (1997).

Freedman, David Noel, et al., eds. *Anchor Bible Dictionary*. 6 vols. New York: Doubleday, 1992.

Gilkey, Langdon. "Nature as the Image of God: Signs of the Sacred." *Theology Today* 51 (1995): 127–41.

Gittins, Anthony J. *Gifts and Strangers: Meeting the Challenge of Inculturation*. New York: Paulist, 1989.

————. *Bread for the Journey: The Mission of Transformation and the Transformation of Mission*. Maryknoll, NY: Orbis, 1993.

————. *Reading the Clouds: Mission Spirituality for New Times*. Liguori, MO: Liguori, 1999.

Gottwald, Norman. *The Tribes of Yahweh: A Sociology of the Religion of Liberated Israel 1250–1050 B.C.E.* Maryknoll, NY: Orbis, 1979.

Griffin, Emilie. *Clinging: The Experience of Prayer*. San Francisco: Harper and Row, 1984.

Gundry-Volf, Judith. "Spirit, Mercy, and the Other." *Theology Today* 51, no. 4 (1995): 508–23.

Gustafson, James. "Spiritual Life and the Moral Life." *Theology Digest* 17 (1971): 296–307.

Gutiérrez, Gustavo. *We Drink from Our Own Wells*. Maryknoll, NY: Orbis, 1984.

Hanson, Paul D. "The Responsibility of Biblical Theology to Communities of Faith." *Theology Today* 37 (1979–1980): 39–50.

————. *The People Called: The Growth of Community in the Bible*. Louisville, KY: Westminster John Knox, 2001.

Hardy, Richard. "Christian Spirituality Today: Notes on Its Meaning." *Spiritual Life* 28 (1982): 151–59.

Hilkert, Mary Catherine. "Bearing Wisdom: The Vocation of the Preacher." *Spirituality Today* 44 (1992): 143–60.

Holder, Arthur, ed. *Blackwell Companion to Christian Spirituality*. Malden, MA: Blackwell, 2005.

Holt, Bradley P. *Thirsty for God: A Brief History of Christian Spirituality*. Minneapolis: Fortress, 1993.

Johnson, Elizabeth A. *She Who Is: The Mystery of God in Feminist Theological Discourse*. New York: Crossroad, 1992.

Johnson, Luke Timothy. *Faith's Freedom: A Classic Spirituality for Contemporary Christians*. Minneapolis: Fortress/Augsburg, 1990.

Kinerk, Edward, S.J. "Toward a Method for the Study of Spirituality." *Review for Religious* 40, no. 1 (1981): 3–19.

Knitter, Paul F. *No Other Name?* Maryknoll, NY: Orbis, 1985.

Kydd, R. *A Charismatic Gift in the Early Church*. Peabody, MA: Hendrickson, 1994.

Langford, Jeremy. *God Moments: Why Faith Really Matters to a New Generation*. Maryknoll, NY: Orbis, 2001.

Macquarrie, John. *Paths in Spirituality*. 2nd ed. Harrisburg, PA: Morehouse, 1992.

Marx, Karl. *A Contribution to the Critique of Hegel's Philosophy of Right*. Translated by Annette Jolin and Joseph O'Malley. Cambridge: Cambridge University Press, 1970.

McBrien, Richard P. *Ministry: A Theological-pastoral Handbook*. San Francisco: Harper and Row, 1987.

————. *Catholicism*. Rev. ed. New York: HarperCollins, 1994.

McFague, Sallie. *The Body of God: An Ecological Theology*. Minneapolis: Fortress, 1993.

McGinn, Bernard, and John Meyendorff, eds. *Christian Spirituality: Origins to the Twelfth Century*. New York: Crossroad, 1985.

McGrath, Alister E. *Christian Spirituality: An Introduction*. Oxford: Blackwell, 1999.

Murphy, Anne. "The Lenses of Gender." *The Way* 36, no. 4 (1996): 323–30.

Newell, Philip. "Spirituality, Community, and an Individualist Culture." *The Way* Supplement 84 (1995): 121–28.

O'Keefe, Mark, O.S.B. "Catholic Moral Theology and Christian Spirituality." *New Theology Review* 7, no. 2 (1994): 60–73.

————. *Becoming Good, Becoming Holy: On the Relationship of Christian Ethics and Spirituality*. New York: Paulist, 1995.

Osei-Bonsu, Joseph. "Biblically and Theologically Based Inculturation." *African Ecclesiastical Review* 32, no. 6 (1990).

Ostini, Anthony H. "Painful Images of God." *Spiritual Life* 41 (1995): 13–19.

Paris, Peter J. *The Spirituality of African Peoples*. Minneapolis: Fortress, 1995.

Peterson, Eugene H. "Eat This Book: The Holy Community at Table with the Holy Scripture." *Theology Today* 56, no. 1 (1999): 5–17.

Pontifical Biblical Commission. *The Interpretation of the Bible in the Church*. Boston: Pauline Books and Media, 1993.

Pope, Alexander. "The Riddle of the World." In *The Golden Treasury of the Best Songs and Lyrical Poems*, edited and revised by F. T. Palgrave and Oscar Williams, 266–67. New York: Mentor Books, 1961.

Principe, Walter. "Toward Defining Spirituality." *Studies in Religion* 12 (1983): 123–41.

Schneiders, Sandra M. "From Exegesis to Hermeneutics: The Problem of the Contemporary Meaning of Scripture." *Horizons* 8, no. 1 (1981): 23–39.

————. "Theology and Spirituality: Strangers, Rivals, or Partners?" *Horizons* 13, no. 2 (1986): 253–74.

————. "Spirituality in the Academy." *Theological Studies* 50, no. 3 (1989): 684.

————. "A Hermeneutical Approach to the Study of Christian Spirituality." *Christian Spirituality Bulletin* 2 (1994): 9–14.

————. "The Study of Christian Spirituality: Contours and Dynamics of a Discipline." *Christian Spirituality Bulletin* 6, no. 1 (1998): 1–12.

————. "Biblical Spirituality." *Interpretation* 56, no. 2 (April 2002): 133–42.

Shannon, William H. "Contemplation, Contemplative Prayer." In *The New Dictionary of Catholic Spirituality*, edited by Michael Downey, 209–14. Collegeville, MN: Liturgical Press, 1993.

Sheldrake, Philip F. *Images of Holiness: Explorations in Contemporary Spirituality*. Notre Dame, IN: Ave Maria, 1988.

————. *Spirituality and History: Questions of Interpretation and Method*. New York: Crossroad, 1992.

————. "Some Continuing Questions: The Relationship between Spirituality and Theology." *Christian Spirituality Bulletin* 2, no. 1 (1994): 15–17.

————. "Befriending Our Desires." *The Way* 35 (1995): 91–100.

————. *Spirituality and Theology: Christian Living and the Doctrine of God*. Maryknoll, NY: Orbis, 1998.

Thomas, Carolyn. *Gift and Response: A Biblical Spirituality for Contemporary Christians*. New York: Paulist, 1994.

Suetonius. *The Life of Domitian*. Translated by J. C. Rolfe. New York: Macmillan, 1914.

Thurman, Howard. *The Negro Spiritual Speaks of Life and Death*. Richmond, IN: Friends United Press, 1975.

————. *Jesus and the Disinherited*. Richmond, IN: Friends United Press, 1981.

————. *Disciplines of the Spirit*. Richmond, IN: Friends United Press, 1987.

————. *The Centering Moment*. Richmond, IN: Friends United Press, 1990.

————. *The Inward Journey*. Richmond, IN: Friends United Press, 1990.

Toolan, David S. "Praying in a Post-Einsteinian Universe." *Cross Currents* 46, no. 4 (1996–1997): 437–70.

Tracy, David. "Theology and the Many Faces of Postmodernity." *Theology Today* 51, no. 4 (1994): 104–14.

Walker, Alice. *The Color Purple*. New York: Washington Square Press, 1982.

Whelan, Michael. *Living Strings: An Introduction to Biblical Spirituality*. New South Wales: Dwyer, 1995.

Wijngaards, J. N. "Biblical Spirituality (1)." *Scripture Bulletin* 9 (1978): 9–14.

————. "Biblical Spirituality (2)." *Scripture Bulletin* 9 (1979): 32–36.

COLLECTED ESSAYS

Fabella, Virginia, Peter K. H. Lee, and David Kwang-sun Suh, eds. *Asian Christian Spirituality: Reclaiming Traditions*. Maryknoll, NY: Orbis, 1992.

Felder, Cain Hope, ed. *Stony the Road We Trod: African American Biblical Interpretation*. Minneapolis: Fortress, 1991.

King, Ursula, ed. *Feminist Theology from the Third World*: A Reader. Maryknoll, NY: Orbis, 1994 (see especially part 5, "A New Emerging Spirituality," 303–94).

Levison, John R., and Priscilla Pope-Levison, eds. *Return to Babel: Global Perspectives on the Bible*. Louisville, KY: Westminster/John Knox, 1999.

Osiek, Carolyn, and Donald Senior, eds. *Scripture and Prayer*. Wilmington, DE: Glazier, 1988.

Segovia, Fernando F., and Mary Ann Tolbert, eds. *Reading from This Place: Social Location and Biblical Interpretation in Global Perspective*. 2 vols. Minneapolis: Fortress, 1995.

Shorter, Aylward, ed. *African Christian Spirituality*. Maryknoll, NY: Orbis, 1980.

Smith-Christopher, Daniel, ed. *Text and Experience: Toward a Cultural Exegesis of the Bible*. Sheffield, England: Sheffield Academic Press, 1995.

Sugirtharajah, R. S., ed. *Voices from the Margin: Interpreting the Bible in the Third World*. Maryknoll, NY: Orbis, 1995.

OLD TESTAMENT

Alonso Schökel, Luis. "Sapiential and Covenant Themes in Gen 2–3." *Theology Digest* 13 (1965): 3–10.

Anderson, Bernhard W. *Out of the Depths: The Psalms Speak for Us Today*. Rev. ed. Philadelphia: Westminster, 1983.

Balentine, Samuel. *The Hidden God: The Hiding of the Face of God in the Old Testament*. New York: Oxford, 1983.

———. "The Prophet as Intercessor: A Reassessment." *Journal of Biblical Literature* 103 (1984): 161–73.

———. "Prayer in the Wilderness Traditions: In Pursuit of Divine Justice." *Hebrew Annual Review* 9 (1985): 53–74.

———. *Prayer in the Hebrew Bible*. Minneapolis: Fortress, 1993.

Barr, James. "Man and Nature: The Ecological Controversy and the Old Testament." *Bulletin of the John Rylands Library* 55 (1972–1973).

Bergant, Dianne. *Praise and Lament in the Psalms*. Atlanta: John Knox, 1981.

———. *Israel's Wisdom Literature: A Liberation-Critical Reading*. Minneapolis: Fortress, 1997.

———. *Genesis: In the Beginning*. Collegeville, MN: Liturgical Press, 2013.

Bird, Phyllis A. "'Male and Female He Created Them': Gen 1:27b in the Context of the Priestly Account of Creation." *Harvard Theological Review* 74, no. 2 (1981): 129–59.

Blank, Sheldon. "The Confessions of Jeremiah and the Meaning of Prayer." *Hebrew Union College Annual* 21 (1948): 331–54.

Boadt, Lawrence. *Reading the Old Testament: An Introduction*. New York: Paulist, 1984.

Boyce, Richard. *The Cry to God in the Old Testament*. Atlanta: Scholars Press, 1989.

Brueggemann, Walter. "From Hurt to Joy, from Death to Life." *Interpretation* 28 (1974): 3–19.

———. "The Formfulness of Grief." *Interpretation* 31 (1977): 263–75.

———. *The Prophetic Imagination*. Philadelphia: Fortress, 1978.

———. "Trajectories in Old Testament Literature and the Sociology of Ancient Israel." *Journal of Biblical Literature* 98 (1979): 161–85.

———. "A Convergence in Recent Old Testament Theologies." *Journal for the Study of the Old Testament* 18 (1980): 2–18.

———. *The Message of the Psalms*. Minneapolis: Augsburg, 1984.

———. "The Costly Loss of Lament." *Journal for the Study of the Old Testament* 36 (1986): 57–71.

———. "The Exodus Narrative as Israel's Articulation of Faith Development." In *Hope within History*, 7–26. Atlanta: John Knox, 1987.

———. *Israel's Praise: Doxology against Idolatry and Ideology*. Philadelphia: Fortress, 1988.

———. "Welcoming the Stranger." In *Interpretation and Obedience*. Philadelphia: Fortress, 1991.

———. "The Book of Exodus." In *The New Interpreters' Bible*. Vol. 1, edited by Walter Brueggemann et al., 657–981. Nashville: Abingdon, 1994.

———. *Texts That Linger. Words That Explode: Listening to Prophetic Voices*. Minneapolis: Fortress, 2000.

Carney, S. "God Damn God: A Reflection on Expressing Anger in Prayer." *Biblical Theology Bulletin* 13 (1983): 116–20.

Clements, R. E. *In Spirit and in Truth: Insights from Biblical Prayer*. Atlanta: John Knox, 1985.

Collins, John J. *The Scepter and the Star: Messianism in Light of the Dead Sea Scrolls*. 2nd ed. Grand Rapids, MI: Eerdmans, 2010.

———. *The Apocalyptic Imagination: An Introduction to Jewish Apocalyptic Literature*. 3rd ed. Grand Rapids, MI: Eerdmans, 2016.

Collins, R. F. "'Male and Female' He Created Them." *Chicago Studies* 32, no. 1 (1993): 9–18.

Craghan, J. F. *The Psalms: Prayers for the Ups, Downs and In-Betweens of Life*. Collegeville, MN: Liturgical Press, 1985.

Davidson, R. *The Courage to Doubt: Exploring an Old Testament Theme*. London: SCM, 1983.

Drane, John. "Defining a Biblical Theology of Creation." *Transformation* 10, no. 2 (1993): 7–11.

Endres, John C., S.J. "Psalms and Spirituality in the 21st Century." *Interpretation* 56, no. 2 (April 2002): 143–54.

Fitzmyer, Joseph A. *The One Who Is to Come*. Grand Rapids, MI: Eerdmans, 2007.

Fraade, Steven D. "Judaism (Palestinian)." *Anchor Bible Dictionary*. Vol. 3, edited by David Noel Freedman, et al., 1054–1061. New York: Doubleday, 1992.

Gnuse, R. *You Shall Not Steal: Community and Property in the Biblical Tradition*. Maryknoll, NY: Orbis, 1985.

Goldingay, J. "The Dynamic Cycle of Praise and Prayer in the Psalms." *Journal for the Study of the Old Testament* 20 (1981): 85–90.

Gordis, Robert. *The Song of Songs and Lamentations*. New York: KTAV, 1974.

Gowan, Donald G. "Wealth and Poverty in the Old Testament: The Care of the Widows, the Orphan, and the Sojourner." *Interpretation* 41 (1987): 341–53.

Greenberg, Moshe. *Biblical Prose Prayer as a Window to the Popular Religion of Ancient Israel*. Berkeley: University of California Press, 1983.

Guinan, Michael D. *The Pentateuch*. Message of Biblical Spirituality 1. Collegeville, MN: Liturgical Press, 1990.

———. *To Be Human before God: Insights from Biblical Spirituality*. Collegeville, MN: Liturgical Press, 1994.

Hanson, Paul D. *The Dawn of Apocalyptic*. Philadelphia: Fortress, 1975.

Hens-Piazza, Gina. "Learning to Curse: Psalms of Lament." *Review for Religious* 53, no. 6 (1994): 860–65.

Heschel, Abraham J. *The Prophets*. New York: Harper and Row, 1962.

———. *The Sabbath*. New York: Farrar, Straus and Giroux, 1975.

Hobbs, T. R., and P. K. Jackson. "The Enemy in the Psalms." *Biblical Theology Bulletin* 21 (1991): 22–29.

Holladay, William L. *The Psalms through Three Thousand Years*. Minneapolis: Fortress, 1993.

———. *Long Ago God Spoke: How Christians May Hear the Old Testament Today*. Minneapolis: Fortress, 1995.

Hovda, Robert. "The Amen Corner: Scripture Has It, Not on Bread Alone Shall Human Beings Live." *Worship* 57 (1983): 255–63.

Jensen, R. A. "Human Experience and the Blessing/Saving God." *Word and World* 1 (1981): 237.

Jodziewicz, Thomas W. "Listening, Hearing, Responding: Hannah, Eli and Samuel." *Spiritual Life* 39, no. 4 (1993): 230–35.

Kim, E. Kon. "'Outcry' Its Context in Biblical Theology." *Interpretation* 42 (1988): 229–39.

Kuthirakkattel, S. "The Man-made Temple and the God-made Sanctuary: Some Aspects of the New Testament Theology of the Temple." *Jeevadhara* 23, no. 134 (1993): 153–70.

Lang, Bernard. "The Social Organization of Peasant Poverty in Biblical Israel." *Journal for the Study of the Old Testament* 24 (1982): 47–63.

Levenson, Jon D. "The Temple and the World." *Journal of Religion* 64 (1984): 275–98.

Martínez, Florentino García, and Eibert J. C. Tigchelaar, eds. *The Dead Sea Scrolls Study Edition*. 2 vols. Grand Rapids, MI: Eerdmans, 1997–1998.

Mays, James L. "The Language of the Reign of God." *Interpretation* (1993): 117–214.

McEleney, Neil J. "Gospel Simplicity." *Spiritual Life* 42, no. 4 (1996): 195–200.

McEvenue, Sean. "The Old Testament, Scripture or Theology?" *Interpretation* 35 (1981): 229–42.

Mendenhall, George E. *The Tenth Generation: The Origins of the Biblical Tradition*. Baltimore: Johns Hopkins University Press, 1973.

———. "The Monarchy." *Interpretation* 29 (1975): 157.

Miller, P. D. "The Blessing of God: An Interpretation of Numbers 6:22–27." *Interpretation* 29, no. 3 (1975): 240–51.

———. *Interpreting the Psalms*. Philadelphia: Fortress, 1986.

———. *They Cried to the Lord: The Form and Theology of Biblical Prayer*. Minneapolis: Fortress, 1994.

Mott, S. C. "The Partiality of Biblical Justice." *Transformation* 10, no. 1 (1993): 23–29.

Murphy, Frederick J. *Apocalypticism in the Bible and Its World: A Comprehensive Introduction.* Grand Rapids, MI: Baker, 2012.

Murphy, Roland E. *The Tree of Life: An Exploration of Biblical Wisdom Literature.* New York: Doubleday, 1990.

———. "Wisdom Literature and Biblical Theology." *Biblical Theology Bulletin* 24, no. 1 (1994): 4–7.

Nickelsburg, George W. E. *Ancient Judaism and Christian Origins: Diversity, Continuity, and Transformation.* Minneapolis: Fortress, 2003.

———. *Jewish Literature between the Bible and the Mishnah.* 2nd ed. Minneapolis: Fortress, 2005.

Nickelsburg, George W. E. , and James C. VanderKam. *1 Enoch: A New Translation.* Minneapolis: Fortress, 2004.

Nowell, Irene. "My Light, My Rock: Images of God in Nature." *The Bible Today* (March 1991): 69–74.

Ochs, Carol. "Exodus: My Spiritual Map." *Cross Currents* 46, no. 4 (1997): 548–51.

O'Connor, Kathleen M. *The Wisdom Literature.* Message of Biblical Spirituality 5. Collegeville, MN: Liturgical Press, 1988.

Pietersma, Albert, and Benjamin G. Wright, eds. *New English Translation of the Septuagint.* New York: Oxford University Press, 2007.

Ramshaw, Gail. "The Place of Lament within Praise: Theses for Discussion." *Worship* 61 (1987): 317–22.

Sakenfeld, Katherine. *The Meaning of Hesed in the Hebrew Bible.* Missoula, MT: Scholars Press, 1978.

Sheriffs, Deryck. *The Friendship of the Lord: An Old Testament Spirituality.* Carlisle, Cumbria: Pater Noster Press, 1997.

Stuhlmueller, Carroll, C.P. *The Psalms I and II.* Old Testament Message 21. Collegeville, MN: Liturgical Press, 1983–1984.

Trible, Phyllis. "God, Nature of, in the OT." In *Interpreters' Dictionary of the Bible Supplement,* 368–69. Nashville: Abingdon, 1976.

———. *God and the Rhetoric of Sexuality.* Philadelphia: Fortress, 1978.

———. *Texts of Terror: Literary-Feminist Readings of Biblical Narratives.* Philadelphia: Fortress, 1984.

———. "Bringing Miriam out of the Shadows." *Bible Review* 5, no. 1 (1989): 14–25, 34.

———. "Subversive Justice: Tracing the Miriamic Traditions." In *Justice and the Holy: Essays in Honor of Walter Harrelson,* edited by Douglas A. Knight and Peter Paris, 99–109. Atlanta: Scholars Press, 1989.

Vogels, Walter, W.F. "The God Who Creates Is the God Who Saves: The Book of Wisdom's Reversal of the Biblical Pattern." *Église et Théologie* (1991): 315–35.

Westermann, Claus. "Salvation and Healing in the Community: The Old Testament Understanding." *International Review of Mission* 6 (1972): 9–19.

———. "The Role of Lament in the Theology of the Old Testament." *Interpretation* 28 (1974): 20–38.

———. *Blessing in the Bible and the Life of the Church.* Philadelphia: Fortress, 1978.

———. *What Does the Old Testament Say about God?* Atlanta: John Knox, 1979.

———. *Praise and Lament in the Psalms.* Atlanta: John Knox, 1981.

———. *Elements of Old Testament Theology.* Atlanta: John Knox, 1982.

Wilson, Robert R. *Prophecy and Society in Ancient Israel.* Philadelphia: Fortress, 1980.

NEW TESTAMENT

Barnhart, Bruno. *The Good Wine: Reading John from the Center.* New York: Paulist, 1993.

Barton, Stephen C. *The Spirituality of the Gospels.* Peabody, MA: Hendrickson, 1992.

———. "The Desert in the Biblical Tradition." *The Bible Today* 31, no. 3 (1993): 134–39.

Borg, Marcus J. *Jesus a New Vision: Spirit, Culture, and the Life of Discipleship.* San Francisco: HarperCollins, 1991.

Bowe, Barbara E. "John 13 and Christian Service: A Study in Christian Spirituality." *The Bible Today* 32, no. 4 (1994): 223–27.

———. "'Many women have been empowered through God's grace' (1 Clem. 55:3): Feminist Contradictions and Curiosities in Clement of Rome." In *A Feminist Companion to Patristic Literature,* ed. Amy-Jill Levine and Maria Mayo Robbins, 15–25. London: T & T Clark, 2008.

Byrne, Brendan, S.J. *Inheriting the Earth: A Pauline Basis for a Spirituality for Our Time.* New York: Alba House, 1990.

Conzelmann, Hans. *The Theology of St. Luke.* Translated by Geoffrey Buswell. New York: Harper & Row, 1961.

Countryman, L. William. *The Mystical Way in the Fourth Gospel: Crossing Over into God.* Philadelphia: Fortress, 1987.

Crosby, Michael. *The Spirituality of the Beatitudes.* Maryknoll, NY: Orbis, 1982.

———. *The Prayer That Jesus Taught Us.* Maryknoll, NY: Orbis, 2002.

Cruz, Hieronymus. "The Conflict Spirituality of Jesus." *Jeevadhara* 23 (1993): 78–86.

Cullmann, O. *Prayer in the New Testament.* Minneapolis: Fortress, 1995.

D'Angelo, Mary Rose. "Images of Jesus and the Christian Call in the Gospels of Mark and Matthew." *Spirituality Today* 36 (1984): 220–36.

———. "Images of Jesus and the Christian Call in the Gospels of Luke and John." *Spirituality Today* 37 (1985): 196–212.

———. "Theology in Mark and Q: Abba and 'Father' in Context." *Harvard Theological Review* 85 (1992): 149–74.

Dickson, Kwesi A., and Paul Ellingsworth, eds. *Biblical Revelation and African Beliefs.* Maryknoll, NY: Orbis, 1969.

DiDomizio, D. "Christological Paradigms in Spirituality." *Chicago Studies* 24 (1985): 87–96.

Donahue, John R., S.J. "Jesus as the Parable of God in the Gospel of Mark." *Interpretation* 32 (1978): 385.

Donnelly, Doris. "Pilgrims and Tourists: Conflicting Metaphors for the Christian Journey to God." *Spirituality Today* 44, no. 1 (1992): 20–36.

Doohan, Helen. *Paul's Vision of Church.* Wilmington, DE: Glazier, 1989.

———. *Prayer in the New Testament: Make Your Requests Known to God.* Collegeville, MN: Liturgical Press, 1992.

Doohan, Leonard. *Luke: The Perennial Spirituality.* Santa Fe: Bear, 1985.

———. *Matthew: Spirituality for the 80's and 90's.* Santa Fe: Bear, 1985.

———. *Mark: Visionary of Early Christianity.* Santa Fe: Bear, 1986.

———. *John: Gospel for a New Age.* Santa Fe: Bear, 1988.

Elliott, John H. "Jesus Was Not an Egalitarian: A Critique of an Anachronistic and Idealist Theory." *Biblical Theological Bulletin* 32, no. 2 (Summer 2002): 75–91.

Fabing, Robert. *Real Food: A Spirituality of the Eucharist.* New York: Paulist, 1994.

Fee, Gordon D. "Some Reflections on Pauline Spirituality." In *Alive to God: Studies in Spirituality Presented to James Houston,* edited by J. I. Packer and L. Wilkinson, 96–107. Downers Grove, IL: InterVarsity Press, 1992.

Flora, J. "New Testament Perspectives on Evil." *Ashland Theological Journal* 24 (1992): 15–26.

Friesen, Steven J. *Imperial Cults and the Apocalypse of John: Reading Revelation in the Ruins.* London: Oxford University Press, 2001.

Galligan, J. S. "The Tension between Poverty and Possessions in the Gospel of Luke." *Spirituality Today* 37 (1985): 4–12.

Hall, Douglas J. *God and Human Suffering: An Exercise in the Theology of the Cross.* Minneapolis: Augsburg, 1986.

Hanson, K. C., and Douglas E. Oakman. *Palestine in the Time of Jesus: Social Structures and Social Conflicts.* Minneapolis: Fortress, 1998.

Hartin, Patrick J. *Exploring the Spirituality of the Gospels.* Collegeville, MN: Liturgical Press, 2011.

Hennessy, Anne. *The Galilee of Jesus.* Rome: Gregorian, 1994.

———. "Holy Land Pilgrims and Ministry to Them." *Review for Religious* 53, no. 4 (1994): 605–16.

Howell-Smith, Arthur Denner. *Jesus Not a Myth.* London: Watts, 1942.

Hultgren, Arland J. "Expectations of Prayer in the New Testament." In *A Primer on Prayer,* edited by Paul R. Sponheim, 23–35. Philadelphia: Fortress, 1988.

Ingram, Kristen J. "Good News for Modern Women: The Gospel of John." *Spirituality Today* 41 (1989): 305–17.

Karris, Robert J. *A Symphony of New Testament Hymns.* Collegeville, MN: Liturgical Press, 1996.

———. *Prayer and the New Testament: Jesus and His Communities at Worship.* New York: Crossroad, 2000.

Koenig, J. *Rediscovering New Testament Prayer.* Harrisburg, PA: Morehouse, 1998.

Koester, Helmut. "One Jesus and Four Primitive Gospels." *Harvard Theological Review* 61 (1968).

Kysar, Robert. *John: The Maverick Gospel.* Atlanta: John Knox, 1976.

Lambrecht, Jan. "The Groaning Creation: A Study of Rom 8:18–30." *Louvain Studies* 15 (1990).

LaVerdiere, Eugene, S.S.S. *Luke.* Wilmington, DE: Michael Glazier, 1980.

Malbon, Elizabeth Struthers. "Fallible Followers: Women and Men in the Gospel of Mark." *Semeia* 28 (1983): 29–48.

Martini, Carlo. *The Joy of the Gospel*. Collegeville, MN: Liturgical Press, 1994.

Metzger, Bruce M. *The Canon of the New Testament*. Oxford: Oxford University Press, 1997.

Meye, Robert P. "Spirituality." In *Dictionary of Paul and His Letters*, edited by Gerald F. Hawthorne, Ralph P. Martin, and Daniel G. Reid, 906–16. Downers Grove, IL: Inter-Varsity Press, 1993.

Minor, Mitzi. *Spirituality of Mark: Responding to God*. Louisville, KY: Westminster/John Knox, 1996.

Murphy-O'Connor, Jerome, O.P. "On the Road and on the Sea with St. Paul: Traveling Conditions in the First Century." *Bible Review* 1, no. 2 (Summer 1985): 38–47.

Oakman, Douglas E. *Jesus and the Economic Questions of His Day*. Lewiston, NY: Edwin Mellen, 1986.

Plymale, Steven F. *The Prayer Texts of Luke–Acts*. New York: Peter Lang, 1991.

Prior, Michael. "Isaiah, Jesus, and the Liberation of the Poor." *Scripture Bulletin* 24, no. 2 (1994): 36–46.

Purvis, Sally B. *The Power of the Cross: Foundations for a Christian Feminist Ethic of Community*. Nashville: Abingdon, 1993.

Race, Marianne, C.S.J. "The Israel Experience. Learning the Bible in the Land." *The Bible Today* 32, no. 4 (1994): 252–57.

Race, Marianne, and Laurie Brink. *In This Place: Reflections on the Land of the Gospels for the Liturgical Cycles*. Eugene, OR: Wipf & Stock, 2008.

Reese, J. M. "Christ as Wisdom Incarnate: Wiser Than Solomon, Loftier Than Lady Wisdom." *Biblical Theology Bulletin* 11 (1981): 44–47.

Reid, Barbara E. *Taking Up the Cross: New Testament Interpretations Through Latina and Feminist Eyes*. Minneapolis: Fortress, 2007.

———. "Reading Luke with the Poor." *The Bible Today* 32, no. 5 (1994): 283–89.

Ringe, Sharon H. *Jesus, Liberation, and the Biblical Jubilee: Images for Ethics and Christology*. Philadelphia: Fortress, 1985.

Rossing, Barbara. *The Choice between Two Cities: Whore, Bride, and the Empire in the Apocalypse*. Harvard Theological Studies 48. Valley Forge, PA: Trinity Press International, 1999.

Schatzmann, Siegried. *A Pauline Theology of Charismata*. Peabody, MA: Hendrickson, 1995.

Schneiders, Sandra M. *The Revelatory Text: Interpreting the New Testament as Sacred Scripture*. 2nd ed. Collegeville, MN: Liturgical Press, 1999.

Schreiter, Robert. *The Ministry of Reconciliation: Spirituality and Strategies*. Maryknoll, NY: Orbis, 1998.

Segovia, Fernando, ed. *Discipleship in the New Testament*. Philadelphia: Fortress, 1985.

Senior, Donald, C.P. *The Passion Series*. Collegeville, MN: Liturgical Press.

Smith, Dennis E., and Hal Taussig. *Many Tables: The Eucharist in the New Testament and Liturgy*. Philadelphia: Trinity Press International, 1990.

Stanley, David. *Boasting in the Lord: The Phenomenon of Prayer in Paul*. New York: Paulist, 1973.

Stendahl, Krister. "Paul at Prayer." In *Meanings*, 152–59. Philadelphia: Fortress, 1984.

———. "Prayer and Forgiveness: The Lord's Prayer." In *Meanings*, 115–25. Philadelphia: Fortress, 1984.

Thurston, Bonnie B. *The Spiritual Landscape of Mark*. Collegeville, MN: Liturgical Press, 2008.

EARLY CHRISTIAN LITERATURE

Bovon, François. "Canonical and Apocryphal Acts of Apostles." *Journal of Early Christian Studies* 11 (Summer 2003): 165–194.

Bowe, Barbara Ellen. *A Church in Crisis: Ecclesiology and Paraenesis in Clement of Rome*. Harvard Dissertations in Religion. Minneapolis: Fortress Press, 1988.

Ehrman, Bart D. *Lost Christianities: The Battles for Scripture and the Faiths We Never Knew*. New York: Oxford University Press, 2003.

Ehrman, Bart D., and Zlatko Pleše. *The Apocryphal Gospels: Texts and Translations*. New York: Oxford University Press, 2011.

Esler, Philip Francis, ed. *The Early Christian World*. Vol. 2. London: Routledge, 2000.

Eusebius. *The History of the Church from Christ to Constantine*. Translated by G. A. Williamson. New York: Penguin Books, 1965.

Gamble, Harry Y. *Books and Readers in the Early Church: A History of Early Christian Texts*. New Haven, CT: Yale University Press, 1995.

Hock, Ronald F., J. Bradley Chance, and Judith Perkins. *Ancient Fiction and Early Christian Narrative*. SBL SymS 6. Atlanta: Scholars Press, 1998.

Holmes, Michael W. *The Apostolic Fathers: Greek Texts and English Translation*. 3rd ed. Grand Rapids, MI: Baker, 2007.

Hurtado, Larry W. *The Earliest Christian Artifacts: Manuscripts and Christian Origins*. Grand Rapids, MI: Eerdmans, 2006.

Jefford, Clayton N. *The Apostolic Fathers and the New Testament*. Peabody, MA: Hendrickson, 2006.

———. *Reading the Apostolic Fathers: A Student's Introduction*. 2nd ed. Grand Rapids, MI: Baker, 2012.

Klauck, Hans-Josef. *Apocryphal Gospels: An Introduction*. London: T & T Clark International, 2003.

———. *The Apocryphal Acts of the Apostles*. Waco, TX: Baylor University Press, 2008.

Lapham, Fred. *An Introduction to the New Testament Apocrypha*. London: T & T Clark, 2003.

Lewis, Nicola Denzey. *Introduction to "Gnosticism."* Oxford: Oxford University Press, 2013.

McCurry, Jeffrey. "'Indeed You Will Have No Enemy': A Spirituality of Moral Vision in the Didache." *Spiritus* 7 (2007): 193–202.

Niederwimmer, Kurt. *The Didache*. Hermeneia. Minneapolis: Fortress Press, 1998.

Norris, Richard. "Apocryphal Writings and Acts of the Martyrs." In *The Cambridge History of Early Christian Literature*, edited by Frances Young et al., 28–35. Cambridge: Cambridge University Press, 2005.

Osiek, Carolyn. *The Shepherd of Hermas*. Hermeneia. Minneapolis: Fortress Press, 1999.

Rhee, Helen. *Early Christian Literature: Christ and Culture in the Second and Third Centuries*. New York: Routledge, 2005.

Schneemelcher, Wilhelm, and R. McL. Wilson, eds. *New Testament Apocrypha*. Vol 2. Louisville, KY: Westminster John Knox Press, 1992.

White, L. Michael. *The Social Origins of Christian Architecture*. Vol. 2, *Texts and Monuments for the Christian Domus Ecclesiae in Its Environment*. Valley Forge, PA: Trinity Press International, 1997.

Young, Frances. "From Suspicion and Sociology to Spirituality: On Method. Hermeneutics and Appropriation with Respect to Patristic Material." In *The Cambridge History of Early Christian Literature*, edited by Frances Young et al., 28–35. Cambridge: Cambridge University Press, 2005.

Zizioulas, John D. "Primitive Christianity: The Original Spirituality." *Church* 3.3 (1987): 10–14.

INDEX OF BIBLICAL NAMES

INDEX OF PROPER NAMES

INDEX OF PLACES

INDEX OF SCRIPTURE CITATIONS AND ANCIENT LITERATURE

3:8, 38
3:12–13, 41
9:8–17, 68
10:21–31, 236
11:1–9, 194–195
11:4, 189
12–50, 68
12:1–3, 68, 76
12:1–9, 235
14:22, 29
15:5–7, 68, 76
15:18–21, 68
16:13, 29
17, 68
18:1–33, 225n14
18:25, 28
21:33, 29
28, 9
28:16, 9, 20
32:22–32, 2, 9
32:26–32, 236
33:19–20, 29
35:7, 29
Habakkuk
2:2–3, 95
2:3, 101, 191
Hosea
2:19, 86
2:19–20, 83, 195
4:1–3, 87
4:4–9, 82
6:4, 87
8:4, 87
11:1–2, 87
11:3-4, 88
11:8–9, 88
11:9, 26
13:7–8, 25, 29
14:4–5, 88
14:5a, 25
14:7–8, 88
14:8c–d, 25
Isaiah
1:12–16, 118
1:14, 91
1:16–17, 92
1:23, 91
2:2–4, 89, 128–129
6:1–8, 2, 91

6:3, 91
6:5, 91
6:6, 101
6:6–8, 91
11:1–3, 92
11:1–9, 139–140
12:3, 13–14
24:1-3, 130
24–27, 130
25:6–8, 129
27:1, 225n12
30:20, 28
40:1–2, 99
40:3, 100
40:8, 100
42:1, 100
42:1–4, 100
42:14, 29–30
43:1–4, 14
49:1–6, 100
49:15, 29–30
50:4–9, 100
52:13–53:12, 100
53:4–5, 100
54:5, 27–28
54:11–12, 28
54:16, 28
55:1, 189
55:8–9, 26
55:10–11, 100
56:6–7, 101
60:16, 28
65:17–18, 123
66:13, 27
Jeremiah
1:5, 93
1:6, 93
1:7–9, 93
1:9, 101
1:10, 79, 80
2:12–13, 82
6:13–14, 82
7:4–7, 93–94
7:9–10, 124
12:1, 106–107
15:16, 94, 193
16:1–4, 94
17:14, 28
18:6, 28

New Testament Bible References

INDEX OF SUBJECTS

IN MEMORIAL:
BARBARA ELLEN BOWE, R.S.C.J.

December 1, 1945–March 14, 2010

Barbara Ellen Bowe was raised in Fonda, New York, the second of four children. She entered the Society of the Sacred Heart, making first vows in 1970 and final vows in 1975. By this time, she wanted to do biblical study. Those who knew her were skeptical, thinking her more interested in sports than study. Nevertheless, she entered the MTS program at Harvard Divinity School, and from there into the ThD program in New Testament and Christian Origins, graduating magna cum laude in 1986.

She then returned to the Philippines to teach for three years at Maryhill School of Theology in Manila. In 1989 she returned to the United States to join the faculty of Catholic Theological Union at Chicago, where she remained for the rest of her life. Teaching was her great passion and relationship her special gift. She gave of herself tirelessly in the classroom in Chicago, in numerous places around the world where she lectured and gave retreats, and in travel programs in biblical lands with groups of adoring students trekking along after her.

Barbara always said that she wrote only in order to teach, that teaching "is what I do best; it is what I love best." Nevertheless, she produced several books and a number of articles, including the publication of her dissertation: *A Church in Crisis: Ecclesiology and Paraenesis in Clement of Rome* (Fortress, 1988). Her most significant publication and the one dearest to her heart was *Biblical Foundations of Spirituality: Touching a Finger to the Flame,* published by Rowman & Littlefield [Sheed & Ward] in 2003. It received two First Place awards from the Catholic Press Association in 2004. Of that book, Barbara said: "It had to be written. But, in a way, I didn't so much write it—it wrote me!" She traced its origins back to her first days of discovery of the power of the Bible and her continuing quest to understand its meaning.

She was a member of the Catholic Biblical Association, the Chicago Society of Biblical Research, the North American Patristics Society, and the Society of Biblical Literature, and served on the editorial board of *The Bible Today* from 1999 to her death. Her love of sports never diminished. One of her friends remembered: "We once went to a Chicago Bulls game on Ash Wednesday with donated tickets. We celebrated Ash Thursday that year and knew God would understand."

In June 2009, she returned exhausted from lectures in Australia and Ireland. Through the summer and early fall, she seemed to be getting better. Then at the end of October came the diagnosis of a very serious brain tumor. At first news of her illness, stacks of mail arrived daily from all over the world. An aggressive treatment of surgery, radiation, and chemotherapy brought little improvement. She moved to California with hope for further treatment at Stanford Medical Center, but she was never well enough for it. As word got around that she was on her last journey, a new round of messages arrived from all over the world. When asked three days before her death, in a semiconscious state, how she wanted to be remembered, she replied without hesitation: "She does the Word of God with her whole life."

—Carolyn Osiek, "Remembering . . ." *The Bible Today*,
Volume 53, Number 1 (January/February 2015).
Used by permission of Liturgical Press.
Photo courtesy of the Society of the Sacred Heart

Lightning Source UK Ltd.
Milton Keynes UK
UKHW04f0618091018
330214UK00001B/132/P

9 780742 559615